T0351229

CORPORATE POWER AND CANADIAN CAPITALISM

CORPORATE POWER

and

CANADIAN CAPITALISM

William K. Carroll

UNIVERSITY OF BRITISH COLUMBIA PRESS
VANCOUVER 1986

This book has been published with the assistance of a grant from the Social
Science Federation of Canada, using funds provided by the Social Sciences
and Humanities Research Council of Canada.

Canadian Cataloguing in Publication Data

Carroll, William K.
  Corporate power and Canadian capitalism

  Includes index.
  Bibliography : p.
  ISBN 0-7748-0246-4

  1. Capital — Canada.   2. Corporations — Canada.
3. Elite (Social sciences) — Canada.   I. Title.
HC120.C3C37 1986   332′.041′0971   C86-091361-9

International Standard Book Number 0-7748-0246-4
Printed in Canada

For Anne

CONTENTS

FIGURES

TABLES

ACKNOWLEDGEMENTS

This book had its origins in a study of corporate and political elites in Canada, conducted in collaboration with John Fox and Michael Ornstein of York University. My doctoral dissertation, which forms the basis for part of the book, developed out of that research and benefited greatly from the assistance of Drs. Fox and Ornstein, as well as Bernard Blishen. In refining my ideas at the University of Victoria I have drawn upon the advice and constructive criticism of Rennie Warburton, Rick Ogmundson, and Charles Tolman.

Others have made more technical but no less valuable contributions. I appreciate the research assistance of Mahbub Ahmed, Lucille Covelli, Ada Donnelly, Katherine Harding, Alome Mendoza, Alejandro Rojas, Alex Roman, Greg Stockton, and Rod Wheeland. Scott Lewis, Moira Glen, and Mirka Ondrack provided programming support in massaging the data into interpretable form. Mollie Arnold, Louise Gendreau, Bill Little and Barbara Millward helped process the text in its successive incarnations. Jane Fredeman and Laura Coles of UBC Press have given careful editorial advice and assistance. Notwithstanding these collective efforts, the usual disclaimer applies: I bear responsibility for whatever deficiencies remain.

I would also like to acknowledge the financial support of the Social Sciences and Humanities Research Council and the University of Victoria. Finally, it should be noted that the present work elaborates upon two previously published papers. Portions of Chapters 2 and 8 incorporate ideas first presented in "Dependency, Imperialism, and the Capitalist Class in Canada," *The Structure of the Canadian Capitalist Class*, edited by Robert J. Brym (Toronto: Garamond Press, 1985). Part of the analysis in Chapters 4 and 5 has been revised from "The Canadian Corporate Elite: Financiers or Finance Capitalists?", *Studies in Political Economy* 8 (1982): 89–114. Permission to reprint portions of these works is gratefully acknowledged.

PREFACE

To a considerable extent, the character of any society is revealed through its dominant class. Although history is a complex product of consciousness and actions that ultimately embrace all classes and myriad other social forces, the dominant class typically plays a hegemonic role in shaping the economic and political structures through which it rules.

The dominant class rules not with complete information about its available options and their likely consequences nor with unanimity about the most propitious courses of action. Nor, for that matter, does the dominant class impose its rule arbitrarily or even directly on subordinate classes. Indeed, within market societies, a state with relative autonomy from particular class interests endeavours to mediate economic contradictions and to contain social conflict within the prevailing mode of production.

Nevertheless, the dominant class does rule. By virtue of its control of society's principal economic resources, it significantly shapes material life and social consciousness. And while an analysis of the ruling class, however thorough, cannot hope to substitute for a comprehensive investigation of classes and class struggle, it can form an important element of such study.

In Canada and other developed market societies, economic resources exist as capital, and the dominant class makes up a bourgeoisie. The class power of capitalists is expressed, through the corporations they control, as corporate power. Disciplined by the ever-present requirement to remain competitive and constrained to some extent by resistance from below, capitalists in the control of corporations decide when, where, and how to invest. Thus, they "set the order of priorities on national growth, technological innovation, and ultimately the values and behavior of human lives" (Hacker 1964, 140). The high degree to which capital in Canada is concentrated in a relatively few giant corporations, most of which are controlled by wealthy families or other corporations, has made the nature of corporate power a topic of prime importance in Canadian studies, in public policy, and in the mass media.

This book is about Canada's bourgeoisie—particularly its most powerful fractions—and that class's relationship to Canadian capitalism. The topic will be recognized as a familiar one, having been explored by scholars such as Gustavas Myers (1972), Donald Creighton (1937), Libbie and Frank Park (1973), Gilles Piedalue (1976), Tom Naylor (1972, 1975a), Wallace Clement (1975, 1977, 1983), Michael Ornstein (1976, 1984, 1985), Jorge Niosi (1978, 1981, 1985a, 1985b), and Jack Richardson (1982, 1985). Naylor and Clement have made particularly influential contributions to scholarship in this area with their studies of Canadian business in the formative era of the National Policy (Naylor 1975a) and in the more recent post-Second World War period (Clement 1975, 1977).

But while the subject matter may be quite familiar, the substantive interpretation in this study departs fundamentally from the arguments of Naylor, Clement, and others who have emphasized certain similarities between Canadian capitalism and the development of capitalism in the Third World. Drawing on the theory of dependency and underdevelopment, these writers suggest that in Canada a bourgeoisie with an accumulation base including the major sectors of industry never arose. Instead, an indigenous merchant class, which had gained economic dominance in the era of the Commercial Empire of the St. Lawrence, maintained its accumulation base in commerce and banking long after the demise of world mercantilism. Alongside it grew a comprador class fraction representing the interests of foreign capital, whose control over much of the country's industrial capital was consolidated in the years following the Second World War. With the decline of British colonialism and the ascent of U.S. foreign direct investment, a continental alliance is said to have been forged in which the indigenous, commercial fraction of the bourgeoisie occupies a subordinate status in servicing the ever-expanding Canadian industrial assets of American corporate capital. Colourful terms such as "silent surrender," "branch plant capitalism," "the staples trap," and even "de-industrialization" have been used by exponents of the dependency perspective to describe the deformed character of Canadian capitalism and its attendant drift toward truncated or underdevelopment.

The alternative interpretation presented here locates Canada in the category of advanced capitalist societies that grew up in the second wave of industrialization in the middle and later decades of the nineteenth century. The establishment of industrial capitalism brought a transformation of indigenous capitalists into a national bourgeoisie with effective control over industrial capital and the emerging home market. In the twentieth century, following closely on industrialization, much of Canadian business was reorganized into a monopoly form. The dominant fraction of the bourgeoisie became centred on a structure of "finance capital," a fusion of large-scale industrial and financial capital. Traced from this perspective, the path of development taken in Canada is not unlike that followed by other advanced capitalist countries: it culminates in the consolidation of a national economy largely under the control of a financial-industrial capitalist elite, in the penetration of foreign economies as domestically based finance capitalists internationalize their investments, and in a concomitant penetration of the domestic economy by foreign-based finance capital.

Ultimately, the validity of these two perspectives rests on the manner in which capital has accumulated in Canada. The accumulation of capital is a multifaceted process in which the basis of bourgeois society is maintained and extended even as its contradictions deepen. Two especially important aspects of this process are: (1) the reproduction of capitalist enterprises, chiefly through concentration, centralization, and internationalization of capital, and (2) the reproduction of the social classes and class fractions which comprise a capitalist society. We are thus led to ask how in Canada corporations have emerged, grown, and reorganized under the control of "indigenous" and "comprador" fractions of the bourgeoisie and how within this process of corporate expansion different capitalist fractions have been inter-related. This study addresses these questions by tracing the accumulation of capital in the largest Canadian corporations, as well as by examining the institutional relations among the same firms, in the period since the Second World War.

Chapter 1 presents the thesis of Canadian dependency in some detail, focusing on the proposition that Canada's traditional hinterland position in world economy engendered an indigenous merchant class that has remained bound within its dependent alliances with stronger metropolitan interests. In Chapter 2, I criticize this thesis on the basis of both theoretical and substantive considerations and show the need for an alternative analysis of Canadian capitalist development. The rudiments of such an interpretation are elucidated in Chapter 3 with a discussion of the political economy of advanced capitalism that draws on the insights of Buk-harin, Hilferding and Lenin about the concept of finance capital. This perspective is then applied to Canadian capitalism, from the late 1800's through the first few decades of the twentieth century, in an attempt to show that the dominant fraction of the Canadian bourgeoisie was trans-formed in this period into a financial-industrial elite. Far from remain-ing ensconsed in commercial activities, leading Canadian capitalists be-came directly involved in the production and circulation of commodities as well as in the financing of capitalist enterprises, through their control of major corporations and financial institutions.

The remainder of the book follows this capitalist fraction in the post-Second World War era. I argue that instead of selling out in a protracted silent surrender to foreign capital, the indigenous monopoly fraction has to a great extent preserved and even consolidated its accumulation base. In Chapter 4, an examination of accumulation in large Canadian firms reveals that indigenous capitalists maintained control of a substantial portion of capital in all economic sectors, throughout the years from 1946 to 1976. After an initial period of great American corporate ex-pansion into Canada, clear trends are found for indigenous industrial capital to enlarge its share of the home market by pursuing business strategies such as diversification into the expanding commodity-producing sectors and predatory takeovers of large foreign-controlled firms. Chapters 5 and 6 consider the institutional relations that weave the dominant Canadian corporations into a social network of interlock-ing directorates. In contrast to the predictions of the dependency thesis, the intercorporate network has been and continues to be focused around Canadian-controlled firms in both the industrial and financial sectors, with foreign-controlled companies occupying decidedly peripheral posi-tions in the structure. Its more recent evolution, charted in Chapter 7, suggests a further consolidation of Canadian-based finance capital into distinct though inter-related financial empires or "interest groups" with substantial international investments of their own.

On balance, the evidence from this analysis suggests that rumors of the Canadian bourgeoisie's demise—or of its stillbirth—have been greatly exaggerated. In a period when American domination is said to have become irrevocably complete, there are compelling indications that Canadian capitalists have maintained their competitive position and ex-panded their investments, both at home and abroad. This observation challenges the view that Canadian capitalism has followed an excep-tional and cumulative course toward the final irony of becoming a rich dependency: a society marked with the characteristics of advanced capitalism and dependent underdevelopment. The empirical evidence against the thesis of Canadian dependency and the conceptual problems in this approach underline the need for an alternative theorizing of Canada's evolving position in the world capitalist system. To this end, in the concluding chapter I offer some notes toward a reinterpretation, emphasizing the general internationalization of capital that has evolved in the era of modern imperialism and the specific regime of accumulation within which Canadian capitalism has matured in the same period.

While this alternative perspective does not counsel complacency in the face of foreign domination, it does question the extent to which such domination constitutes the focal point of political contention in Canadian society. The struggle against capitalism in Canada takes place within a national class structure in which Canadian monopoly capital is ascendent and within a global system in which the internationalization of capital breeds greater interdependencies, even as the deepening economic crisis breeds greater rivalries among both capitalists and states.

1

THE THESIS OF CANADIAN DEPENDENCY

The image of Canada as a resource hinterland dominated by powerful foreign interests in concert with a local elite of commercial capitalists is a familiar one among Canadian social scientists. Its intellectual roots can be traced to the historical studies of Harold Innis and Donald Creighton and to their basic notions of staple production at the margin of western civilization (Innis 1970, 385) and the commercial empire of the St. Lawrence (Creighton 1937; see also Naylor, 1972, 1). It was not, however, until the appearance of Kari Levitt's *Silent Surrender,* (published as a monograph in 1968 and expanded to a book in 1970) that a "thesis of Canadian dependency" found its first fully articulated expression.

In *Silent Surrender,* Levitt builds on Innis's (1956, 1970) conception of the Canadian economy as a staple-producing hinterland. But Levitt also incorporates the dependency theorists' claims about the connection between foreign direct investment and underdevelopment (see, for example, Baer 1962; Furtado 1964), along with a Schumpeterian notion of capitalist enterprise as "entrepreneurship." A key metaphor uniting each of these ideas is that of the "new mercantilism," which Levitt associates with multinational corporations:

> The central thesis of our argument is that the subsidiaries and branch plants of large American-based multinational corporations have replaced the operations of the earlier European-based mercantile venture companies in extracting the staple and organizing the supply of manufactured goods. In the new mercantilism, as in the old, the corporation based in the metropole directly exercises the entrepreneurial function and collects a "venture profit" from its investments. It organizes the collection or extraction of the raw material staple required in the metropolis and supplies the hinterland with manufactured goods, whether produced at home or "on site" in the host country (1970, 24–25).

As an external force acting on the penetrated society, the new mercantilism breaks down national ties which integrate economic and cultural life, leaving in its wake a politically balkanized and culturally homogenized hinterland, increasingly dependent on the metropole. The process embraces both the older peripheral countries like Canada, which gradually regress toward underdevelopment, and the new ones, which gain political independence but "cannot easily escape from their colonial status of economic satellites" (ibid., 25). In the former case, Levitt recognizes three historical periods:

> Canada was discovered, explored and developed as part of the French, and later the British mercantile system. It grew to independence and nationhood in a brief historical era in which goods, capital and people moved in response to forces operating in relatively free, competitive international markets. Present-day Canada may be described as the world's richest underdeveloped country (ibid).

Levitt concentrates on an unravelling of the specific manner in which Canada has been recolonized.

Levitt ascribes a particularly important role to the changing character of foreign investment, which has always played a key role in the' financing of Canadian enterprise. Financing from foreign sources may take the form of portfolio investment: that is, the selling of bonds or other credit instruments on foreign money markets, usually entitling the creditor to a fixed rate of interest over a long time period but denying the creditor any direct control over the financed enterprise. This internationalization of loan capital is the classical form of foreign investment. In combination with domestic savings, it was used to good advantage in the late nineteenth century by Canadian entrepreneurs in building a national economy on the basis of railroads, western wheat, and associated manufacturing (Levitt, 1970, 60–62).

According to Levitt, the developmental implications of the second form of foreign financing, foreign direct investment, are quite different. In this case the investor is not a money capitalist but a multinational corporation intent on controlling the production process (and of course the profits) in the "branch plants" that it establishes or takes over in hinterland countries. This form of foreign investment has become predominant in the twentieth century, particularly since the First World War. Thus, Canada's brief respite from colonial domination ended, as the United States gained power, Great Britain declined, and direct investment replaced portfolio investment in international capital flows. Levitt describes the "silent surrender" of indigenous capital which culminated in the postwar incorporation of the Canadian economy into the American empire:

> In Canada economic resources are allocated primarily to suit the requirements of large scale private corporations, and the majority of these are under United States control. The constellation of the east-west economy and strong central government has largely been destroyed by the economic forces of corporate centralization and corresponding regional political fragmentation. The Canadian entrepreneurs of yesterday are the coupon clippers and hired vice-presidents of branch plants of today. They have quite literally sold out the country (ibid., 39–40).

The data from which Levitt infers this "sell-out" are official statistics on foreign control of Canadian industry, which show dramatic increases between 1948 and 1963. Moreover, the specific industries in which foreign, mainly American, control predominates are the strategic sectors "in which metropolitan taste-formation and technological and product innovation are crucial" (ibid., 121): automobiles, rubber, chemicals, electrical products, aircraft. Canadian-controlled industries, in contrast, "are characterized by either small production units, such as sawmills, construction concerns or certain food-processing industries or, as in the case of textiles, by thoroughly dim prospects" (ibid., 123). Hence, in the distribution of indigenous industrial assets there is little basis for domestic control of the portion not yet committed to branch plants. Rather, foreign direct investment produces a peculiar economic structure in which Canada serves the United States both as a hinterland for raw materials and as a market for American manufactured goods (ibid., 60).

The coming of branch-plant capitalism carries with it a transformation of the hinterland bourgeoisie. The pervasively dependent character of Canadian capitalism is reflected in a business elite that retains the trappings of economic dominance without any semblance of effective power. This is because:

> The executives of branch plants are managers, not entrepreneurs. They dispose of funds, equipment and personnel within the means allocated to them. They do not formulate policy, they administer it....An economy composed of branch-plant industry must of necessity lack the self-generating force which characterizes successful entrepreneurship. To the degree that Canadian business has opted to exchange its entrepreneurial role for a managerial and rentier status,

Canada has regressed to a rich hinterland with an emasculated, if comfortable, business elite (ibid., 77).

The regression, furthermore, is cumulative. Lacking its own indigenous entrepreneurship, the branch-plant economy depends increasingly on imported technology: less and less research and development are carried out in Canada. By the same token, the predominance of foreign-owned industry "chokes the development of local capitalists and inhibits the development of a local capital market" (ibid., 109). As was mentioned earlier, branch plants tend to locate in the most dynamic sectors, diminishing opportunities for local capitalists to develop these industries. The domestic capital market is likewise crippled since control of branch-plant profits rests with the parent firm. Even where profits are reinvested in the hinterland they function merely as an extension of the metropolitan economy: the appropriated domestic savings of the hinterland. As Levitt notes, "the structure of ownership and control is such that there are barriers to the flow of Canadian savings to finance new Canadian enterprises" (ibid., 119).

When she turns her attention to the issue of Canada's position in world economy, Levitt grants that there are more extreme cases of dependency and underdevelopment. Some other countries actually serve as hinterlands of Canada. With this analysis, she anticipates Wallerstein's (1974) notion of a world capitalist system composed of core, peripheral, and semi-peripheral economies, as well as Galtung's (1971) concept of "go-between" powers in a structure of global imperialism, characterizing the world economic order as

a system of corporate empires, most of them centred in the United States. They extend into hinterland countries through branch plants and subsidiaries. Where the subsidiaries and affiliates are located in countries which are not themselves in a relation of metropolis to other countries, there is extreme technological, financial and organizational dependence. But there exists a range of intermediate situations where a country stands, at one and the same time, in a metropolitan relation to some countries and in a hinterland relation to others. Canada falls into this category. Both her resource and her manufacturing industries are dominated by foreign-controlled concerns. At the same time, her financial institutions, which have always been highly concentrated and powerful, have extended to the Caribbean and other countries through affiliated branches. So have some of her resource industries, such as the aluminum industry (ibid., 103).

In the context of world economy, then, Canada is both advantaged and dependent. But for Levitt it is clearly the latter attribute that has been ascendant since the Second World War. In her analysis, Levitt describes a range of tendencies that portend increased dependence over time. The domination of domestic industry by foreign interests, the economic, political, and cultural dependence that foreign control engenders, the continued emphasis on staple production for export, the prospects of economic stagnation as indigenous entrepreneurship disappears while branch-plant profits are remitted to parent corporations are phenomena that dependency theorists have associated with the so-called Third World (Amin 1974; Frank 1979; Cardoso and Faletto 1979).

Levitt's documentation of these features in Canada was both intellectually intriguing and politically momentous. There was a definite radical edge to the identification of Canada as "the world's richest underdeveloped country." This radicalism, however, was based not on a concept of class exploitation but of national oppression. As such, Levitt's analysis played an important part in providing a coherent theoretical framework for the Waffle, a left-wing movement that formed within the New Democratic Party in 1969, emphasizing the need to combine the struggle for socialism with the struggle for Canadian independence from American imperialism. As Penner suggests, "there is no doubt that by the time the Waffle Manifesto was drawn up, most of the signatories, and certainly all of the authors of that Manifesto, were fully acquainted with Levitt's study, and were enormously influenced by it" (1977, 240).

In a more academic vein, *Silent Surrender* was equally influential, setting the terms of reference for a considerable volume of critical scholarship on Canadian political economy that emerged in the ensuing decade. Indeed, in introducing the thesis of Canadian dependency I have focused directly on Levitt's essay precisely because it has been paradigmatic to the formation of "a Canadian Marxist school of political economy" (Drache 1977, 26), whose major strength has been described as "its ability to situate Canada's dependency within the world system and the power of this to account for internal development" (Clement 1983, 142).

Contributing in no small measure to this ability was the more general dependentist approach to world political economy which formed a major current in critical western scholarship in the late 1960's and throughout the 1970's (Howe and Sica 1980). "Dependency theory"—an eclectic combination of models converging around the concepts of dependency and underdevelopment (Weeks and Dore 1979, 67–68)—sought to present a comprehensive critique of foreign capitalist domination in less developed countries and colonies. The theory had its origins in two sources: (1) the radical structuralism of Prebisch (1950) and ECLA (the United Nation's Economic Commission for Latin America), cited by Levitt in *Silent Surrender*, and (2) Paul Baran's (1957) neo-Marxist analysis of the political economy of backwardness, which Andre Gunder Frank (1966) drew heavily upon in his seminal essay on the "development of underdevelopment." This second stream of dependency analysis proved particularly influential in the Canadian literature subsequent to Levitt[1] and therefore merits closer examination.

In Frank's (1967, 30–38) original formulation, underdevelopment on the periphery was attributed to three contradictions of capitalism: (1) the hierarchical chain of metropolis-satellite relations, (2) the extraction of surplus from satellite to metropolis, and (3) historical continuity in change, conserving basic structures of dependency in spite of such apparent transformations as political independence. In later accounts Frank injected a class element into his analysis with the claim that the metropolis-satellite relation transforms the class structure of the periphery, creating a close alliance between the metropolitan power (such as the colonial administration, transnational corporations) and the local reactionary interests (composed of merchants and landowners, [1972, 1979]). Thus, for Frank, as for Baran (1957), the peripheral bourgeoisie is essentially dependent on external forces and therefore is unable to play a progressive role in national development (Angotti 1981, 127).

In the 1970's, this notion of a sustained metropolis-hinterland alliance of ruling classes became a pivotal element in the emerging Canadian dependency school. At that time, analyses moved away from Levitt's descriptive periodization of Canadian economic history into colonial, national-developmental, and neocolonial eras, toward a stronger claim that the capitalist class in Canada has had a "colonial character" throughout its history. The works of Drache (1970, 1977), Naylor (1972, 1975a), Clement (1975, 1977) and Marchak (1979) developed this theme at some length.

In "The Canadian Bourgeoisie and its National Consciousness" (1970) Daniel Drache asserted that the roots of Canadian dependence are very deep indeed, ultimately devolving to the historically comprador mission of the Canadian bourgeoisie as a mediating agent of foreign colonial powers:

> The disintegration of the country cannot be seen and studied in isolation from the historic mandate of the bourgeoisie to rule Canada....The bourgeoisie are in the process of dismantling the Canadian state economically, socially and culturally. By this process,

Canadian history has come full circle—from a colony to a colonial dependency (1970, 4–5).

Buttressing his argument with citations of Innis, Creighton, Levitt, and Watkins, Drache argued that the Canadian bourgeoisie is different from that of Britain or the United States. Instead of aggressively searching after world markets and imperial domination, the Canadian capitalist class in the nineteenth and twentieth centuries consistently pursued as its national goal "protection, preference, entry and accessibility into imperial markets" (1970, 9), forgoing indigenous industrialization for the safety of colonial status (ibid., see also Bliss 1970, 39). According to Drache, this form of "nationalism" is consistent with the description of the "colonial bourgeoisie" offered by Franz Fanon (1965), a bourgeoisie devoted to pacification of a subject people in the service of draining economic surplus from colony to imperial centres (Drache 1970, 20).

A more detailed historical account consistent with this interpretation was given by Tom Naylor (1972), who followed Creighton (1937) in depicting Canadian economic history as the rise and fall of three "commercial empires." The first coincided with the era of French colonialism and ended with the British conquest of New France. The second spanned the period of direct British control, from 1760 to 1846, during which the British merchant class gained and maintained control of the land, the staple trade in fur and timber, and the emerging financial institutions. The mercantile character of this class inhibited industrial development by focusing on primary staple extraction, which maximized the surplus appropriated by Britain while minimizing local capital formation (Naylor 1972, 6).

For Naylor, Confederation and the National Policy were merely political devices to effect the third era, one of dependent alliance with the emerging American metropole:

> Far from being the response of a rising industrial capitalism striving to break down intercolonial tariff walls, Confederation and the national policy was the work of the descendents of the mercantile class which had aligned itself with the Colonial Office in 1837 to crush the indigenous petite bourgeoisie and nascent industrialists. As we indicated earlier, the direct line of descent runs from merchant capital, not to industrial capital but to banking and finance, railways, utilities, and speculation, and so on (ibid., 16).

The linchpin of the new dependency was the tariff, whose purpose was not to protect existing industry but to expand the scale of the economy and thus the volume of commercial activity (ibid., 20). Following Bliss (1970), Naylor claimed that what the tariff actually accomplished was an interiorization of the mercantile nexus. Instead of American-produced goods being mediated by Canadian merchants via the St. Lawrence, the new intermediation would be internal. The branch plants merely shifted the locus of metropolitan production inside the border. Produced commodities, as before, were circulated within the mercantile system "by the same merchant class in a slightly new guise" (ibid., 21).

Throughout the twentieth century this continental system of U.S. industrial capital and Canadian commercial capital has developed, in step with the decline of Britain as a metropolitan centre. Canadian capitalists' commercial predilections led them to reproduce their wealth in the form of merchant and financial capital, while joining with American monopolies offering safe investments. Canadian investments abroad have taken on a character of "branch plant quasi-imperialism," centred around the same nonindustrial sectors that the Canadian bourgeoisie retains under its control: banking, life insurance, transportation and utilities (ibid., 34).

Naylor's general conclusions were similar to Levitt's and were wholly pessimistic regarding the future of the Canadian bourgeoisie. The advance of branch-plant industry engenders more and more north-south linkages, decimating the east-west axis of national development by fragmenting national markets and balkanizing the state structure. Ultimately, "a Canadian capitalist state cannot survive because it has neither the material base nor the will to survive, the former contributing substantially to the latter" (ibid., 36).

This, then, is the final implication of Naylor's thesis. His account of Canadian political economy integrates Levitt's more descriptive analysis of "silent surrender" to the new mercantilism with a dependentist interpretation of the Canadian bourgeoisie as an essentially mercantile class, inherently receptive to, and even dependent on, such foreign domination for its own wealth.

Three years after the appearance of his seminal essay on the "Third Commercial Empire," Naylor published a copiously documented two-volume study whose main purpose was to elucidate "the roots of contemporary economic structures" in Canada through investigation of Canadian business in the period of the National Policy (Naylor 1975, I, p.xvi). In this densely empirical work Naylor attempted to lay bare what he termed the "logic of Canadian development strategy": a history of colonialism and mercantilism whose legacy is dependent integration within the American economy. Using official statistics and a plethora of sources in the contemporary business press, Naylor characterized the era as one of "industrialization by invitation," as patent regulations and tariffs closed the border to commodity flows while keeping it open to the influx of "factors of production": first American entrepreneurs and pirated patents, later, and increasingly, direct investment (ibid., II, p.276).

Meanwhile, Canadian capitalists busied themselves with the financing, transportation and trade of staples such as wheat and forest products. The enormous works of infrastructure necessary to the commercial economy—canals and railways—were funded mainly by long term foreign debt, while Canadian capital flowed into short term investments in commerce and staple transport, a pattern that would persist thereafter (Naylor 1975, I, pp.21, 68). In the "commercial" sectors of railways, utilities, commercial banking and finance, Canadian entrepreneurs were quite successful in consolidating control and even exporting capital in the same form to the United States, West Indies, and Latin America. Yet,

> this strength was not matched by industrial efforts. Rather the strength of the commercial sector went hand-in-hand with industrial weakness, by virtue of the absence of funds due to the twisting of the capital market so that funds flowed freely into commerce and staple movements, and away from industry, and because of the absence of independent innovative capacity (1975, II, pp.282–83).

In this work, Naylor assigned less importance to the conscious metropolitan-hinterland alliance of ruling classes than to the complementary division of Canadian and American investment interests (Ryerson 1976). However, the thrust of the study was consistent with earlier Canadian dependency analysis. The themes were familiar: the hinterland economy, specialized in staple production, the hegemony of commercial capital; and the emphasis on "industrialization by invitation" instead of the accumulation of industrial capital under domestic control. Further, they are structural features that, within the confines of Naylor's conceptual framework, would seem to have determined Canada's pattern of development throughout the twentieth century.

In *The Canadian Corporate Elite* (1975) Wallace Clement investigated the consequences of this pattern of development in the post-Second World War period, as reflected in the composition and structure of dominant Canadian corporations and their directors. Clement's work is of particular importance because of its novel synthesis of two traditions in social inquiry. On the one hand, *The Canadian Corporate*

Elite replicated Porter's (1965) study of the directors of 183 dominant corporations in the early postwar period, focusing on elite social backgrounds, recruitment patterns, and interlocking directorships among 113 dominant corporations. On the other hand, Clement's systematic analysis of corporate directors was influenced by the concepts and concerns of the Canadian dependency school.

For Clement, the legacy of the new mercantilism is visible in Canada's social structure: "Primarily using the multinational corporation, U.S. economic elites have penetrated the Canadian power structure and created a distorted elite formation at the top of the economic hierarchy" (1975, 117). The formation is distorted in the sense that foreign-owned corporations are directed not by citizens and residents of Canada but by a "comprador elite" made up of their senior management and directors. The companies are ultimately controlled by a "parasitic elite": the directors and executives of foreign parent firms. Thus, on the level of the economic elite, the massive influx of U.S. direct investment has brought "compradorization," creating a situation "where capital, entrepreneurial talent and investment potentials are eliminated from the 'host' country with the effect of decreasing, rather than increasing, autonomy with development" (ibid., 119). Ordinarily, one might expect conflict between an indigenous economic elite and a growing comprador elite, as the former attempts to defend its home market from foreign penetration. Yet in Canada,

> the position of the traditional indigenous elite is reinforced by the industrial development occurring with U.S. direct investment. It is the smaller entrepreneurs based in industries which have not established themselves as dominant who feel the squeeze of U.S. penetration (ibid., 121).

This congenial relationship between the two dominant elite fractions results from their specialization in different spheres of economic activity, the indigenous elite in circulation, the comprador in production. Clement echoed Naylor in claiming that the indigenous elite's specialization in unproductive pursuits such as finance, transportation and mass media

> has stifled the development of indigenous social forces in most manufacturing and resource activities—the sectors which are actually engaged in the creation of surplus within a capitalist society. In the process, [the indigenous elite] has become allied with foreign capitalists in these surplus-creating sectors....This rather unique de-

velopment of elite configurations makes the Canadian corporate elite atypical compared to other industrialized liberal-democracies.... [T]he Canadian bourgeoisie is primarily a commercial one, engaged in circulation rather than production while in other nations the bourgeoisie is typically both industrial and financial (ibid, 355).

Clement elaborated on his thesis about the uniqueness of Canada's corporate elite in his comparative study of the American and Canadian political economies. As a major hypothesis, Clement suggested that:

What has been forged over the past century is an alliance between the *leading* elements of Canadian and U.S. capital that reinforces mutually the power and advantage of each. The particular type of economic development Canada has experienced has occurred in the context of two overriding factors: the dominant place of financial capitalists in Canada and the presence of the world's largest industrial giant immediately adjacent (1977, 6).

Clement endeavored to document the emergence of this continental alliance through parallel accounts of Canadian and American economic histories.

The dominance in Canada of a financial elite and the concomitant "underdevelopment" of industrial and resource entrepreneurs were presented in stark contrast to more balanced and diversified patterns of American economic development (ibid, 8). Arising in the early mercantile period, the indigenous capitalist class in Canada comprised a commercial elite whose mission was to intermediate in the staples trade. With further development of world commerce, and with the decline of mercantilism, Canada's leading capitalists moved into both financial institutions, and the transportation of goods (canals and railways). Their strategy for industrialization, however, was quite different. Following Naylor, Clement suggested that the commercial elite "sought out and found foreign capitalists willing and able to enter the sphere of production in Canada" (ibid., 17), laying the framework for the development of a continental economy.

In the United States, industrialization occurred from within, and its hallmarks—the introduction of technological innovations particularly in expanding industries and the concentration and centralization of capital—were evidenced earlier. American capitalists were not encumbered by a colonial, commercial status, so the coming of the railways greatly encouraged indigenous industry by spurring production of primary metals, locomotives, and so forth, and by opening markets, particularly in the northeastern and northcentral areas (ibid., 45). As these industries arose, financial capitalists such as J.P. Morgan became interested in them, and a tightly knit structure of interlocking directorates emerged between financial, railway, and manufacturing companies (ibid., 46). In contrast to Canada, where a commercial elite "stultified indigenous entrepreneurs by dominating them" (Clement 1975, 93), major financial and industrial interests in the United States effectively merged with the development of railways and heavy industry.

Although the structure of foreign ownership was already largely in place by the early 1900's, Clement followed Levitt in viewing the Second World War period as a watershed for Canadian development. During the war, the economy experienced rapid industrialization with the assistance of state aid, only to have most of the new means of production sold to U.S. industrialists at the war's end (Clement 1977, 18). American penetration of Canadian industry intensified in the early postwar years. In 1946, 35 per cent of Canadian manufacturing and 38 per cent of mining and smelting were foreign-controlled; by 1957, 56 per cent and 70 per cent of these industries were under foreign control (ibid., 80).

According to Clement, American ownership of Canadian industry, together with strong trade relations, provides the economic basis for a continental alliance of Canada's leading commercial capitalists and the major financial-industrial interests in the United States. But the alliance is also discernable, and is cemented, through interlocking corporate directorships:

> Since the Canadian elite has overdeveloped the sphere of circulation and allowed the sphere of production to become U.S. dominated, it has put itself in the position of having to find outlets for its capital and services. This is done in part through joint directorships, and it is clear that a good many of the indigenous members have been successful in forging these relations (ibid., 287–88).

Clement examined the extent of corporate interlocking among dominant Canadian corporations, dominant American corporations, and between the two sets of firms. He compared the density of interlocking within and between major economic sectors in each country, and found the financial sector to be densely connected to other sectors in both countries. In the U.S., the manufacturing sector is equally integrated with other sectors while in Canada the transportation-utilities sector is especially well integrated. Clement also found greater interlocking within the financial sector in Canada than in the U.S., and greater interlocking within U.S. manufacturing than within Canadian manufacturing. From these results he concluded that

> in Canada, elite members in the sphere of circulation are thoroughly integrated with each other but have tenuous connections with the sphere of production, which is foreign controlled. They have consolidated their position only in circulation, while members of the U.S. economic elite have effectively maintained control of all economic activities in their society (ibid., 167).

Moreover, within the Canadian elite, Clement reported that "many of those who hold indigenous positions simultaneously hold comprador positions," suggesting that "a high degree of interconnection exists in Canada between indigenous and comprador fractions of the elite" (ibid., 287).

Finally, the pattern of interlocking between dominant American and Canadian companies showed two kinds of ties: (1) those between U.S. parents and Canadian subsidiaries and (2) those between firms controlled in Canada and firms controlled in the U.S., many of which lead from Canadian financial institutions or lead to U.S. manufacturers. These interlocks were seen as manifestations of a "continental elite" in which "the exchanges, because of the particular historical development of each nation, occur in such a way that they are mainly from Canadian finance to U.S. manufacturing and from U.S. manufacturing to Canadian finance—from strength to strength" (ibid., 179). Clement was led by these observations to an interesting conclusion which will be contested in this study. The dependent, commercial orientation of Canada's elite, in continental alliance with the autonomous corporate interests in the United States, has produced a peculiar situation in which "the financial-industrial axis is continental for Canada but national within the United States" (ibid.).

To be sure, Naylor's and Clement's detailed investigations of the capitalist class present the most compelling empirical evidence for the thesis of Canadian dependency. Together they evoke an image of remarkable consistency in the character of the Canadian bourgeoisie, reaching from the period of the emergence of capitalism in Canada to the present day. The key element that has steered Canadian development along its exceptional path is the mercantile or commercial nature of the country's dominant capitalist fraction, itself a product of prolonged colonial status.

Other contributions to the study of Canadian dependency also adopt this line of argumentation in one form or another (see, for example Watkins 1977; Drache 1977; Hutcheson 1978; Marchak 1979; Clement 1983). Still, several recent works have de-emphasized the role of ruling class alliances and agency in favour of structural features which have limited or distorted Canadian development, such as the "externalities" surrounding the social and economic relations of colonialism (Drache 1983, 34) and the stultifying dependence on American technology (Britton and Gilmour 1978; Williams 1983, 22–40). In general, however, the claim that Canada occupies an unusual location in the world capitalist system, in large part owing to the commercial proclivities of its ruling class, retains considerable popularity in academe.

More than exceptional, however, dependency analysts consider Canada's position in world capitalism to be unviable. The cumulative, long-range effects of dependency bring a host of distortions and deficiencies to the Canadian economic and social structure. Instead of a balanced, diversified industrial structure, the economy is comprised of a truncated, branch-plant manufacturing sector—whose concentration in the golden triangle of southwestern Ontario exacerbates regional disparities—and an overextended raw materials sector precariously based in nonrenewable resources and vulnerable to fluctuations in world markets (see Watkins 1973, 1977; Drache 1977, 23; Hutcheson 1978, 134; Clement, 1983, 77). The leakage of capital in the form of patriated dividends, the lack of domestic research and development, and the tendency for the employment priorities of U.S. multinationals to favour American workers lead to flagging international competitiveness, economic stagnation, and even deindustrialization (see Levitt 1970; Gonick 1970, 65; Watkins 1970, xii; Laxer and Jantzi 1973; Clement 1977, 89–90, 1983, 83; Drache 1977, 21–25; Britton and Gilmour 1978; Marchak 1979, 262). The economic costs of dependency are great, but the social price may be even steeper: political balkanization, cultural homogenization toward metropolitan values and tastes, and the regression of the Canadian state to "a relatively dependent position within the system of U.S. hegemony" (Clement 1983, 84; see also Levitt 1970; Naylor 1972; Clement 1977; Marchak 1979, 127–28).

To summarize this thesis of Canadian dependency: (1) the "new mercantilism," whereby Canada supplies the American metropole with raw material for its industries and provides a market for manufactured goods from the metropole or its branch plants is said to have emerged on the basis of a peculiar bourgeois class formation, and to have the effect of reinforcing that formation. (2) The Canadian bourgeoisie, or more properly its dominant fraction, is claimed to have been overwhelmingly commercial in its orientation, eschewing an interest in domestic industry. (3) By implication, an essential element in Canada's dependency is the deeply rooted disarticulation of indigenous financial and industrial capital, which has engendered an uneven pattern of capitalist accumulation by "overdeveloping" the financial and service sectors in tandem with the underdevelopment of domestic industry. (4) Concomitantly, the dominant commercial fraction has allied with foreign industrial interests, represented by the "comprador fraction," and has become dependent for its own wealth on these surplus-producing clients. Finally, (5) Canada's branch-plant economy may well contain the seeds of economic stagnation and politico-cultural decay: a bitter "harvest of lengthening dependency" (Levitt 1970).

   The task of this study is not to evaluate all of these claims. Rather, our empirical analysis focuses on the basic issues of class and capital accumulation. I will attempt to refute the claims of Naylor, Clement and others about the commercial character of the dominant bourgeois fraction, its disarticulation from indigenous industrial capital, and its dependent alliance with American interests in the period since the Second World War.

   But a strictly empirical critique of so wide-ranging a thesis is clearly insufficient. Indeed, the Canadian dependency school has already provoked numerous critiques that question the particular relevance of dependency analysis to Canada (see MacDonald 1975; Moore and Wells 1975; Ryerson 1976; McNally 1981; Panitch 1981; Schmidt 1981; Niosi 1981, 1983). In these works, however, the copious international literature which questions the validity of dependency as a general theoretical construct has not been systematically brought to bear on the Canadian case, nor has much attention been devoted to the articulation of a theoretical alternative capable of integrating the patterns of Canadian capitalist development within a qualitatively different perspective on world capitalism. To understand the problems of the Canadian dependency interpretation and to formulate a more adequate account, we must widen the scope of our analysis beyond the North Atlantic Triangle that has formed the focus of Canadian dependency analyses. We must, in short, situate the Canadian political economy within a framework that faithfully reflects the general dynamics of world capitalist development. These are the concerns of the following two chapters.

2

RETHINKING CANADIAN DEPENDENCY

At its core, the concept of "dependency"—whether in its general or Canadian-specific version—is both appealingly simple and widely applicable. It refers to any external relation of international (or interregional) dominance, which distorts the internal functioning of the dependent social formation (Browett 1981, 14). Dependency is observable as a syndrome of economic conditions in the hinterland, including the predominance of foreign capital, the use of foreign, capital-intensive technologies in a relatively small industrial sector, and export specialization in primary products (Lall 1975, 803). The argument is that these features have an inner coherence; one can speak of dependence on foreign capital, foreign technology or trade as inter-related aspects of "dependent capitalism," with the implication that this dependence acts as a break on development and distorts whatever development occurs. The value of dependency theory rests on the extent to which the symptoms of dependence are systematically inter-related in the empirical world as well as on the link between dependence as a specific condition and blocked or distorted development as a dynamic tendency.

Critics of dependency theory in the past decade have pointed to two sorts of inherent difficulties: (1) *conceptual* problems which limit the extent to which the theory provides a consistent, well-defined framework of explanation, and (2) problems of *empirical fit* between the theoretical contours of dependency analysis and the concrete reality of a developing capitalist world system. To the extent that these problems impeach the dependency framework in general, its capacity to aid analysis of Canadian capitalism is likewise undercut. The burden of this chapter is to provoke a rethinking of Canadian dependency by linking general critiques of dependency theory to the specific case of capitalism in Canada.

CONCEPTUAL PROBLEMS

Heterogeneity in the World System

The first major problem that one encounters in attempting to apply the concept of dependency to concrete national economies is the tremendous heterogeneity with which the purported symptoms of dependency are actually distributed within the world system. As a result, many of the general characterizations of peripheral capitalism made by dependency theorists cannot be sustained by reasonable empirical description (Little 1975, 226). In particular, the diversity of conditions among the less developed economies is so great that in order to be adequately inclusive, concepts such as dependency and underdevelopment must be framed so broadly as to have little meaning in empirical analysis. (Leys 1977, 95). Cypher, for instance, notes that less developed countries (LDCs) display a wide range of recent growth records, and that the high-growth LDCs are themselves a diverse category. Occasionally, high-growth LDCs exhibit some of the supposed symptoms of dependency, but often they do not. In export-platform economies such as Hong Kong and South Korea there is a substantial indigenous bourgeoisie controlling most of the manufacturing sector and such elaborate use of advanced technology that, by the late 1970's Taiwan and Singapore were competing head-to-head as major exporters of machine tools to the United States (Cypher 1979a; Barone 1983).

According to Lall (1975; see also Lipietz 1984 pp. 94, 103), attempts to form a general category of dependency do not seem to have been successful, since countries classified as non-dependent inevitably show some characteristics of dependence, and vice versa. Foreign capital, for instance, is massively present in many LDCs, but this appears to be part of a more general phenomenon in which all countries within the capitalist ambit are increasingly penetrated by international capital. Thus, Canada and Belgium are more ''dependent'' on foreign investment than India or Pakistan, yet in Lall's view they are not among the dependent countries. Similarly, on the matter of technological dependence, it is clear that LDCs obtain most of their technology from abroad, but so do a number of advanced countries such as Denmark.

In consequence, ''it is ultimately impossible to draw a line between dependence and non-dependence...without falling into the basic error of *defining* underdevelopment to constitute dependence (i.e., arguing that these features constitute dependence only when found in underdeveloped countries)'' (Lall 1975, 802–3). This resolution, of course, is unsatisfactory because of its logical circularity. But the alternative—arguing that the same features constitute dependence *wherever they are found* — is no more satisfactory, since in practice it eliminates the possibility of discerning "truly" dependent from non-dependent countries.

Studies of Canadian dependency have tacitly followed this second course: they have *assumed* the internal coherence of dependency as a construct and have proceeded — on the basis of observations about foreign investment, trade patterns, and so forth — to subsume Canada under the same rubric of dependency as supposedly applies to LDCs. But in light of the stubborn refusal of many countries to conform to the neat categories of "dependent hinterland" and "autonomous metropole," an alternative interpretation can be suggested. It may well be the case that Levitt's (1970) description of Canada as a "rich dependency" attests less to an exceptional condition in need of special explanation and more to the analytic incoherence of dependency as a general construct.

The Inversion of Modernization

A second conceptual problem arises from dependency theory's etymology as a radical, "Marxified" structuralism which developed through a series of revisions of orthodox economic analysis, beginning with Prebisch's critique of international trade theory and his advocacy of import substitution as a means of overcoming structural barriers to development (Leys 1977, 97). In the course of its own genesis, dependency theory never broke decisively from the problematic of orthodox development theory which posited modernization as a process which flowed from developed to developing countries. It simply inverted diffusionist concepts and propositions to arrive at the diametrically opposed conclusion that capitalist penetration engenders *under*development. This innovation might seem to mark a radical departure toward a qualitatively different understanding of world capitalism. In a deeper sense, however, dependency analysis remains squarely within the same domain assumptions as the diffusionist paradigm (see Cueva 1976; Brenner 1977; Leaver 1977; Browett 1981; Henfrey 1981): the "polemical inversions" of developed/underdeveloped, centre/periphery, and dominant/dependent are merely substituted for analogous pairings within liberal development theory, such as traditional/modern, rich/ poor, and advanced/backward (Leys 1977, 95). As such, the two approaches present a false dialectic, with the strengths of one appearing as the weaknesses of the other, while *both* occupy the same metatheoretical terrain of non-Marxist political economy (Cueva 1976, 12).

In the Canadian context we can see this "dialectic" at work in Naylor's (1972) seminal attempt to, in his words, "stand Creighton on his feet." Donald Creighton's (1937) sympathetic account of Canadian economic development emphasized the progressive role of Canadian merchants in forging an "empire of the St. Lawrence" around the trans-Atlantic trade in staples. In his dependentist interpretation, Naylor reverses Creighton's tribute to Canada's commercial capitalists yet retains the idea that they were the driving force in Canadian (under)-development. While giving the appearance of radical departure, Naylor remains trapped within Creighton's problematic of Canadian development as he substitutes for Creighton's eulogy what Schmidt has termed a "moralistic apportionment of blame" for Canada's blocked development (1981, 76).

Idealism, Teleology, Moralism

The example of Naylor brings up a third ground on which dependency theory has been challenged, namely the extent to which its core concepts are imbued with such normative, ideological content as to result in distorted empirical analysis. At the heart of the theory is a contrast between the *ideal types* of autonomous development and dependent underdevelopment. Many critics have pointed out the difficulties in the empirical use of these categories.

Consider first the couplet "autonomous development," which attempts to encapsulate the course followed by advanced capitalist countries. By turning the variety of Western historical experiences into an ideal type, the concept

> disregards the fact that capitalism grew up in the various countries in a variety of ways, under different historical settings, and with a varying degree of world market integration. To the extent that development in the peripheral economies does not correspond to this model, countries are judged to lack an "autonomous capacity" and are hence "dependent" (Marcussen and Torp 1982, 144–45, see also Swainson 1977, 55; Henfrey 1981, 44; Johnson 1981, 73).

"Autonomous development" is thus set up as a normative, teleological category, which serves as a standard by which dependent underdevelopment can be recognized (Phillips 1977, 11). Autonomous development implies a fully independent national capitalist class, a full range of manufacturing industries, an indigenous capacity to develop and implement technologies, in short an ideal state of economic well-being and national autonomy, carrying a strong positive moral connotation (Chinchilla and Dietz 1981, 142; Johnson 1983, 90–91). "Dependent underdevelop-

ment" provides just the opposite idealization and carries an appropri
ately negative connotation. Dependent countries are bound to core
countries by economic and political relations such that the structures and
movements of the latter determine those of the former in a fashion detri
mental to their own economic progress (Warren 1980, 59). The theory
posits a fundamental unconformity between the results of capitalist pen
etration (dependence) and a hypothetical situation which *could* have oc
curred if locally produced surplus had been utilized rationally to meet
indigenous needs (Browett 1981, 15). This posing of "autonomous de
velopment" as an option abstractly available to LDCs but blocked by
foreign domination is *idealist* in that it ignores the lack of material con
ditions for such a process, substituting a hypothetical "alternative his
tory" driven by the motor of "mere intention" (Henfrey 1981, 44).

The polar opposites of autonomous development and dependent un
derdevelopment give rise to curious distortions when one attempts to
deploy them empirically. This is so because the conceptual structure of
dependency theory "idealizes social relations by fitting reality into *a
priori* categories (core/periphery; development/underdevelopment) rath
er than developing categories from observation and scientific analysis of
history" (Angotti 1981, 134). The categories of dependency theory thus
serve as "ideological molds for reshaping the raw materials of history in
the single preordained direction" of dependency and underdevelopment
on the periphery (Henfrey 1981, 37). A sense of how these distortions
occur can be gained by examining the concepts of dependency and un
derdevelopment.

In the literature on dependency, there is a striking lack of attempts to
define the term in a rigorous way. In light of this, several authors have
argued that "dependency" is a poorly formed descriptive concept that
masquerades as an explanation of underdevelopment. Leaver, for in
stance, holds that

> the notion of dependence really implies nothing more or less than
> the lack of some factor. Technological dependence is simply the
> lack of technology, financial dependence the lack of finance
> etc....But to invoke dependence as an explanation for under
> development seems to me to be profoundly mystifying; all that we
> are doing is stating what we already know in a different way. The
> task of naming should not be confused with that of explanation
> (1977, 113).

For Colin Leys, the question arises whether the concept of dependency
is not "a fairly arbitrary way of sensitizing us to one set of relationship

at the cost of anaesthetising us to others—i.e. sensitising us only to one dimension of a more complex *inter*dependency" (1977, 95). This argument has been made quite succinctly by Carlos Johnson (1981, 73), who notes that the very superficiality of dependency as an inter-relationship makes it inherently bidirectional. Against the arbitrary claim that "Latin America is dependent on the United States," one could just as easily substitute the reverse (Johnson 1983, 87). For Johnson it is not a question of "who depends on whom" but of concrete social relationships and their contradictions (ibid., 89). In contrast, by setting up "autonomous development" as an ideal type to be politically realized in the LDCs through gaining independence from a particular class's or country's dominance, dependency theory obscures the important reality that "social relations precisely mean specific kinds of relationships, independent, dependent, and interdependent at specific moments" (Johnson 1981, 73).

The concept of "underdevelopment" has fared no better than "dependency" when subjected to critical scrutiny. "Underdevelopment" in the hinterland is said to have occurred in tandem with "autonomous development" in the metropolis. Rarely, however, is underdevelopment assigned a precise definition. Instead, Lall (1975, 808) is able to recount three quite distinct usages: (1) underdevelopment as immiseration, (2) underdevelopment as market constriction, and (3) underdevelopment as marginalization and subservience. What ultimately unites these disparate themes are the undesirable conditions such as lack of domestic innovation and subjection to international fluctuations, which are seen as inherent consequences of dependency. At the core of "underdevelopment," then, is not a scientific concern with the concrete process of social and economic reproduction in LDCs, but a *moral* condemnation of capitalism's inability to "fully" develop its periphery (see ibid.). The problem with proceeding from such a moral premise is that there is in the final analysis no *scientific* way to distinguish "normal" from "distorted" or "under"-development (Phillips 1977, 12). As a result, "underdevelopment" becomes "an empty concept into which any subjective-normative criterion may be fitted so as to expound an apparent historical alternative, or even more important, a *better* alternative" (Warren 1980, 169).

As we saw in Chapter 1, in Canadian studies the concept of dependency has been employed in a variety of ways to emphasize the lack of indigenous industrial capital and technological innovation, the trade imbalance in manufactured goods, and especially the absence of effective capitalist entrepreneurship. In the twentieth century the combination of a commercial bourgeoisie uninterested in local industry and a foreign-controlled industrial sector geared to production of raw materials for export and manufactured goods for domestic consumption is said to have resulted in a pattern of "distorted development" (Clement 1977; 1983b), "advanced resource capitalism" (Drache 1977), "truncated development" (Britton and Gilmour 1978; Ehrensaft and Armstrong 1981), "de-industrialization" (Jim Laxer 1973a), and so forth.

These various descriptors draw upon the concept of underdevelopment to encapsulate the undesirable effects of Canadian dependency. The implicit comparison is always with an idealized condition of autonomous development, often represented by the metropoles of Britain and the United States. A serviceable example is provided by the notion that Canada's commercially dominated bourgeoisie "caused economic distortions" by overdeveloping the sphere of circulation and services while underdeveloping indigenous industry, especially manufacturing (Naylor 1972; Clement 1977, 1983a, 151; Marchak 1979; see also Drache 1970, 9). This characterization tacitly borrows from orthodox development theory (Fisher 1935, 1952) in assuming a "normal" transition from primary through secondary to tertiary economic activities. It therefore *appears* anomalous that

> no clear progression from primary to secondary to tertiary activities took place in Canada as it had in the United States. In Canada the economy changed from primary to tertiary without developing the area of secondary production. Here again can be seen the uneven nature of Canada's development and the effects of external control (Clement 1977, 96).

The failure of Canadian capitalists to achieve a diversified manufacturing economy is viewed as a direct consequence of their longstanding dependency on stronger external forces (Schmidt 1981, 77; see also Drummond 1978, 93).

The pitfalls of this approach to understanding Canadian capitalism are clear in the results of Singelmann's comparative study of labour force distributions in seven advanced capitalist economies. According to Singelmann, "the early industrialized countries themselves do not follow one common pattern of labour force transformation" (1978, 14). Rather, they can be described in terms of three distinct types of sectoral change. In the United States, employment in manufacturing has never been greater than 27 per cent of the labour force; relative to other developed capitalist nations, the American economy has long been highly "service-intensive" (Walker 1985, 82). By 1970 Singelmann's (1978, 145–53) data show that the U.S. has the most "overdeveloped" circulation and service sector while Italy, Japan and France seem saddled with especially "overdeveloped" primary sectors (see also Richardson, 1982, 290–91). In short, the hypothetical ideal of "normal," "balanced" capitalist development just doesn't exist in concrete history. Given this, Canada's slightly smaller manufacturing sector is no more indicative of "distorted," "truncated," or "arrested" development than are France's or Italy's large primary agricultural sectors and their associated agrarian petty bourgeoisies (see Burris 1980).

Empiricism

A fourth conceptual criticism of dependency theory focuses on the empiricist tendency to mistake the appearance of social reality for its essential relations and dynamics. The basic issue for dependency theory is not how fundamental class relations are reproduced within concrete social formations, but how immediately observable phenomena such as multinational corporations (MNCs) and international trade patterns have distorted or blocked development. The perspective is empiricist in that it displaces theorization of capitalism "from the abstract realm of capital and value in a commodity system to the more concrete and empirical realm of 'nations,' 'agriculture,' 'industry,' and 'international relations' " (Howe and Sica 1980, 247). Rather than penetrating these immediately perceivable forms of empirical reality to reveal real relations such as class (Mepham 1979, 147–48), dependency theory appropriates as real the superficial categories of capitalism and proceeds to erect explanations that account for some categories (for example, the unemployment rate, growth rate, size of manufacturing sector) in terms of others (such as domination by MNC's, importation of technology, international trade relations). By remaining primarily at this empiricist level of discourse, dependency analyses inevitably pursue "the common features of conjunctures rather than the structural features of generic systems" (Howe and Sica 1980, 249; see also Berberoglu 1984, 401–2).

Two particularly telling instances of this empiricism are an overwhelming concern for spatial relations and a view of production relations as defined by exchange relations (Brenner 1977; Browett 1977). The former entails a "fetishism of space" (Anderson 1973, 3), as relations between social groupings and classes are depicted in terms of antagonistic metropolis-hinterland linkages between nation-states or regions (Brenner 1977, 91; Howe and Sica 1980, 240; Szymanski 1981, 15–16). The latter tends to reduce classes from active historical agents to passive "*categories* resulting from the structural evolution of underdevelopment or dependent development" (Leys 1977, 95; see also Henfrey 1981; Schmidt 1981, 77).

Class relations are also obscured by the tendency among dependency theorists to adopt Adam Smith's model of capitalist development as the rise of a world market in which international exchange relations transferred the economic surplus of the periphery to the core (Brenner 1977, 38). The empiricism of this approach is discussed by Weeks and Dore who note that"a surplus arises in production and appears in circulation (if exchanged). By dealing with countries only, one considers the appearance of reality, not reality itself. What is missing is the concept of mode of production" (1979, 65). When the concrete production relations that have predominated at the periphery of capitalism are examined (as in Laclau 1971), we find an abundance of pre-capitalist relations, articulated with the capitalist mode of production by means of commodity exchange. Many scholars have concluded that at the root of the syndrome of dependency in much of the Third World is this articulation of pre-capitalist and capitalist modes and *not the specifically foreign character of capital nor the commercial connection with the metropole* (Kay 1975; Brenner 1977, 85; Weeks and Dore 1979; Chincilla and Dietz, 1981; Weeks 1986).

Empiricism in the Thesis of Canadian Dependency

The central thesis of Canadian dependency—that Canada's economic development has comprised a succession of "staple trades" with more advanced metropolitan economies, in which the dominant fraction of Canadian merchants and bankers has stultified local industry while allying with foreign interests—presents an especially revealing example of the empiricism that generally characterizes dependency-theoretic analyses. As David McNally has noted, by equating capitalism with exchange, the staples thesis attends mainly to phenomenal appearances in the sphere of commodity circulation. It fails to consider the specific manner in which labour and means of production have been combined within concrete modes of production. Staples analyses thus "abstract the market, the sphere of circulation, from the total circuit of capital and treat it as the general determinant of economic and social phenomena" (McNally 1981, 41; see also Cuneo 1982, 61–62; Clement 1983, 175–77). The particular *things* produced and exchanged in the economy are held to have conditioned development in peculiar ways, such that "the history of Canada...is the history of its great staple trades: the fur trade, the cod fisheries, square timber and lumber, wheat, and the new staples of this century—pulp and paper, minerals, oil and gas" (Watkins 1973, 116). As McNally (1981) emphasizes, it is this fetishism of commodities, of materialized labour circulating on the world market and abstracted from the social relations in which labour is appropriated, that provides the empiricist premise for a view of Canadian capitalist development as a continuous process of "staple-ization" (Drache 1977). Indeed, only superficially can the fur trade of the seventeenth century be likened to the so-called "new staples" of twentieth century Canada, which for various writers include forest products, base metals, minerals, energy products, electricity, and even aluminum (see Easterbrook and Aitken 1956, 520; Gonick 1970, 59; Levitt 1970, 127; Drache 1977, 19; Marchak 1979, 107), all of which are produced within capitalist relations using sophisticated technologies.

Against this eclectic grouping of semi-processed and processed goods, Marx's concepts of industrial and commercial capital can be instructively counterposed. For Marx, industrial capital is capital engaged directly in the generation of surplus value. It is "not a thing but rather a definite social production relation" (1967, III, p.814) which is continually reproduced as a "circuit describing process" involving the successive metamorphosis of value across money, productive and commodity forms, and resulting in the expansion of value (ibid., II,p.48).

In essence, the industrialist purchases labour power and means of production in the sphere of circulation and supervises the subsequent production of new use-values. Into these is incorporated the value of the means of production, as well as the socially necessary labour expended in the production process. The capitalist then returns to the sphere of circulation and sells the new use-values as commodities which, *ceteris parabus*, fetch money sums equivalent to their values, that is, to the socially necessary labour that has been materialized in them. This exchange leaves the industrialist with funds enough to cover the costs of means of production and labour power consumed in the production process, plus an increment of surplus value which results from the difference between workers' creative power in the production process and their subsistence needs as bearers of labour power (see Figure 2.1). Industrial capital, then, refers to *any* process in which wage labour is purchased and consumed in the production of new use-values, whose exchange brings to the industrialist a reflux of surplus value realized as profit. Concretely, this includes farming, resource extraction, manufacturing, as well as transportation (Marx 1967, II, pp.149–50).

Much of capitalist economy devolves to the interlacing of these industrial circuits in the production and circulation of means of production and articles of consumption. But inserted between many of these industrial circuits are various circuits of merchant capital and interest-bearing or loan capital. Merchant capital moves in the circuit M-C-M': the

Figure 2.1
The Formal Circuit of Industrial Capital

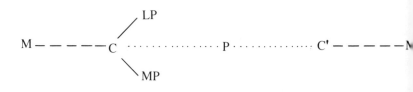

Legend

M   money capital
C   commodity capital
LP   labour power
MP   means of production
P   productive capital
ʼ   capital containing newly produced surplus value

merchant exchanges money-capital (M) for commodity-capital (C) and then sells the latter at a profit (M′). This serves to decrease the time and cost of circulation (a deduction from aggregate profit) by centralizing and rationalizing the circulation process. Since capital is mobile across industrial and commercial sectors, merchant capital "exhibits a tendency to earn an average rate of profit even though it is not itself the source of surplus value (which can only be created by productive labor engaged by industrial capital)" (Fine 1986, 390).

In this way, merchant capitalists and industrial capitalists share in the total appropriated surplus value. Interest-bearing capital, which has the circuit M-M′, facilitates capital accumulation by providing money-capital on loan to industrialists and merchants in need of financing. Both merchant capital and interest-bearing capital operate solely in the sphere of circulation but articulate closely with production. Although merchant profit and interest are deductions from the surplus-value generated in industrial production, Marx does not posit a fundamental antagonism between these forms of capital. "Commercial capital" is in fact necessary to the production and circulation of surplus value and therefore to the reproduction of capitalism (Kay 1975, 86–93). Merchant capital promotes circulation in general and provides for the realization of surplus value in the sale of commodities to "ultimate consumers''; interest-bearing capital promotes accumulation by financing new or expanded enterprise.

As capitalism develops, new forms of industrial and commercial capital emerge, such as railways, hydro-electric or nuclear power stations, and corporate share capital. Their location in the global process of capitalist accumulation can be determined through analysis of their function in the production and circulation of surplus value. For example, with growth of a world market linking distant centres of production and consumption, "there is a simultaneous growth of that portion of social wealth which, instead of serving as direct means of production, is invested in means of transportation and communication and in the fixed and circulating capital required for their operation" (Marx 1967, II, p.251). The growth of this form of industrial capital has particular relevance in the case of Canada, where creation of a modern transportation system was inextricably tied to the development of industrial capitalism (Pentland 1981).

The *empiricism* of the Canadian dependency school is especially evident in the superficial and eclectic grounds on which its exponents have defined industrial and commercial capital. In Naylor's view, for instance, under the National Policy "industrial capital formation was retarded relative to investment in staple development and the creation of the commercial infrastructure necessary to extract and move staples" (1975, I, p.15; see also Clement 1977, 17; Drache 1977, 25). Guided by the image of a staple-producing hinterland, Naylor equates industrial capital with the manufacture of finished products (1975, II, p.78). All other forms of industry in the Marxist sense of capitalist production of use-value—resource extraction, the transportation industry, public utilities—are eclectically defined as part of the dominant "commercial bloc" which is supposed to have stultified industrial development. But if we are to take Marx's analysis of capitalism seriously we must conclude that the notions of "industrial underdevelopment" and "commercial domination," so central to the Canadian dependency school, betray a profound misunderstanding of what capitalist industrialization is. They result in a serious under-rating of Canada's industrial development (Ryerson 1976, 42).

The confusion surrounding the meaning of industrial capital spills over into another principal contention of the Canadian dependency school, namely that Canada's commercial bourgeois fraction has remained historically *detached* from indigenous industrial interests, thereby stultifying domestic industrialization. As we have seen, Canadian dependency analysis interprets railway investments in the nineteenth century as a drain of funds from industrial development to mercantile pursuits (Naylor 1972, 1975; Clement 1977; Marchak 1979). If, however, we accept the Marxist analysis of capitalistically operated railways and other means of transportation as *industrial* capital,

> then, on the distinction between parasitic merchants and productive industrialists, we are forced to admit that a mass of mercantile funds was really flowing into production as industrial capital. The prominent men associated with railways would be industrialists. And since railways were such a large part of the economy the general complexion of nineteenth-century Canada would not be mercantile at all but, if anything, over-invested in industry (MacDonald 1975, 267).

Nor are the problems of the dependency thesis confined to its misconstrual of the railway's economic significance. Naylor, for instance, (1975, 38) entirely misreads the significance of the ties that emerged in the late nineteenth century between Canadian financial capital and indigenous manufacturing. He describes in some detail the close relations between the banks and manufacturers of cotton, sugar and steel. Yet, instead of recognizing in these examples an intermingling of financial and industrial interests, Naylor sees only a commercial elite, refusing to fund small-scale industry in southern Ontario and diversifying into industries such as cotton manufacturing, sugar refining, and iron and steel, which become "stamped" with the same mercantile character (1975, I, p.109). Eschewing an historical conception of capital, Naylor continues to "detect" his commercial elite well into the twentieth century—long after Canadian bankers have actively intervened in circuits of industrial capital in transportation, resource extraction, and manufacturing.

As MacDonald (1975, 270–75) points out, the one piece of evidence apparently in support of Naylor's thesis—the detachment of the Montreal financial community from manufacturing in southern Ontario—is probably spurious. These manufactures were of small scale until manufacturing capital began centralizing in the 1890s, so they did not require major long term financing. The exceptions to this description of nineteenth-century manufacturing—the sugar refineries, cotton mills, rolling mills and distilleries, which did have high fixed capital requirements—were the very industries in which financial interests were most involved.

Clement (1977), for his part, draws several misleading comparisons between Canadian and American economic history in arguing the case for the dominance of Canadian commercial capital. He describes the involvement, at the turn of the century, of Canadian financiers in consolidating "smaller manufactories into corporate complexes through promotion, takeover, and merger" as a process through which budding industry fell under the control of "financial forces" (ibid., 52). When he turns to developments in the United States, Clement reports that financial capitalists played an identical role "in combining various manufacturing firms into corporate complexes" (ibid., 56). For Clement, however, the same tendency in the two countries for financial capitalists to become directly involved in centralizing industrial capital has quite different historical implications: in Canada it indicates the continued domination of a commercial elite to the detriment of domestic industry, a symptom of dependency; in the United States it signals the merging of financial and industrial interests, a transformation of competitive into advanced or corporate capitalism (ibid.).

Clement's analysis of interlocking directorates in the U.S. and Canada suffers from a serious misreading of his findings. On the basis of a comparison of interlock densities Clement concludes that in the U.S. the financial and manufacturing sectors are strongly interlocked with each other as well as with other sectors of the economy. In Canada, however, he discerns only "tenuous connections" between elite members in the sphere of circulation and those in the sphere of production (1977, 167). In fact, the interlock density between the financial and manufacturing sector in Canada is *higher* than the corresponding density in the U.S. (0.62 vs. 0.50), as is the density of interlocking between financial and resource sectors (0.59 vs. 0.23) (ibid., 166). As of the 1970's, the connections between Canadian financial and industrial capital were hardly "tenuous"; they were actually stronger than their counterparts in the United States.

Nor does other research lend support to the disarticulation of indigenous finance and industry that the Canadian dependency school posits. A host of studies have documented the close connection and interpenetration of financial and industrial interests in Canada since the coming of the railways (Myers 1972; Ryerson 1973) and most decisively since the industrial merger movement that preceded the First World War (Park and Park 1973; Piedalue 1976; DeGrass 1977; Sweeny 1980; Carroll 1982, 1984; Carroll, Fox and Ornstein 1982; Richardson 1982, 1985).

In short, not only is the dependency approach hampered by an empiricism that is superficial and misleading, but also the formulation is, in the Canadian case, empirically suspect. This observation raises the larger issue of the empirical adequacy of dependency theory in general.

THE PROBLEM OF EMPIRICAL FIT

Bill Warren has perhaps provided the most resolute empirical criticism of the dependency perspective. He accepts the fact of uneven world development of the forces of production, but disputes the "fiction of underdevelopment" as a process. In terms of concrete productive forces, there is in Warren's view no evidence of any systematic, general process of underdevelopment on the periphery since western contact. Rather, the evidence indicates capitalist development, especially since the Second World War. Consequently, as Warren puts it, the quality of postwar literature on dependency has suffered from "ascribing rising significance to a phenomenon of declining importance" (1980, 114–15).

To begin, consider the postwar records of economic growth among LDCs. Per capita Gross Domestic Product (GDP) has in general grown at a faster rate than in the prewar period, often faster than the rates for advanced capitalist economies (Warren 1980, 190–99). Even without the oil-producing countries, the economies of LDCs as a whole grew much faster than the most advanced capitalist economies in the 1960's and 1970's (Cypher 1979a; Szymanski 1981). The same period witnessed the rapid growth of manufacturing, again faster than in the advanced capitalist countries (Warren 1980, 241; Petras 1984b, 188–90). For LDCs as a whole, the proportion of GDP devoted to manufacturing grew from 14.5 per cent in 1950–54 to 20.4 per cent in 1973; for developed capitalist economies the figure in 1973 was 28.4 per cent. These trends point to a rapidly diminishing world division of labour between primary production in the periphery and manufacturing in the core.

Ironically, one of the major forces propelling capitalist industrialization in certain LDCs has been foreign investment by "core" capitalists. From the mid-1960's to the late 1970's, twice as much total wealth was transferred to LDCs as was repatriated to the United States, a trend also evident for other advanced capitalist countries (Szymanski 1981, 292). Between 1970 and 1977, LDCs with the highest ratio of service payments to GDP grew at *faster* rates than LDCs less afflicted by such "surplus drainage." Contrary to the predictions of dependency theory, *"the development of underdevelopment is in fact linked to the relative absence of MNCs, not their relative presence"* (Andreff 1984, 76; emphasis in original). In the present system of world capitalism the more foreign investment a country secures the more rapid is its rate of growth (Szymanski 1981, 335; see also Barone 1983). This is not to say that the Third World is now uniformly on the road to "modernization." In fact, the uneven pattern of international investment has split the Third World into a large group of *least* developed countries which transnational capital has abandoned to impoverishment and a smaller group of high-growth countries to which foreign capital is attracted for a variety of reasons (Andreff 1984, 72; Petras 1984b, 186).

These empirical tendencies, and the numerous conceptual inadequacies reviewed earlier, seriously call into question the interpretations of world capitalism that have been cast within the problematic of dependency. The implications for political-economic analysis in Canada are far-reaching. Analyses that begin from the moral premise of dependency may have political value in sensitizing Canadians to the immediate problems posed by Canada's insertion in the world capitalist system. Their scientific merit, however, is seriously jeopardized by the superficial and idealist character of dependency theory's core concepts. In light of these conceptual deficiences it is not surprising that the gap between theory and reality is so wide—both at the level of the world system and in the specific case of Canada. As economic crisis engenders further restructuring of world capitalism this gap can only be expected to grow[1]. In the circumstances, if we are not to be continually overtaken by "unpredictable" developments such as the "coming of age of Canadian capital" (Resnick 1982, 15) or even the "LatinAmericanization of the United States" (Barnet and Muller, 1974, 213) we shall have to break decisively with the problematic of dependency and situate Canadian capitalism and its bourgeoisie on the basis of an alternative conceptualization of the world capitalist system.

3

MONOPOLY CAPITALISM
AND CANADIAN FINANCE CAPITAL

If dependency theory is, as we have claimed, unequal to the task of understanding international capitalist relations, and if the Canadian bourgeoisie has not been dominated by a commercial elite mediating the international trade in staples, how may we properly describe Canadian capitalism and its dominant class? An alternative to the dependentist interpretation can be derived from Marx's account of capitalist development. Marx shows how the accumulation of capital under competitive conditions leads to the development of huge concentrations of capital and to the emergence of a credit system whose function in the accumulation process expands as the scale of production is enlarged.

It is in the light of Marx's analysis that Hilferding's, Bukharin's, and Lenin's observations on modern capitalism should be viewed. The concentration and centralization of capital into relatively few giant enterprises and the increasing importance of financial capital in industrial accumulation are inherent tendencies that culminated around the turn of the century with the emergence of "finance capital." A symbiotic relationship arose at that time between large industrial enterprises and major financial institutions. It was a relationship manifested in financial, directorship, familial, and other inter-capitalist ties. This "merging" of the most dominant financial and industrial interests in the advanced economies created within each society a "financial-industrial elite," whose interests and activities took in much of the total social capital, in both its productive and circulating forms.

To the extent that large-scale capital exists in Canada in an advanced and relatively independent state (that is, as an indigenous finance capital), we should be able to discern a financial-industrial elite of Canadian capitalists, controlling large industrial and financial concerns. Likewise, to the extent that such an indigenous fraction can be shown to dominate the Canadian economy, the thesis of Canadian dependency, with its pivotal assumption about the commercial character of the Canadian bourgeoisie, must be considered empirically dubious. At the close of this chapter the development of finance capital in Canada is traced, and in the chapters that follow, the concepts of finance capital and a financial-industrial elite are applied to Canada in the post-Second World War period.

MARX'S ANALYSIS

Writing in the era of "classical" or "competitive" capitalism—after the industrial revolution and before the emergence of monopoly capital—and in the country where capitalist production was most developed—Britain—Marx was able to identify both the historical prerequisites of capitalism (1967, I, pp.714, 750ff) and its trajectory toward monopoly form (ibid., 624–26; 1967, III, pp.435–41, 544–45).[1]

At its most abstract level, the latter is implicit in the tendency for capital to be continually reproduced on an expanded scale. Capitalism is defined not merely in terms of its principal contradiction between dominant and subordinate classes, but by the peculiar, market-mediated conflict that characterizes economic relations among members of the dominant class: by intercapitalist competition. The surplus value appropriated in production by each capitalist is only realized as profit when the capitalist's commodities find buyers on the market. Competition for purchasers induces each capitalist to maximize the rate of profit by cheapening costs of production. In the long run, each capitalist's accumulation rests on continual improvements in the productivity of labour, accomplished by improving the efficiency and the sophistication of production. Thus, the battle between capitalists for maximal profits is waged chiefly through reinvesting profits in expanding, retooling, and revolutionizing the means of production.

This process of accumulation culminated in the nineteenth century with the development of "modern industry," characterized in a technical sense by large-scale production units, complex division of labour, and sophisticated machinery (Marx 1967, I, pp.371–507). Two especially important tendencies in the accumulation of capital promoted the rise of "modern industry" and the emergence of monopoly capital. · Marx calls these "concentration" and "centralization" of capital. Concentration is a direct result of reinvestment of profits, which increases the mass of wealth controlled by individual capitalists, "and thereby widens the basis of production on a large scale and of the specific methods of capitalist production" (ibid., 624–25). Centralization, in contrast, is a violent form of competition between capitalists (Aglietta

1979, 219), in which capitals lose their independent existence and are merged into fewer and larger concerns, with the vanquished capitalists being expropriated by the victorious ones (Marx 1967, I, pp.625–26).

It is not at all by coincidence that a sophisticated credit system emerged with the concentration and centralization of industrial capital. The profound relation between these developments further underlines the lack of fundamental conflict between industrial and financial forms of capital. Prior to development of modern industry and of the credit system, individual capitalists were required to self-finance their accumulation. Surplus value was hoarded as "latent money capital" until it attained a size sufficient to enable purchase of additional elements of productive capital, that is, new means of production and labour power (ibid., pp.78, 492).[2] As the concentration of capital pressed more forcefully against the limitations of this system (ibid., 492), the latent money-capital of individual capitalists became centralized in banks and related financial institutions as loan capital, and made generally available to capitalists in need of financing. With this transformation of scattered hoards into concentrations of interest-bearing capital, the modern credit system was born (ibid., 493).

The subsequent development of this system was necessitated by the changing composition and further concentration of industrial capital. Increasingly sophisticated technologies, introduced to increase productivity and expand surplus value, had the effect of converting "what was formerly variable capital, invested in labour power, into machinery which, being constant capital, does not produce surplus value" (Marx 1967, I, p.407). This shifting composition of capital had important implications for the financing of capitalist enterprise. As industrial capital accumulates, each capitalist's production depends on the ability to purchase greater quantities of the means of production from other capitalists. These outlays increasingly assume the form of fixed capital, such as labour-saving tools and machinery (ibid., II, pp.234–35). Much of the impetus for the credit system thus stemmed from the need to finance these purchases.

There is, then, a symbiotic relation between accumulation of industrial capital and expansion of credit. Capitalist development leads to enormous concentrations of *both* industrial and financial capital. Because of their central location *vis-à-vis* the industrial and commercial circuits comprising capitalist economy, the banks take on an important function as "representatives of social capital" (ibid., III, p.368) or "general managers of money-capital" (ibid., 402). Marx foresaw an increasingly powerful role for the banks, with the further concentration of financial capital and its application to industry and commerce. For example, he suggested that with the development of bank credit, "the banker, who receives the money as a loan from one group of the reproductive capitalists [that is, industrialists and merchants], lends it to another group of reproductive capitalists, so that the banker appears in the role of a supreme benefactor; and at the same time, the control over this capital falls completely into the hands of the banker in his capacity as middleman" (ibid., 506).

But the modern credit system extends beyond concentrations of money-capital in banks. An important complement to bank credit is the formation of joint-stock companies. These limited-liability corporations enable enormous expansion of the scale of production by combining the money capital of several capitalists into the "social capital" of directly associated stockholders (ibid., 436). In this way the corporation further centralizes money capital in the form of corporate shares and channels that capital directly into large-scale production. In turn, the corporate form of organization is well suited to even greater centralization, through transfers of shares on the stock exchange (ibid., 440).

In the concentration and centralization of capital and in the development of the credit system, Marx saw a deepening of the basic contradiction between socialized production and private ownership of the means of production. The growth of banks as "general managers" of money-capital, and the emergence of corporations as loci of the "social capital" of directly associated capitalists do effect an enhanced socialization of production, but that production remains firmly under control of the private owners of banks and corporations and, thus, still "ensnared in the trammels of capitalism" (ibid.).

THE THEORY OF MONOPOLY CAPITALISM

As Mandel (1968, 394) notes, a strong stimulant to further concentration and centralization of industrial capital was provided by the second industrial revolution at the end of the nineteenth century. The first industrial revolution had been based on steam power, cotton, and coal and had spurred development of capitalist production in Europe and North America. The second would be based on technological advances in production of metals, chemicals and energy; it would see the emergence of whole new industries such as automobile production. This revolution would ultimately become one of the forces behind the development of monopoly capital. Concomitantly, the crises of 1873 and 1900 increased the pace of capital centralization, as smaller, often bankrupt businesses were acquired at discount prices by the emerging industrial giants (Jeidels 1905, 108).

The huge enterprises born at this time held the possibility of co-operation and co-ordination among small groups of ostensibly competing capitalists. Their very size provided a strong motivation toward such practices, as the largest firms "found themselves confronted with risks which had increased in the same proportion as their business had expanded" (Mandel, 1968, 398). To prevent any steep decline in prices and profits, and to ensure rapid and regular depreciation of the great amounts of fixed capital they owned, major capitalists reached agreements to restrict price competition. These arrangements took, and continue to take, a variety of forms: informal "gentlemen's agreements," price regulating associations, pools, cartels, trusts, and so on (ibid., 401–3).

In 1917, Lenin, who examined the development of monopolies in Germany and the United States, concluded that:

> ...at a certain stage of its development concentration itself, as it were, leads straight to monopoly, for a score or so giant enterprises can easily arrive at an agreement, and on the other hand, the hindrance to competition, the tendency towards monopoly, arises from the huge size of the enterprises. This transformation of competition into monopoly is one of the most important—if not the most important—phenomena of modern capitalist economy....(1970, 680; see also Bukharin 1973, 65–70).

The same process of concentration and monopolization characterized the banking sector (Lenin 1970, 698), which also became dominated by a very few large concerns. Thus, around the turn of the century, in the capitalist countries where the productive forces were most developed and capital most concentrated (Bukharin 1973, 65), monopoly organizations emerged, controlling large proportions of the total social capital.

Lenin and Bukharin draw critically on the arguments of Hilferding (1923) and Hobson (1965) in pursuing the epoch-making implications of monopoly capitalism. Their central insights concern the form that monopoly capital takes, that of "finance capital" and its tendency to accumulate on a world scale through the export of capital. These characteristics, the essence of modern imperialism, intensify capitalism's contradictions, by producing (1) inter-imperialist rivalries among leading capitalist powers over spheres of investment and influence and shares of the world market, and (2) the most extreme forms of exploitation and national oppression in the colonies and semi-colonies, which call forth anti-imperialist movements of national liberation.

This theory of monopoly capitalism and modern imperialism presents a clear alternative to dependency analysis, both in terms of its model of accumulation and its conception of the international system (Weeks 1981, 118). It incorporates Marx's model of accumulation as the extended reproduction of a capital-labour relation. Capitalist accumulation occurs as both an exploitative and a competitive process which compels individual capitalists to concentrate and centralize their capital while they develop the productive forces of society. Capital also expands in a spatial sense, first in the form of trade but later as the export of money capital and productive capital. This theory, then,

> converts its theory of accumulation into a theory of the world economy by locating it explicitly in the context of *countries*. What makes a political territory a "country" is that the territory is controlled by a distinct ruling classes the vehicle for such rule being the state. Materialists identify their theory of the world economy as "the theory of imperialism," which can be defined as the theory of the accumulation of capital in the context of the struggle among ruling classes (ibid., 121).

Apart from the capital-labour relation itself, the focus here is not on bilateral relations between "metropolis" and "satellite". Rather, it is on the process of accumulation and the relations it engenders *among* capitalist ruling classes (inter-imperialist rivalry/co-operation), *between* advanced capitalist ruling classes and ruling classes in backward countries (the articulation of modes of production) and *between* ruling classes and oppressed peoples (national oppression/liberation; [ibid., 121–22; see also Brewer 1980, 80; Howe and Sica 1980, 241]).

For present purposes, consider what the theory asserts about the *form* in which capital is organized in the advanced societies, and the implications of this for the structure of the Canadian bourgeoisie. According to Hilferding, the most obvious outcome of accumulation—concentration of enormous amounts of capital in industrial corporations and banks—creates a "community of interests" between directors of the largest banks, who control much of the available money-capital, and the directors of the largest corporations, who require great quantities of money-capital to finance the expansion of their industrial capital (Hilferding 1981).

Hilferding's analysis is based primarily on the example of Germany, where a tightly cartelized banking sector directly controlled leading industrial enterprises through stock ownership (see, for example, Hussein 1976; Thompson 1977; Noisi 1978). The German economy actually exemplifies one particular form of finance capital: bank control of industry. More generally, finance capital comprises "the merging or coalescence of the banks with industry" (Lenin 1970, 704), a consolidation of leading financial and industrial interests.

This coalescence is manifested in a number of ways. Certainly the principal material element is the banks' financing of industrial and commercial enterprise, through issuing loans, buying stocks and bonds and directly promoting corporations (Bukharin 1973, 71). Another typical form noted by Lenin (1970, 706) is the "holding system," which enables finance capitalists to control a range of individual companies by owning a small minority of the total share capital. But a key sociological aspect of finance capital is the "special form of higher management" in which "the representatives of the industrialists manage the banks, and vice versa" (Bukharin, 1973, 72). In the era of monopoly capital:

> There is formed a circle of persons who, thanks to their own possession of capital or as representatives of concentrated power over other people's capital (bank directors), sit upon the governing boards of a large number of corporations. There thus arises a kind of personal union, on the one hand between the different corporations themselves, on the other between the latter and the banks, a circumstance which must be of the greatest importance for the policy of these institutions since among them there has arisen a community of interests (Hilferding 1923, quoted in Sweezy 1970, 261).

The development of finance capital therefore brings with it the domination of a financial-industrial elite (Lenin 1970, 704),[3] composed of leading bankers and industrialists, whose interests, investments, and corporate positions interpenetrate extensively. With the formation of this elite, the concentration of capital reaches enormous proportions, as "a small number of financially 'powerful' states stand out among all the rest" (ibid., 714).

The fraction of finance capital in these powerful states, of which Lenin distinguished four in 1917,[4] accumulates an enormous "surplus of capital" which is exported abroad to the most profitable outlets, initially as financial capital in the form of loans and corporate shares (portfolio and direct investments), more recently as productive capital (the internationalization of the production process itself [Palloix 1977; Cypher 1979a; see also Bukharin 1973]).

The reasons for this capital export include both opportunities and exigencies that emerge as capital becomes monopolized. On the one hand, the development of finance capital breaks down institutional barriers to international capital mobility. The corporate form of organization and the close links between industrial and financial capital allow foreign subsidiaries to be established and financed without the capitalist having to migrate. On the other hand, protective tariffs erected by other capitalist states discourage the expansion of domestic production for export while encouraging establishment of branch plants behind tariff walls (Hilferding, 1981), a significant fact in the Canadian case (Naylor 1975; Clement 1977). Also, monopolized price structures in the domestic economy can usually only be maintained through reinvestment of profits in nonmonopolized sectors, where there is no danger of eroding monopoly positions through overproduction in the home market (Szymanski 1981, 38; Bukharin 1973, 122–23). Thus, a portion of the surplus value produced within large domestic enterprises is capitalized elsewhere. The low wages and rent on land in less developed countries and colonies serve as a strong magnet for investment as capital becomes fully internationalized (Lenin 1970, 715).

All these constraints and opportunities give rise to an "international network of dependence on and connections of finance capital" (ibid.), in which national monopoly fractions jostle for spheres of investment and shares of the world market. In the process of competing for profits on an international scale, monopoly capitalists internationalize their investments. By exporting capital they also "export" capitalist relations and forces of production to each other's home markets and to the developing periphery.

The accompanying development process, however, is not one of harmonious modernization. Rather,

> the inherent contradictions of capitalism are now expressed in terms of an ever more dramatic uneven development of capitalism and a radical re-structuring of class relations. A dominant financial oligarchy backed by "financially powerful states" buys labour peace in the 'core' countries by encouraging the formation of a "labour aristocracy," while the rest of the world is driven deeper and deeper into states of dependency, subservience and rebellion. Competition within the financial oligarchy and between the financially powerful states is heightened rather than diminished. The end result: inter-imperialist rivalries and wars (Harvey 1982, 289).

Put in this frame of reference, the question of Canada's (or any country's) location in world economy hinges significantly on whether its bourgeoisie is headed by an independent fraction of finance capital: a financial-industrial elite that controls a large proportion of the total social capital and that accumulates its capital both within the home market and internationally. The burden of this study is to demonstrate the development and consolidation of such a fraction in Canada.

Further Development of the Concept of Finance Capital

Elaboration of the concept of finance capital as a tool in the study of advanced capitalism has proceeded in step with the further development of monopoly capital itself. We may distinguish two streams of contributions after the work of Hilferding, Bukharin and Lenin: (1) a longstanding empirical tradition, examining the concrete means through which large-scale industrial and financial capitals are articulated into "financial groups" or "interest groups" in the advanced capitalist economies; and (2) a more recent set of theoretical contributions. It is of use to review this literature, considering first the recent theoretical advances and then some empirical studies.

A diagrammatic representation of finance capital as "an articulated combination of commercial capital, industrial capital, and banking capital" is given by Thompson (1977, 247) and is shown here as Figure 3.1. On this abstract level of the production and circulation of surplus value, finance capital appears as the integration of the three primary circuits of industrial, interest-bearing, and merchant capital, described in Chapter 2. With Thompson, we can work our way through this circuit from left to right,

noting that diagonally arrowed lines represent "exchanges" of money or commodities between the constituent circuits. Hence, money capital is lent to the industrial capitalist (M[B] → M[I]) which, after passing through the cycle of production appears in the form of commodities with an enhanced value (C'[I]). Given that commercial capital (as well as banking capital) exists as a separated circuit, taking the form of a specialized trading activity, commodities C'[I] are purchased by the commercial capital with M[C] money. This M[C] money "realizes" the circuit of industrial capital (C'[I] → M'[I]). The merchant capital's capital now takes the form of commodities, which it sells to realize its capital in the form of M'[C]. Commodities now drop out of the immediate circuit as money (M), enters it. These commodities could either now enter

Figure 3.1
The Formal Circuit of Finance Capital*

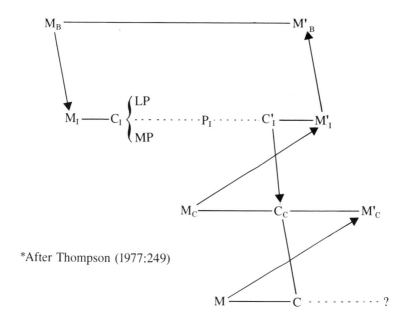

*After Thompson (1977:249)

another productive cycle in the form of means of production (exchanges from Department I) or they could enter a consumption cycle, thus dropping completely out of the circuits, as commodities (exchanges from Department II) (ibid., 248–49).

In this light, finance capital appears as the "highest form" of capital, in which huge concentrations of capital are fully articulated into circuits of production and circulation that push capital's self-expansive character to the limit, in terms of the financing of enlarged production and the realization of surplus value.

The specific institutional expression of finance capital depends on historical circumstances. External financing of industrial production, for instance, may occur in three main ways, through issue of shares, through issue of loan capital (bonds and debentures), and through bank loans (ibid., 250). Athar Hussein (1976), in his essay on Hilferding's *Finance Capital*, makes a similar observation. In some economies, such as Germany, the centralization of financial capital under control of a few large financial institutions has given them a key role in the financing of means of production and hence in the overall accumulation process; in others, like Britain, the market for financial assets—the stock exchange—has been of paramount importance, and formal "merging" of bank and industrial capital may be less evident.

Thompson's and Hussein's discussions of finance capital provide insights at an abstract level. It is equally important, however, to specify the concrete historical conditions under which the articulation of circuits of capital occurs:

> By finance capital we mean the integration of the circuits of money capital, productive capital and commodity capital under the conditions of monopolization and internationalization of capital by means of a series of links and relationships between individual capitals.
>
> The integration of these circuits takes on a durable structural character which is expressed in a network of relations between individual capitals, into which state organizations are incorporated to the extent that state intervention in the economy is developed (Overbeek 1980, 102).

A shortcoming in the abstract analysis of finance capital is its somewhat limited notion of accumulation, resulting from microeconomic analysis of existing capital circuits. The crucial role of finance capital in *reorganizing* and centralizing capital is emphasized by Michel Aglietta, who holds that centralized control of capital can be established only through creation of new structural forms, chiefly the giant corporation and the financial group (1979, 220). Centralization operates "by way of massive transfers in the sphere of financial circulation" (ibid., 225). Consequently, it requires financial institutions controlling large amounts of money-capital. Indeed, the role of investment bankers, in ushering in the era of monopoly capital by merging many small companies into giant corporations, is well documented in both the United States (Kotz 1978, 31ff) and Canada (Niosi 1978, 48–60; 1981, 26–28).

At issue in the centralization of capital is control over productive property itself, which is achieved in the modern era by ownership of money capital in one form or another, typically that of corporate shares. For this reason, financial centralization is the dominant characteristic of capital centralization. When the valorization of productive capital in industrial enterprises can no longer occur without the formation of vast associations that hold money capital and convert wage-earners' savings into money capital, ownership is formally partitioned into rights represented by share titles, and its unity takes the legal form of the joint-stock company. This is why the question of the capitalist power of disposal over production takes the form of the control over property exercised in the enterprise by coalitions of capitalists who wield the weapon of financial centralization to their own advantage. The name finance capital is properly given to the mediation by which coalitions of capitalists exercise proprietary control over the structural forms necessary for the continuing cycles of valorization of productive capital, thanks to the centralized money capital at their disposal. Finance capital is no abstraction. It takes concrete forms in *financial groups* which are systems of interrelation effecting the cohesion of finance capital (Aglietta 1979, 252–53).

Financial groups are the supra-corporate units in which monopoly capital is organized. In class terms they comprise coalitions of capitalists whose ownership of money capital, most often in the form of shares, affords them effective control over inter-related circuits of finance capital. In institutional terms, financial groups comprise the financial, industrial and commercial firms through which control is wielded and in which accumulation actually occurs. These capitalist alliances may be loose and are not immune to restructuring. Often the structure of control is ambiguous, in which case the group's *raison d'être* devolves to a co-ordination of accumulation based on a certain community of interests (Menshikov 1969, 202; Overbeek 1980, 103). Nevertheless,

> the same structure is discovered to exist in the majority of the capitalist countries: a handful of financial groups possessing control over a large proportion of industrial and financial activity; some 60, 125 or 200 families placed at the apex of the social pyramid, who wield their power sometimes as individuals but often as a more or less compact collective group (Mandel 1968, 411).

Capitalists and the companies they control are united into financial groups by virtue of financial, institutional, familial, service, and informal ties. To some extent all these relations are evident in advanced capitalist countries, but "due to specific historical and legal conditions in different countries, different types of relations have been particularly prominent'' (Overbeek 1980, 102–3). Certainly the single most power-ful basis for coalescence of capitals into a financial group is a *financial relation,* which may appear in two forms: the intertwining of share capital and longstanding financial ties (Menshikov 1969, 158–83). The first of these involves ownership by financial institutions of the stock of industrial firms, or vice versa, or simultaneous ownership of both com-panies' stock by third persons or institutions. The second includes own-ership of bonds, a bank's granting of term loans or its underwriting of securities. Concentrated ownership of corporate bonds by financial in-stitutions such as banks and life insurance companies is a particularly important form of the circuit of finance capital. These longterm credits often involve specific agreements such as release of the company's right to pay dividends if it falls into financial difficulty (ibid., 175; see also Aaronovitch 1961, 38–42; Jalee 1972, 126).[5]

After financial relations, the most important means of integration is the interlocking of corporate directorships. Just as financial ties effect an interpenetration of capitals, overlaps in directorships create an ''interpenetration of capitalists,'' thus permitting direct intercorporate co-ordination of accumulation. The two relations complement each other and often occur together, so much so that Menshikov, in his study of finance capital in the United States, asserts that ''personal union, i.e., the personal representation of bankers in industrial corporations and vice versa, is a result of the intertwining of the capital of banks and industries and also of their long-standing financial ties'' (1969, 184). While this claim probably overstates the case, the pattern of directorate interlocking among large corporations in a number of advanced capitalist economies is strikingly consistent with the hypothesis that many interlocks function as institutional arrangements for the combined management of financial and industrial capital. Fennema and Schijf, in their comprehensive review of research on interlocking directorates, summarize the observed pattern as follows:

> In all cases financial institutions, banks, and insurance companies have central positions in the network of interlocking directorates. Another very general result is that in all studies so far almost all the companies are directly or indirectly connected with each other (1979, 327).

Most large capitalist enterprises are integrated into national networks of interlocking directorates, and financial institutions play a leading role in that integration. What is less clear, however, is the extent to which these intercorporate networks are easily divisible into functioning financial or interest groups. The well-researched case of the American network presents a useful example. Although a number of studies of the financial, institutional, and familial relations that connect large American corporations have found evidence of the bank-centred capitalist interest groups (first discerned by Paul Sweezy [1939]; see also Perlo 1957; Menshikov 1969; Levine 1972; Knowles 1973; Sonquist and Koenig 1975; Pastre 1981), other findings question the extent to which neat boundaries can be drawn around groups of interlocked industrial and financial companies.

Interest Groups and Forms of Financial Power

In his study of the American transformation to a full-fledged corporate economy between 1886 and 1905, Roy reports that banks and finance capitalists played an increasingly integrative role in a network that was, from its inception, characterized *not* by equally central clusters but by a singular dimension of *centrality* (1983, 256).[6] According to Mizruchi (1982), by 1904 the American network was dominated by the financial empire of J.P. Morgan, but competing interest groups are not structurally discernible from the pattern of corporate interlocking. Rather, Mizruchi's study of the network from 1904 to 1974 reveals several small cliques of densely connected firms, with most companies on the borders or between multiple cliques. These findings prompt the conclusion that "the concept of separate, specific interest groups is not very relevant for understanding the American corporate system" (1982, 174). This verdict is shared by Mintz and Schwartz (1981a, b), whose analysis of the network of U.S. corporations in the 1960's places financial institutions—especially banks—at the centre, with major industrial firms positioned as bridges connecting the financial hubs of the system. This pattern contradicts the notion of bank-centred financial groups but is consistent with "a modified finance capital theory which locates the importance of banks and insurance companies in their domination of capital flows and not in discrete spheres of influence" (1981a, 866).

The importance of these flows is evident in case studies of American banks and corporations. Ratcliff's (1980) analysis of the lending practices of seventy-seven banks in St. Louis demonstrates a strong tendency for banks closely interlocked with large corporations to be most engaged in lending to capitalist (as opposed to state or residential) borrowers. Thus, partially underlying the network of interlocks is the flow of loan capital and interest between banks and corporations. The *allocative* power of financial instutions to gather surplus capital from various sources and redistribute it among capitalists in need of money capital is illustrated in Glasberg's study of Leasco Corporation's bid to take over the Chemical Bank in 1969. The attempt was opposed not only by Chemical's management but by a host of allied financial institutions, which unloaded their substantial institutional holdings in Leasco, causing the price of the company's stock to plummet and thereby eliminating the economic basis for the takeover bid (1981, 102). Power, in this case, was exercised not through the voting of stock to determine corporate management but through the disposal of stock onto the financial market.

Allocative power is the characteristic form in which large financial institutions exert influence over productive capitalist and other economic agents, including the state. As industrial capital has become further concentrated, the financing needs of the largest U.S. corporations have outgrown the capacities of individual banks. Financial institutions have thus moved away from single-handed financial relations with corporations, toward a system of "collective bank control" (Gogel and Koenig 1981). Simultaneously, in the American case, a structure of reciprocal share ownership has developed among the largest banks, so that the major shareholders in any one are typically other large banks (Eitzen, Purdy and Jung 1985, 46). Hence, large financial institutions act increasingly as a group, allocating loan capital to major industrial corporations and collectively setting guidelines for corporate decisions through their interlocked directors (Mizruchi 1982, 181; see also Menshikov 1969, 218).

The power of finance capital in its allocative form, however, ought not to be overestimated. Ultimately, the forces of supply and demand for interest-bearing capital drive the interest rate toward an equilibrium position defined in terms of sustained accumulation:

> An imbalance in the power relation between industry and finance will force departure from equilibrium and so threaten accumulation. From this it follows that the survival of capitalism depends upon the achievement of some kind of proper balance of power between industrial and financial interests. This...suggests that the power of finance capital...is necessarily a constrained power, and can never be unlimited or totally hegemonic (Harvey 1982, 299).

There is, moreover, a second form of financial power which complements and may even counterbalance the allocative power of financial institutions. This is the *operational* power to directly control the management of several corporations by owning decisive blocs of share capital. As Hussein (1976, 12) points out, corporate shares constitute a peculiar type of financial capital in which the stock market "combines individual loans in an unending sequence: the loan itself is never paid back but an individual shareholder can recover his capital by selling the share." Furthermore, unlike bank loans and bonds, share ownership entitles the holder to a vote in determining the corporation's board of directors. Capitalists who are able to accumulate concentrated shareholdings, often through investment companies, can build financial empires around the operational power that accrues to them as major shareowners, although they may remain dependent on the allocative power of financial institutions for financing key share purchases (Pastre 1981, 115–129).

An important and largely unresolved question is the manner in which allocative and operational forms of financial power are distributed and articulated within the structure of contemporary monopoly capital.[7] The absence of discrete, bank-centred financial groups in the American network, for instance, does not necessarily preclude the existence of capitalist interest groups organized around the operational power of concentrated share ownership. Our examination of corporate interlocking in Canada will attempt to shed light on this issue, among others.

THE DEVELOPMENT OF FINANCE CAPITAL IN CANADA

The theory of imperialism and monopoly capital is important for analyzing the development of capitalism in Canada. Contrary to the dependency theory, quite a number of studies provide evidence of the emergence of closely articulated financial and industrial interests around some of the country's largest capitals in the late 1800's, and of the further elaboration of indigenously controlled finance capital in the decades since. To focus attention on the history of Canadian finance capital is not to deny the significant role of foreign (mainly American) interests in the history of Canadian capitalism, since the establishment of the first branch plants in the 1870's (Bliss 1970, 30–34; Naylor 1975, II, pp.71–73). The place of foreign investment in Canadian capitalist development will be discussed in the last chapter. In charting the course of indigenous finance capital, it will be demonstrated that the growth of foreign investment proceeded not in alliance with a commercial Canadian business elite but in conjunction with the emergence of a financial-industrial capitalist elite.

Preconditions of the Formation of Finance Capital in Canada

Nineteenth-century Canada may be roughly divided into two eras of capitalist development. The early and middle decades comprise the formative period of classical "industrial capitalism." It was in these years that the basis was laid for the emergence of finance capital, which began in the final two decades, with the formation of industrial combinations and the close interpenetration of railway and banking interests.

The first period was one in which the capitalist mode of production took root in Canada, based on both economic and political premises.[8] Its political origins involved the attainment of political autonomy, first with responsible government in 1849 and ultimately with Confederation in 1867. Its economic premises were: (1) production of a reliable agricultural surplus, a prerequisite for capitalist division of labour; (2) formation, mainly through immigration, of a class of propertyless wage-workers; (3) growth of small-scale manufactories in the emerging cities and towns; and thus (4) formation of an integrated home market wherein commodities could circulate with some facility, satisfying the needs of the population while enabling the continuous renewal of various industrial and commercial circuits. Creation of a modern transportation system, especially the railways, themselves industrial investments, spurred all of these developments. In the process, they served as a crucial impetus to concentration of capital in urban centres and in fewer hands (Pentland 1981; Ryerson 1973; Kealey 1982; Palmer 1983, 9–12, 60–66).

In the same period, financial intermediaries emerged. The first chartered bank appeared in 1817, the first life insurance company in 1847, and the first mortgage loan company in 1855. Banks chartered in the early decades of the century were formed by prominent merchants to relieve the chronic shortage of currency and to carry on the business of merchant banking (Neufeld 1972, 71–76). By mid-century, however, sufficient industrial capital had accumulated that several of the newly chartered banks were established and directed by industrial interests.[9] By 1867, there were 33 chartered banks with 123 branches, whose assets accounted for 78 per cent of all financial capital. The remainder of the capital was distributed among 28 building societies, 6 savings banks, 1 large life insurer, 30 fire insurers, and the state. In all, the assets of these financial intermediaries equalled one-third of the Gross National Product (GNP) in 1867 (Neufeld 1972, 43–44). By the later decades of the nineteenth century then, a basis for the development of a dominant fraction of finance capital had been laid in both the accumulation of industrial capital and the emergence of a credit system.

The Development of Canadian Finance Capital

The period from the 1870's to 1910 was one of very rapid growth for financial capital, as new forms of financial intermediaries emerged, such as trust companies, trusteed pension plans, and specialized bond dealers. As well, the assets of banks and especially life insurance companies grew rapidly, and stock exchanges expanded their corporate share listings and volumes (Neufeld 1972, 47–49, 55, 495). The same period brought tremendous concentration and centralization of industrial capital, first in the railway sector, and later in manufacturing, mining, and electric utilities.

In this era of the National Policy, "Canadian private venture capital flowed freely from railway enterprises into the financial sector and into manufacturing industries, including those supplying steel and rolling stock to the railway, fertilizer and farm equipment to the Western farmer" (Levitt 1970, 51–52; see also Drummond 1962, 222). With the diversified accumulation of capital came the full development of a national bourgeoisie in control of the expanding domestic market. The Canadian state facilitated this development in various ways, most tangibly with its protective tariff, designed to encourage industrial production at home by discouraging the importation of commodities. In general, the national bourgeoisie — the industrialists, bankers, railway barons and merchants — were

> either directly dependent on the success of the National Policy or indifferent to it. The pulp and paper and mining industries could exist in the absence of industrial Canada: the Canadian Pacific Railway and Bank of Montreal could not. Industrialists in general considered the profitability and vitality of manufacturing activity to be critical to Canada's future, whether or not they were themselves directly involved in manufacturing activity. And critical to the profitability and vitality of manufacturing, in their view, was the protective tariff (Craven and Traves 1979, 15; see also Kealey 1982).

Concurrent with the rapid growth of a domestic manufacturing sector, the later decades of the nineteenth century were marked by another very significant development in the structure of Canadian capital: the coalescence of the railways and chartered banks, which were the major industrial monopolies and financial institutions of the day. In this period manufacturing was not yet centralized into giant corporations but was organized as small- and medium-sized individual proprietorships and partnerships, whose needs for fixed-capital financing could be satisfied internally (Canada 1937, 14; MacDonald 1975, 270). Quite the opposite applied to the railways, which represented capital-intensive industry *par excellence*. Much of the capital required for railway financing was raised on the money-markets of London, with the federal government often serving as a benign "financial intermediary," granting enormous sums to the railway companies and issuing state bonds that were in turn heavily subscribed by London investors. But part of railway financing was provided by the domestic credit system, revolving around the big chartered banks. A tightly knit community of interests arose between leading bankers and railway capitalists (who quite often were the very same people, such as Peter McGill and Donald Smith) [Ryerson 1973, 270]).

Certainly the most momentous coalescence of bank and railway capital occurred with the incorporation of the Canadian Pacific Railway Company:

> founded in 1881 with very concentrated capital: nine shareholders held 79 percent of the initial offering of shares. Among them were George Stephen, Richard B. Angus and Donald Smith (Lord Strathcona) of the Bank of Montreal, all of whom remained for many years on the railway company's board of directors. Later, they were to bring other directors to the company from the bank, but also from Stelco, Royal Trust and Sun Life. The founding directors bought a major portion of subsequent stock offerings (Niosi 1978, 87).

The close financial and directorate relations between the Bank of Montreal and the Canadian Pacific Railway were to form an axis for the country's major financial group, a cluster of corporations that thereafter comprised the bedrock of Canadian finance capital (see Ashley 1957; Johnson 1972; Chodos 1973; Park and Park 1973).

As Anderson points out, the creation of the CPR furnishes an important example of how "Canadian capitalists and the Canadian state...responded entirely rationally to opportunities afforded by the latest developments in the logic of the reproduction of capital" (1985, 126). The enormous financial needs of such an undertaking required that financial capital be mobilized on an international basis. While the CPR would be effectively controlled by Canadian capitalists (Chodos 1973; Niosi 1978), its 1881 charter allowed for a capital structure that included a large bloc of shares owned by American, British, Dutch, French, and German banking houses, many of which were also represented on the

CPR board of directors (Anderson 1985, 123–124).

Following on the heels of the financing of the transcontinental railway came the first thrusts toward centralization of manufacturing capital: the combination movements of the 1880's and 1890's. In these decades, competing manufacturers and wholesalers transcended their differences and formed associations—at first "gentlemen's agreements," later to be formalized as output pools and price-fixing cartels—with the aim of maximizing their profits as associated capitalists. Three economic conditions lay behind this flight from competition. The National Policy spurred development in trade, transport and industry, creating in an integrated home market the objective basis for inter-capitalist co-ordination of the accumulation process. By the same token, the protective tariff introduced an element of extra-market price regulation and encouraged domestic capitalists to maximize their profits by setting prices just below those of imports. Finally, the crisis of 1882–86 drastically reduced sales and profits, intensifying price competition and eliminating weaker firms. The stronger capitalists emerged from the crisis with a conviction that cut-throat competition was wasteful, to say nothing of dangerous.They resolved that a more rational system of regulated prices and output should take its place (McLennan 1929, 8ff; see also Bliss 1974, 33–54). Hence, for example:

> By 1898 output pools were formed in the manufacturing and distributing of iron and steel goods and took the form of "income and profits" pools. A definite proportion of production was allocated to each firm and each member was required to pay from 15 to 25 percent of the value of his excess sales to the organization (McLennan 1929, 23).

The closing years of the nineteenth century and the early years of the twentieth also witnessed the emergence of large manufacturing corporations, as numerous small firms amalgamated, particularly in the cotton and steel industries. So it was that "By 1907, Canada was already dominated by a few large corporations. The CPR, Bank of Montreal, and so on were already dominant in the economic situation in Canada....Cross-directorships were already common among the larger corporations" (De Grass 1977, 88).

The concrete manifestation of finance capital in financial groups was not limited to the Bank of Montreal-Canadian Pacific interests, however powerful that combination may have been. In Toronto, concentration of finance and industry produced a similar network of corporations which in 1906 included George A. Cox's Canada Life Assurance, the Canadian Bank of Commerce, National Trust Company, Imperial Life, Dominion Securities, Dominion Iron and Steel, Canadian General Electric, and Mackenzie Mann and Company (Drummond 1962, 211).

Between 1908 and 1913, there was a consolidation of this nascent monopoly fraction, as an intense merger movement centralized industrial capital into many of the corporations (or their predecessors) that presently dominate the Canadian economy. In this period there were 52 important mergers absorbing 229 firms (McLennan 1929, 41). Bank capital also centralized as the number of chartered banks fell from 34 in 1907 to 22 in 1914 (De Grass 1977, 111). Mergers in the steel industry, an essential sector in the development of advanced capitalism, were especially noteworthy. Both vertical and horizontal amalgamations produced a highly centralized and rationalized industry, with "considerable interlocking directorates and communities of interest...between the iron and steel industries, banks and transportation companies" (McLennan 1929, 47).

De Grass's (1977, 115) study of the forty-four men who in 1910 controlled "the main banks, railways, steamship lines, manufacturing plants, insurance companies, stock brokerages, and mining companies in the country" gives a convincing account of the leading role this financial-industrial elite played in centralizing capital under its control. Many of the mergers in this period listed by Stapells (1927) directly involved members of this elite, who then took up positions on the boards of the merged companies (DeGrass 1977, 115–23). The same capitalists, led by Senator George A. Cox, were principals of the Electric Development Company syndicate, which brought large-scale hydroelectricity to the industrial heartland of southern Ontario.[10] Individual members of this elite were highly integrated by means of interlocking directorships: the 44 capitalists held 616 directorships in 1910, 387 of them on boards manned by other members of the same elite group. Furthermore, 36 held directorships in both financial and mining or manufacturing companies, and another 4 interlocked with financial and transportation companies. Indeed, only one of the country's leading corporate directors in this period fits Naylor's "commercial bourgeoisie" stereotype, with directorships in financial and merchandizing firms only (ibid., 116, 131; see also MacDonald 1975, 274–75). Similarly, a majority of the 164 members of the Toronto economic elite of the 1920's, studied by Richardson (1982, 287), had directorship ties to *both* industrial and commercial sectors.

By the second decade of this century, then, an advanced form of capitalist production, circulation, and finance was in place in Canada. At the apex of this bloc of finance capital was a small elite of Canadian capitalists whose interlocking interests and corporate positions effectively fused big industry with high finance.

The ensuing decades witnessed both the preservation of this bloc of finance capital and its elaboration in several ways. An indigenous capital market dominated by a few large investment banks arose with the closing of the London financial market during the First World War: although between 1904 and 1914 only 18 per cent of Canadian bond issues were floated in Canada, by 1915–20 the proportion had risen to 67 per cent. The major investment banks that underwrote these issues—Wood Gundy and Nesbitt Thomson in particular—invested their profits in industrial sectors, in many cases establishing positions of control in leading firms such as Massey-Harris, Consolidated Paper, and much of the hydro-electric industry (Niosi 1981, 26–28).

In the same period, intertwining of share capital was institutionalized in the form of investment companies such as Power Corporation, itself controlled by Nesbitt-Thomson. Through these holding companies, Canadian finance capitalists pyramided their concentrated shareholdings to exercise operational power over multiple companies. By 1932, 10.5 per cent of the assets of the 276 largest non-banking corporations were located in pure holding companies, and another 16.2 per cent were claimed by firms that functioned primarily as holding companies (Canada 1937, 19).

Monopoly capital also expanded abroad, in both financial and industrial forms (see, for example, Nuefeld 1969; Park and Park 1973, 122–61; Niosi 1985a, 67–81); it underwent further centralization in a second wave of mergers between 1921 and 1930. In this period, for instance, 49 pulp and paper mills were absorbed into 9 companies, 61 liquor firms were merged to form 13, and 52 fruit and vegetable preparation concerns were consolidated into 3 companies (Canada 1937, 333f).

Gilles Piedalue (1976), in a study of large Canadian corporations and their interlocks from 1900 to 1930, documents the dramatic growth of institutional relations from 1900 to 1910 and their preservation thereafter. In 1900, 80 per cent of the country's largest firms shared at least one director with another large company. By 1910, the percentage had increased to 89 and by 1930, to 91. On average, these interlocked corporations were directly linked to eight firms in 1900, thirteen in 1910, and fifteen in 1930 (Piedalue 1976, 22).[11]

The strongest interlocks, those involving three or more directors, tended by 1923 to be focused on the three big chartered banks—the Bank of Montreal, Bank of Commerce, and Royal Bank—which according to Piedalue formed the centres of integrated financial groups (ibid., 22–34). Throughout the period, most of the directors of the largest firms were Canadians, and the percentage of Canadian directors increased from 73 per cent in 1900 to 81 per cent in 1930 (ibid., 24–25). Although he does not distinguish the national locus of controlling interest for the large corporations studied, Piedalue does provide detailed documentation of a fraction of finance capital composed largely of Canadian capitalists. The key question concerns that fraction's fate in subsequent years, most importantly in the period since the Second World War.

The Postwar Dilemma: Capitulation or Consolidation?

There are at least three different opinions on this matter. First, and least plausibly, the tremendous flow of U.S. capital to Canada, especially in the postwar years, has been interpreted as part of the fulfilment of a colonial destiny by a commercial Canadian bourgeoisie (see Drache 1970; Naylor 1972; Clement 1975, 1977). The problem with this version of the dependency thesis is the general lack of evidence for a "commercial" bourgeoisie uninterested in industry after the industrial revolution. Still, the trend toward "continentalism"—in foreign direct investment (see Levitt, 1970), in interlocking directorships (see Clement 1977), and in trade relations (see Laxer 1973a)—might signal capitulation of Canadian finance capital to stronger monopoly interests invading from the south. This shift would have telling implications for the long-term survival of an indigenous Canadian bourgeoisie.

This is the position adopted by Levitt (1970, 50–52), who recognizes the rise of a national bourgeoisie in the period of the National Policy but identifies the postwar era with its "silent surrender." It is also accepted by Buck (1970, 79), who describes the bourgeoisie in postwar Canada as both dependent and imperialist. Buck locates the political origins of this transformation in 1947–48, with the introduction of the Abbott Plan by the St. Laurent government: "the legal lever by which finance capital and its government of the day in Canada brought about a radical change in the relationship of Canada to the United States literally overnight" (ibid., 81). The goal of the Abbott plan was to integrate the United States and Canada into a continental economy in which the latter would play a dependent role as resource supplier to the former. American direct investment in the postwar years was an important concomitant of this policy; it had the effect of intensifying Canadian dependence, as the economic base of the Canadian bourgeoisie became physically controlled by American-based monopolies (Buck 1970, 87).

Buck's thesis was applied by Libby and Frank Park in a study of Canadian finance capital in the late 1950's. These writers advocate a second opinion about finance capital, arguing that the accumulation strategies of Canadian finance capital continually draw Canada "into the orbit of U.S. capital as a junior partner, away from national development" (1973, 37). The Parks examine interlocking directorates among large Canadian corporations in 1958. Their analysis documents (1) the existence in Canada of a corporate network centred on leading financial institutions, indicating a fraction of finance capital, and (2) a variety of alliances between Canadian and American capitalists, whereby U.S. interests are furthered through Canadian participation. The clearest example of these features is given by the segment of finance capital

> centered around the Bank of Montreal and a group of financial and producing companies closely associated with the bank. These include the Canadian Pacific Railway and its subsidiary, Consolidated Mining and Smelting, the Steel Company of Canada, Dominion Textile Company, to take examples from the companies considered truly Canadian. But to stop there would be to ignore the influence within the bank of the big U.S. financial groups, the Morgan, Mellon, Rockefeller and other interests controlling Aluminum Ltd., International Nickel, Canadian General Electric, all U.S.-controlled companies in close relationship with the groups working through the bank (ibid., 15, 100–21).

The Parks view the postwar era as one in which a strong continental alliance has been consolidated, not between Canadian commercial capitalists and American industrialists, as Clement (1977) holds, but between Canadian and American finance capital. The circuits of finance capital in Canada have come to involve interests based in both countries, but it is the bigger and stronger American capitalists who dominate the Canadian economy more and more. Although they view the precise nature of the relationship differently, Clement (1977) and Park and Park (1973) agree that an unequal alliance has emerged between leading Canadian and American capitalists, an alliance that reflects "a structural dependence of the Canadian economy on that of the United States" (ibid., 13).

The third interpretation of the trajectory of Canadian finance capital in the postwar era emphasizes the *preservation* of the country's major financial-industrial interests and points to certain secular trends suggesting a further *consolidation* of indigenous monopoly in the context of ongoing capitalist internationalization. Two kinds of evidence have been cited in favour of this interpretation: (1) comparative economic statistics, indicating the evolving position of Canadian capitalists in their home market and in world economy and (2) interlocking directorates among large Canadian firms, indicating the institutional relations that unite the country's leading capitalists.

The first of these is used by Moore and Wells in their study of Canadian imperialism. The general thesis advanced is that

> While Canada is a predominantly dependent country today, the economic trends indicate that Canada will play an increasingly imperialist role in the coming decades. In short Canada is not moving towards colonial status in the American Empire; it is moving towards a greater imperial role in the world imperialist system (1975, 11).

Moore and Wells grant that the high levels of foreign investment in Canada are a source of dependence, but they also note that such dependence has been increasingly experienced by quite a number of advanced capitalist nations, and is not in itself antithetical to imperialism (ibid., 29). Nevertheless, "dependency and imperialism cannot statically co-exist forever as equal partners" (ibid., 92). Therefore, a dialectical analysis of Canadian capitalism must determine the historical trajectory of the country's ruling class. Through a series of economic comparisons, Moore and Wells attempt to demonstrate that:

> Canadian monopoly capitalism is well developed and highly concentrated; that the Canadian bourgeoisie is holding its own in home market expansion; that Canada's industrial growth statistics are comparable with other imperialist countries; that there is a substantial Canadian-controlled section of the bourgeoisie that has large numbers of branch plants abroad; that Canadian investment is rapidly increasing in the Third World; and that there has been a much more rapid increase in Canadian investment abroad than in foreign investment in Canada (ibid., 92–93).

The more recent work of Jorge Niosi (1981, 1985a) lends considerable support to these claims. Characterizing the 1970's as a period of declining American hegemony and increasing Canadian nationalism, Niosi shows that between 1970 and 1978 foreign control of non-financial assets in Canada fell from 36 per cent to 29 per cent, as crown corporations and Canadian capitalists purchased control of numerous foreign-controlled companies, thus contributing to "the decline of the comprador bourgeoisie" (1981, 47). Niosi's study of Canadian multinationals identifies Canada as one of the world's major exporters of capital throughout most of the twentieth century, ranking seventh as of 1976 in foreign direct investments (1985a, 44–45). Since the late 1960's, moreover, Canadian direct investment abroad has grown more rapidly than its American counterpart and has been directed particularly into less developed economies. Consequently, Canadian foreign invest-ments, which were heavily concentrated in the United States immedi-ately after the Second World War, are "now spread all over the globe" (ibid., 44). Control of most of this capital is concentrated in a handful of Canadian-controlled oligopolies, well suited to international expan-sion (ibid., 170). Indeed, in 1976 nearly two-thirds of Canadian direct investment in other countries was held by just sixteen multinationals op-erating in a wide range of industries (ibid., 50, 127, 165; see also Lit-vak and Maule 1981). There is clear evidence in these economic statistics of a strengthening or consolidation of Canadian monopoly capital in both its home market and the world market, particularly since 1970.

Considering the institutional relations that integrate capitalists and corporations, several researchers have suggested that interlocks between Canadian financial and industrial companies have been preserved or have even multiplied since the Second World War, providing a basis for preservation and further consolidation of domestic finance capital. Robert Chodos points to an interesting development in Canadian inter-locking that seems to parallel the American trend toward increased bank hegemony:

> While the banks as a group have increased their control, the dividing lines between the different networks have become more and more blurred. A large corporation will maintain a primary rela-tionship with one bank, and secondary relationships with one or more of the others (1973, 136).

For instance, Canadian Pacific Limited, the subject of Chodos' study, is linked by five directors to the Bank of Montreal, by four to the Royal Bank, by two to the Canadian Imperial Bank of Commerce, and by one director to both the Toronto-Dominion Bank and the Bank of Nova Scotia.

A study by Sweeny (1980) of bank-centred interlock networks in 1948, 1958, 1967, and 1977 replicates Piedalue's findings in suggesting the continued presence of "financial groups" focused around the three largest Canadian banks. Sweeny used listings of corporate directorates in the Financial Post *Directory of Directors* and other sources to con-struct networks of firms linked by at least three shared directors to one of the "big five" chartered banks, or to another corporation tied as strongly to one of the big banks. In this way a snowball sample of companies having significant interlocks with one or more of the major banks was constructed for each year of the study. This methodology carries an obvious bias toward exaggerating the centrality of the sample's core members—the banks—so Sweeny's findings must be interpreted with caution (see Fennema and Schijf 1979, 305). Even so, the large number of industrial and financial corporations that make up the resulting networks is clear testimony to the continuity of finance capital in Canada throughout the post-Second World War period. Sweeny's sample increases in size from 76 firms in 1948, to 104 in 1957 and 1967, and to 118 in 1977, supporting Johnson's (1972, 155) claim that the network of monopoly capital has widened over the years. Most significantly, Sweeny reports that relatively few foreign-controlled companies participate in the network, suggesting that the indicated financial groups are composed of predominantly Canadian interests.

In a study of the 250 largest Canadian corporations of 1972, Michael Ornstein reports a strong relationship between firm size and number of bank interlocks: the largest corporations have the most ties to banks, while firms without any bank interlocks are concentrated in small asset and sales categories. Financial institutions (such as life insurers and trust companies) show the greatest number of bank interlocks. Transportation, communications, utility, wood and paper, and mining companies—all with large fixed capital investments—also rank high in interlocks with banks. On the crucial issue of national locus of control, Canadian-controlled firms are reported to average 2.4 bank interlocks, while the means for firms controlled in the U.S. (1.1), Britain (1.3), and other countries (2.2) are lower (1976, 428–29).

Carroll, Fox and Ornstein's (1982) examination of directorate interlocks among the largest one hundred Canadian corporations of 1972 provides further evidence of the postwar preservation of a bloc of finance capital, centred around the big financial institutions, particularly the banks. Ninety-seven of the one hundred firms studied form a single connected network in which 12 per cent of all pairs of firms are directly interlocked and another 53 per cent are tied at one remove. Within the network, companies controlled in Canada tend to occupy more central positions than foreign-controlled firms, especially those held in the U.S. Moreover, a tendency is observed for the five big banks to share directors with the *same firms*, suggesting again the parallel with the advanced form of finance capital found in the United States, in which large corporations maintain multilateral financial ties with several banks (see, for example, Menshikov 1969, 216–21; Gogel and Koenig 1981;

Mintz and Schwartz 1981a; Mizruchi 1982). The authors conclude that the structural features of the network provide evidence of the existence of an independent national bourgeoisie centred in both industry and finance and integrated with foreign capital through the boards of financial institutions (Carroll, Fox and Ornstein 1982, 62).

Issues to be Explored

There are indications both in the economic trends and in the patterning of corporate interlocking that the years since the Second World War have witnessed not a "silent surrender" to foreign capital but the preservation and further consolidation of an indigenous fraction of finance capital. To the extent that this is so, several of the key propositions within the thesis of Canadian dependency must be rejected. The available evidence, however, is open to competing interpretations.

For example, the conclusion reached by Carroll, Fox and Ornstein on the "existence of an independent national bourgeoisie" could be countered with Park and Park's (1973) argument that Canadian finance capital operates through the chartered banks in a dependent alliance with U.S.-based monopolies. Clearly, an historical analysis of corporate interlocking is required in order to delineate the evolving relationship between the indigenous monopoly fraction and the foreign interests that continue to control much of the country's industrial capital.

The longitudinal approach taken by Sweeny (1980) would seem to hold promise in this connection. However, in addition to the methodological problems arising from the snowball sampling technique, Sweeny's structural analysis does not take into account the impact of capital accumulation over time on the economic position of the indigenous monopoly fraction, nor does it explicitly consider the position of foreign-controlled corporations in the interlock network. It is not inconceivable that even though the corporate *network* has expanded in the post-Second World War years, the indigenous *capital* controlled within it now comprises a smaller proportion of the total social capital, while that claimed by foreign interests—whether attached to or detached from the network—has been correspondingly augmented. From a structural analysis of interlocks, even one with a longitudinal dimension, it is difficult to reach definite conclusions regarding the historical trajectory of a capitalist fraction. What is missing from this sort of study is an explicit examination of the changing *accumulation base* of the corporate elite's indigenous and comprador fractions.

The historical trajectory of Canadian finance capital needs to be documented in two ways: through an economic analysis of accumulation within the large Canadian corporations controlled by each of these fractions; and by a structural analysis of directorate interlocking among the same firms. The chapters that follow provide these analyses, drawing upon the most systematically observable features of finance capital in the economic boom period from the mid 1940's to the mid-1970's. The analysis centres on: (1) the concentration and centralization of capital in large corporations, and (2) the institutional relations through which that capital has accumulated in the control of finance capitalists. It may be helpful at this point to summarize some of the key issues to be addressed.

On the subject of the corporate elite's accumulation base, it will be shown that a substantial amount of large-scale industrial and financial capital has been controlled in Canada throughout the post-Second World War era. There has thus been an economic basis for an indigenous monopoly fraction to accumulate capital within predominantly self-contained circuits of finance capital. Several processes are described through which the indigenous monopoly fraction appears to have consolidated its position within the Canadian economy. These include takeovers and mergers, shifting of investments to expanding industries, and repatriation of control of specific firms from foreign to Canadian interests. A number of the major companies involved in this concentration and centralization of capital have extended their accumulation bases *internationally*, particularly since the 1960's. Finally, the consolidation of Canadian finance capital is apparent in the growth of several diversified investment companies, which have emerged as important vehicles for the assertion of operational power through concentrated ownership of corporate shares.

This expanding accumulation base has been institutionally reinforced by a network of corporate interlocks: a social structure in which circuits of industrial, financial, and commercial capital may articulate, legally distinct capitals may be controlled, accumulation strategies may be coordinated, and a consciousness of kind may be cultivated. A stable component of indigenous monopoly capital—based largely in Toronto and Montreal and integrated under the control of a financial-industrial elite through interlocking directorates—appears to have been sustained throughout the period. Conversely, ties to foreign controlled capital tend to be weaker and less stable. Moreover, as indigenous capital has concentrated and centralized within new enterprises, these have been drawn into the network, reflecting the reproduction of Canadian finance capital under changing conditions of accumulation. Similarly, as industrial firms have grown larger indigenously controlled corporations have tended to establish multilateral interlocks with several banks, suggesting a trend for *allocative* financial power to be exercised increasingly by groups of large financial institutions. Finally, the growth of major diversified investment companies, interlocked with their subsidiaries and affiliates, as well as with allied financial institutions, suggests a further development of interest groups within which finance capitalists wield *operational* power while relying on banks for allocations of loan capital to finance further concentration and centralization.

4

THE ACCUMULATION OF MONOPOLY CAPITAL
1946–1976

A study of monopoly capital across three decades presents challenging methodological problems, particularly in the areas of sampling and measurement.[1] Consider, for example, the question of sampling. In compiling a set of large corporations for longitudinal analysis the issues of corporate reorganizations and differential rates of capital accumulation loom especially large. Monopoly capital is hardly a static entity. Firms judged to be among the largest at one time may later disappear in takeovers, mergers, or bankruptcies, or may grow at a rate insufficient to warrant their inclusion in a sample of dominant firms. Other firms may grow very rapidly, taking the place of the former companies among the largest corporations. This developmental issue was broached by selecting cross-sectional judgement samples of the largest firms in Canada at five-year intervals from 1946 through 1976.

Using total assets as an indicator of capital controlled, the seventy largest industrials, twenty largest financial intermediaries, and ten largest merchandizing firms were selected for the years 1946, 1951, 1961, 1966, 1971, and 1976, to produce successive "Top 100s." In the case of the merchandizing sector, only three firms in 1946 and five firms in 1951 were judged to be of a size sufficient to qualify for membership in a sample of large-scale capitals. Similarly, in the case of the property-development sector—an industry in which capital has only recently reached enormous concentrations—the sample was restricted to firms of size comparable to the 70th ranked industrial corporation in each selection year. In all, seven property developers were included in the sample.

Several firms were added to the financial sector after the quantitative selection procedures. Three trust companies—Montreal Trust, Royal Trust, and National Trust—controlling a great amount of capital in the form of assets under administration and known to have had longstanding ties to certain chartered banks, were included as dominant financial institutions for all years of the study. Similarly, ten investment companies controlling other firms in the sample were selected on qualitative grounds. These companies form a distinct subsector of financial capital: they control share capital but do not engage primarily in financial intermediation as do the chartered banks, insurance, trust, mortgage, and loan companies. This distinction is of some practical importance. As we have seen, the *operational* power to manage companies that accrues to investment companies differs in kind from the *allocative* power of financial institutions to direct funds toward capitalists in need of financing. Investment companies in the sample include well-known holding companies such as Argus Corporation, Power Corporation, and Canadian Pacific Investments, as well as less prominent firms such as Anglo-Canadian Telephone, Bowater Canadian Limited, Canadian General Investments Ltd., and the Investors Group Limited.

These procedures yielded a sample of 194 firms, each dominant in the Canadian economy at one time or another in the postwar period. Our analysis of monopoly capital involves the study of successive sets of ''Top 100'' companies, each part of the larger sample of 194 corporations.

CONCENTRATION OF CAPITAL

A key issue preliminary to any discussion of accumulation within fractions of monopoly capital is the level of capital concentration in the entire economy. The concentration of most Canadian financial capital within a handful of chartered banks and life insurers—each included in our sample—is well established (Neufeld 1972; Clement 1975, 132–35) and requires no further comment. A number of studies of industrial concentration have appeared since the Second World War (Porter 1956; Brecher and Reisman 1957; Rosenbluth 1961; Canada 1978), evidencing generally high levels of concentration. Niosi has recently commented that in comparison with other major international investing countries "if there is one feature that characterizes the Canadian economy, it is precisely the high level of industrial concentration in the production of goods and services" (1985a, 41).

The purpose here is mainly to test the plausibility of our methodology, by assessing the extent to which the group of firms designated as ''dominant'' do in fact dominate Canadian industry. In this section we also examine concentration of capital *within* the Top 100 by determin-

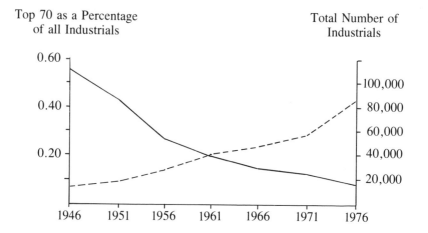

Top 70 as a Percentage
of all Industrials

Total Number of
Industrials

——— Top 70 Industrials as a Percentage of All Canadian Industrials (left hand scale)
- - - - Total Number of Industrial Firms (right hand scale)

Figure 4.1
Dominant Industrial Corporations Compared with All Canadian
Industrials, 1946–1976

ing how much of the capital of the seventy largest industrial and twenty largest financial firms is located in a handful of giant corporations.

Figures 4.1 and 4.2 compare the Top 70 industrials with all industrial corporations in Canada at five-year intervals beginning in 1946. The figures include data from four broad sectors of industry: mining and oil and gas production; manufacturing; "utilities," including transportation, communications, and power generation; and construction. In the construction sector only one corporation, Comstock International Limited, ever numbers among the dominant industrials, ranking 69th in 1971. By and large, capital has remained less concentrated in construction than in other sectors, because of the localized nature of construction markets.[2]

Examination of Figure 4.1 reveals that, with the rapid expansion of the Canadian economy after the Second World War, the proportion of Top 70 industrials in all industrial firms decreased. In 1946, the Top 70 made up 0.55 per cent of all industrials; by 1976, the corresponding figure is only 0.08 percent. Over the same period the total number of industrial firms in Canada expanded from 12,663 to 83,566, as a result of

Percent of
All Assets

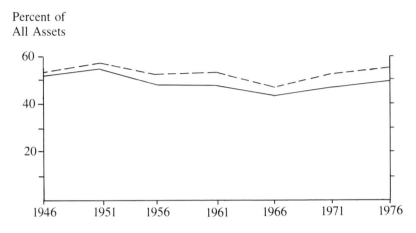

———— Top 70 Industrial Assets as a Percentage of All Industrial Assets
- - - - - Top 70 Industrial Assets as a Percentage of All Non-Construction Assets

Figure 4.2
Assets of Dominant Industrial Corporations as a Percentage of Total
Canadian Industrial Assets, 1946–1976.

the postwar economic boom. Any analysis of concentration in the
1946–76 period must take into account the generally favourable context
in which capital, big and small, accumulated, particularly from the mid-
1950's to the mid-1970's.

Figure 4.2 considers the percentage of Canadian industrial assets
owned by the Top 70 industrials. Overall, the Top 70 make up a declining portion of the total industrial capital from 1946 to 1966 and an increasing proportion thereafter, rising back to 50 per cent in 1976. The
same trend is found in the construction industry (in which small and me-
dium capital predominates) but the percentage declines only to 46 per
cent in 1966 and rises back to 55 per cent by 1976. Clearly, the sample
firms account for a great deal of industrial assets, and a fairly constant
proportion of these assets, throughout the period of study.

The secular trend observable in Figure 4.2 does not support a hypothesis that industrial capital has progressively concentrated within the Top
70, leaving a diminishing share for smaller firms. We should, however,
recall the results of Figure 4.1 when drawing interpretations of this
kind. An alternative method of assessing aggregate concentration, em-

ployed by the Royal Commission on Corporate Concentration (Canada 1978, 30–31), considers what proportion of industrial assets is tied up in the largest companies comprising a constant fraction of all firms. This approach takes into account the great expansion in the total number of firms in the Canadian economy. In 1976, the Top 70 industrials accounted for 50 per cent of all industrial assets and made up 0.08 percent of all industrial firms. Applying the latter percentage to the 12,663 firms that constituted the industrial sector in 1946, we find that the top 0.08 per cent of all industrials in that year (that is the 10 largest firms) accounted for 30.2 per cent of all industrial assets. In this sense, the 1946–76 period witnessed a marked increase in the extent to which productive capital is concentrated in the very largest firms, but this increase occurred in the context of a booming economy favouring the formation of many new firms.[3]

A second dimension of concentration is the distribution of capital among dominant firms: the extent of concentration *within* the monopoly fraction.[4] The distributions of assets among the largest industrials in each year are compared in Table 4.1. Panel A shows the distribution in constant (1976) Canadian dollars,[5] illustrating a great accumulation of capital in the three decades. The smallest of the top industrials in 1946 had assets of $74.9 million; the corresponding company in 1976 claimed $384 million in assets, nearly a fivefold increase. The largest firm shows much less dramatic growth, from $4.2 billion in 1946 to $6.0 billion in 1976. The median firm evidences a rate of growth comparable to the smallest one. Therefore, within the dominant industrial corporations we may note (1) an enormous accumulation of large-scale capital, and (2) faster growth among the smaller firms and somewhat sluggish accumulation at the very top.

Panel B in Table 4.1 considers what proportion of dominant industrial assets is contained in the ranges between the different quantiles of the asset distribution. The smallest firm in each year shows a gradual increase in its share of dominant industrial assets, from 0.37 per cent in 1946 to 0.56 per cent in 1976. The largest firm in 1946—Canadian Pacific Railway Company Limited—represents a remarkable 20.30 per cent of top industrial assets in 1946. The same firm is fifth-ranked in 1976, with 3.74 percent of top industrial assets.[6] It is this marked decline in the relative prominence of the CPR that largely explains the asset redistribution occurring from larger to smaller firms. Not including the CPR, the top decile in 1946 contains 24.04 per cent of top industrial assets; in 1976 it contains 25.14 per cent. Even in 1976, great disparities are apparent among the leading industrial companies. The largest corporation, for instance, is eighteen times the size of the small-

Table 4.1 Asset Distributions for Top Industrial Firms, 1946–1976*

A. Distribution of Firms**

Percentile	1946	1951	1956	1961	1966	1971	1976
Maximum	$ 4,164.4	$ 2,459.8	$ 3,331.7	$ 3,537.1	$ 4,383.6	$ 5,939.8	$ 5,952.0
90	713.4	881.4	1,177.1	1,522.9	1,753.6	2,143.8	2,202.0
75	260.7	264.6	442.6	681.0	845.7	1,116.1	1,182.9
50	151.8	143.1	271.8	378.0	521.7	714.9	720.5
25	97.3	102.2	171.9	246.1	379.7	492.2	515.6
10	85.4	82.8	143.3	208.2	286.8	396.0	452.2
0	74.9	75.9	132.7	187.0	241.8	353.5	384.8
Total Assets	$20,518.6	$18,646.3	$30,360.1	$40,505.3	$53,432.3	$69,185.9	$68,718.7

B. Percentage Distributions of Firms' Assets

Percentile	1946	1951	1956	1961	1966	1971	1976
Maximum	20.30	13.19	10.97	8.73	8.20	8.59	8.66
91–99	24.34	28.08	29.62	28.44	24.03	22.32	21.57
76–90	22.24	23.29	21.67	22.87	25.07	23.90	24.93
51–75	16.70	16.67	17.89	19.17	19.33	21.19	20.32
26–50	9.65	11.28	11.78	12.26	14.08	14.43	13.83
11–25	4.37	4.97	5.41	5.65	6.37	6.42	7.01
1–10	2.04	2.11	2.23	2.40	2.47	2.65	3.11
Minimum	.37	.41	.44	.46	.45	.51	.56
Total	100.0	100.0	100.0	100.0	100.0	100.0	100.0

* Excluding in all years six firms missing financial data in the early years.

**In millions of 1976 dollars, inflated using Wholesale Price Index annual averages. Each value refers to the assets of a firm at the corresponding percentile. For instance, in 1946 the smallest industrial firm had assets of $74.9 million, and the median industrial had assets of $151.8 million.

Table 4.2 Top 10 Industrial Corporations, 1946–1976

Name	Rank			
	1946	1956	1966	1976
Canadian Pacific Limited	1	1	3	5
Brascan Limited	2	5	9	–*
Inco Limited	3	6	5	2
Alcan Aluminum Limited	4	2	2	4
The Seagram Company Limited	5	7	6	7
Bell Canada	6	4	1	1
Imperial Oil Limited	7	3	4	3
International Petroleum Company	8	9	–	–
Shawinigan Water and Power Company	9	10	–	–
Abitibi Paper Company Limited	10	18	33	56
Massey-Ferguson Limited	27	11	7	6
Noranda Mines Limited	34	32	23	8
Gulf Canada Limited	24	8	8	9
Steel Company of Canada, Limited	17	12	11	10
Shell Canada Limited	–+	–+	10	11

*No longer an industrial corporation.

+Privately owned, assets not available.

est. Clearly, the "Top 70" is not a homogeneous group but is itself dominated by a smaller set of giant corporations. The identities of these latter firms are revealed in Table 4.2. Not surprisingly, the ten largest corporations are rather stable in composition: six of the 1976 Top 10 were also among the ten largest of 1946, namely Canadian Pacific Limited, Inco Limited, Alcan Aluminum Limited, Bell Canada, The Seagram Company Limited, and Imperial Oil Limited. Of the four other firms in the 1946 Top 10, Abitibi Paper Company failed to grow rapidly enough to remain among the very largest after that year, Brascan became a *bona fide* investment company with the acquisition of John Labatt Limited in 1967, The Shawinigan Water and Power Company was nationalized by the Province of Quebec, and International Petroleum Company, Limited became a private subsidiary of ESSO Standard (Inter-America) Inc. after 1956 and was ultimately wound up in 1976. The four firms that replace these in the Top 10 of 1976 all numbered among the seventy biggest industrial corporations of 1976—they merely grew at especially rapid rates. Massey-Ferguson Limited, Gulf Canada Limited, and The Steel Company of Canada Limited improved their relative standing in the first postwar decade, while Noranda's assets expanded quickly in the third decade.

The same pattern of disparities in the distribution of capital among the largest firms and of stability in the composition of corporations claiming the largest share of assets is also notable for financial intermediaries. As Panel A of Table 4.3 shows, the total assets of the Top 20 financial intermediaries increase from $41 to $156 billion (1976) over the three decades, comprising roughly twice the total assets of the dominant industrials—a tremendous concentration of financial capital. Both the twentieth-ranked and first-ranked financial institution show great asset growth, the former by a factor of 9.5, the latter by 3.6, and the median firm by about 3. Panel B of Table 4.3 indicates that the largest financial institution in each year, the Royal Bank of Canada, accounts for a fairly stable proportion of top financial assets, ranging from 17 per cent to 19 per cent of the total. The minimum value of the distribution claims a greater share after 1946, growing to represent about one per cent of the total. The two biggest financials (those above the tenth decile) claim a steady 35 per cent of Top 20 assets; the top five approximately 65 per cent to 70 per cent.

Finally, Table 4.4 lists the top five financial intermediaries in 1946, 1956, 1966 and 1976. The hierarchy is headed in all years by the "big three" chartered banks: the Royal, Bank of Montreal, and Canadian Bank of Commerce, (which merged with the Imperial Bank of Canada to become the Canadian Imperial Bank of Commerce in 1961). Sun

Table 4.3 Asset Distribution for 20 Top Financial Intermediaries, 1946– 1976

A. Distribution of Firms*

Percentile	1946	1951	1956	1961	1966	1971	1976
Maximum	$ 7,881.8	$ 5,366.4	$ 8,111.4	$ 1,088.2	$13,695.5	$ 22,895.5	$ 28,831.6
90	6,668.4	4,635.1	6,242.8	9,928.6	12,790.5	19,931.7	25,542.8
75	2,303.3	1,684.1	3,005.5	4,905.0	6,107.7	10,393.9	13,562.7
50	1,239.5	921.1	1,322.2	1,738.1	2,168.9	2,974.6	3,505.7
25	581.3	436.4	734.6	836.1	1,168.7	2,328.6	2,333.5
10	277.9	318.8	552.4	639.9	1,052.5	1,452.1	1,866.9
Minimum	180.4	249.9	527.7	550.1	1,034.2	1,322.5	1,713.8
Total Assets	$41,029.5	$29,921.2	$45,507.1	$62,772.5	$81,132.6	$128,372.4	$156,400.4

B. Percentage Distribution of Firms' Assets

Percentile	1946	1951	1956	1961	1966	1971	1976
Maximum	19.21	17.94	17.82	17.34	16.88	17.84	18.43
91–99	16.62	15.84	13.89	16.04	16.05	15.70	16.69
76–90	31.36	30.47	28.87	30.44	29.58	32.77	35.08
51–75	16.58	17.09	20.43	20.00	20.26	16.50	14.27
26–50	12.09	13.15	12.24	10.53	10.59	10.31	9.17
11–25	3.04	3.62	4.39	3.79	4.07	4.75	4.08
1–10	.66	1.06	1.20	1.00	1.29	1.11	1.18
Minimum	.44	.84	1.16	.88	1.27	1.03	1.10
Total	100.0	100.0	100.0	100.0	100.0	100.0	100.0

*In millions of 1976 dollars, inflated using Wholesale Price Index annual averages. Each value refers to the assets of a financial institution at the corresponding percentile. For instance, in 1946 the smallest financial institution had assets of $180.4 million and the median financial institution had assets of $1,239.5 million.

Life Assurance Company, another longstanding institution, ranks fourth in 1946 but slips to a ranking of seven in 1976. Its position in the top five is taken up by the Toronto-Dominion Bank, product of a merger of the Dominion Bank and Bank of Toronto in 1955. By 1976, the top five is completely composed of chartered banks, two of which represent a post-war centralization of financial capital.

CONTINUITY AND CHANGE IN THE TOP 100

A limitation of the analysis so far has been its insensitivity to the dynamics of accumulation, to the manner in which the concentration and centralization of capital continually reshape the contours of corporate power. The issue of stability and change in the composition of dominant firms, save at the very highest levels, remains unprobed. To address this question, it is necessary to move beyond the description of successive cross-sections of the largest firms, to view the dominant corporations of 1946–76 in longitudinal perspective.

Clement (1975) provides a method for gaining such a perspective in his follow-up analysis of the 183 dominant corporations of 1948–50 identified by Porter in *Vertical Mosaic* (1965). In the two decades between Porter's and Clement's studies no less than forty-one of Porter's corporations were reduced to seventeen dominant firms through acquisitions and mergers (Clement 1975, 26). Other firms that Porter judged as dominant in 1948–1950 show different records of subsequent accumulation (ibid., 1975, 390–95). Some remained economically dominant without undergoing amalgamation with other large companies; others remained intact but were not considered dominant in 1972.

Using these distinctions, it is possible to summarize the changes that occur over time in the corporate elite's accumulation base, as capital concentrates and is centralized into larger units. Dominant corporations may (1) retain their identity as independent firms and grow at a rate that ensures their continued dominance in the economy, (2) retain their identity as independent firms but fail to grow quickly enough to maintain a dominant position or (3) lose their independence as units of capital through bankruptcy, nationalization, or amalgamation with other large firms. In this way, the changing accumulation base of the corporate elite may be described *prospectively* in terms of the subsequent fate of companies considered dominant at the beginning of the period. Similarly, a set of dominant corporations can be categorized *retrospectively* into those that have maintained a consistently dominant and independent position in the economy and those that have become dominant by growing at an especially rapid rate.

Table 4.4 Top 5 Financial Intermediaries in 1946, 1956, 1966 and 1976

Name	Rank			
	1946	1956	1966	1976
Royal Bank	1	1	1	1
Bank of Montreal	2	2	3	3
Canadian Bank of Commerce	3	3	—	—
Sun Life Assurance Co. of Canada	4	4	5	7
Bank of Nova Scotia	5	6	4	4
Canadian Imperial Bank of Commerce	—	—	2	2
Toronto-Dominion Bank	6	5	6	5
Imperial Bank of Canada	8	7	—	—
Bank of Toronto	10	—	—	—
Dominion Bank	—	—	—	—

To apply these longitudinal categories, companies were classified according to four kinds of "corporate survivorship": (1) firms consistently in the set of dominant corporations; (2) firms extant throughout the period of study but not always among the top-ranked corporations; (3) firms incorporated after 1946 and thus representing either new or reorganized capital; and (4) firms that were defunct by 1976, whether as a result of bankruptcy, merger with another dominant firm, or takeover by private or state corporations. This classification of corporate survivorship divides monopoly capital into three components: one which remains very stable (firms consistently in a dominant position and not subject to major reorganization), a second that is stable in its social organization but variable in relative dominance (companies extant throughout), and a third which is most variable (firms incorporated after 1946 or defunct by 1976). By examining these categories in each major economic sector, we can gain a sense of continuity and change in the composition of dominant corporations. Thus we can see how monopoly capital has been perpetuated and reshaped in the context of an expanding economy (see Table 4.5).[7]

Nearly two-fifths (twenty-seven) of the top industrials of any given year are dominant throughout the period under study. These companies form a stable core of big industry and represent many sectors of production including mining, various manufacturing industries, transportation-communications, and power production.

Around this stable core, however, big industry undergoes substantial restructuring across the three decades. Fifty-three of the industrial firms retain their independence as units of capital throughout the period but are dominant only in certain years. Twenty-three of these, including Domtar Inc., Falconbridge Nickel Mines Limited, George Weston, Pacific Petroleums Limited, Dominion Foundries and Steel Limited, and Canadian Utilities Limited, rise from outside the Top 70 to very prominent positions in 1976; twenty-four, such as Imasco Limited, Carling O'Keefe Limited, Dominion Textile Limited, MacLaren Power and Paper Companies, and Hollinger Mines Limited, decline in relative size over the period, dropping out of the Top 100 by 1976. But the restructuring of large-scale Canadian industry is particularly apparent in the cases of "new" and "defunct" firms.

There are twenty-eight "new" industrials, including nineteen firms representing productive capital that did not exist prior to 1947 and nine companies that are reorganized versions of previously extant capital. For example, Dupont of Canada Limited and Canadian Industries Limited were incorporated in 1954 as a result of a U.S. Securities and Exchange Commission ruling that forced their predecessor, Canadian

Table 4.5 Crosstabulation of Dominant Firms, 1946–1976, by Corporate Survivorship and Sector

Sector	Consistently dominant	Extant throughout, inconsistently dominant	Formed after 1946	Defunct by 1976	Total
Industrial	27[1]	53	28[2]	24	132
Financial Intermediaries	15[3]	7	5	4	31
Investment Companies	5	0	4[4]	1	10
Commercial	3	8	3	0	14
Property Development	0	1	6[5]	0	7
Total	50	69	46	29	194

1. Including Brascan Limited, classified as a diversified investment company from 1971 forward.

2. Including: (a) Reed Paper Limited, classified as an investment company from 1961 through 1971 and Genstar Limited, classified as an investment company from 1951 through 1961; (b) Churchill Falls (Labrador) Corporation Limited, nationalized in 1974 and Northern and Central Gas Corporation Limited, merged in 1975.

3. Including three trust companies with longstanding ties to key chartered banks (Royal Trust, Montreal Trust, and National Trust).

4. Including Canadian Chemical and Cellulose Company Limited, defunct in 1959 and International Utilities Corporation, no longer a Canadian corporation in 1971.

5. Including Cadillac Development Corporation, merged in 1974.

Industries Limited, to segregate into two firms. Two giant forest products firms, Consolidated-Bathurst Limited and MacMillan Bloedel Limited, are the product of mergers in the postwar period, as are two oil and gas companies, Norcen Energy Resources Limited and BP Canada Limited.[8]

Industrials that actually started up in the 1946–76 period, forming new means of production which then served as a basis for further accumulation, are heavily weighted toward the oil and gas and associated pipelines industries. Altogether, thirteen new firms that rank in the Top 70 at some time were formed in these sectors after 1946, including Husky Oil Limited, Dome Petroleum Limited, Pan Canadian Petroleum, Alberta Gas Trunk Line Limited, Northern and Central Gas Corporation Limited, Aquitaine Company of Canada Limited, Trans-Canada PipeLine Limited, and Westcoast Transmission Company Limited. This long list underlines the importance of the oil and gas sector for the formation and accumulation of big industrial capital in the 1946–76 period.

Finally, 24 of the 132 industrial firms ever in the Top 70 were defunct by 1976. Only one of these, Barcelona Traction, Light and Power Company Limited, was declared bankrupt—by the government of Spain—and this case was vigorously disputed at the time.[9] The other 23 were reorganized in one of four ways: (1) through mergers; (2) through takeovers by another dominant firm and eventual consolidation with the latter; (3) through nationalizations, usually in the public utilities sector and through the agency of crown corporations;[10] and (4) through court-ordered segregation (in the case of Canadian Industries). In all, four of the defunct industrials merged to form new firms which also ranked in the Top 100, seven were taken over and fully consolidated with their parent firms, eleven were nationalized (in one case—Mexican Light and Power Company Limited—the state involved was a foreign one; the other ten were takeovers by crown corporations or provincial ministries), one was ordered segregated, and one was declared bankrupt and expropriated by the government of Spain. All but three of these mark a centralization of industrial capital under the control of private capitalist interests or the Canadian state.

We witness, then, considerable change in the composition of dominant industrials, as capitals form, concentrate, and reorganize. This in itself is a noteworthy finding inasmuch as it illustrates the fact that the largest firms do not comprise a fixed and unchanging bloc of capital, insulated from the competitive rigours of the market. The monopoly fraction has been subject to significant change over time, reflecting the changing conditions of accumulation in specific firms and industries, as well as the enlarged role of state enterprises in the accumulation process.[11]

Interestingly, most of the industrial mergers and takeovers among the largest firms in the 1946–1976 period involved Canadian-controlled companies, such as MacMillan-Bloedel Limited, Consolidated-Bathurst Limited, and Howard Smith Paper Mills Limited. These reorganizations have served further to centralize industrial capital under the control of Canadian capitalists. There is no clear pattern of foreign penetration through direct takeovers of the largest indigenous industrials. The only case that satisfies this description is Royal Dutch Shell's wresting of Canadian Oil Companies Limited in 1962 from a Canadian group that included Power Corporation of Canada. The other industrials that were reorganized under foreign control were all under foreign control in 1946 and hence do not constitute clear cases of new foreign penetration. Control of Dominion Steel and Coal Corporation Limited was acquired by British-controlled Hawker-Siddeley in 1957, but DOSCO was subsequently nationalized by the Province of Quebec, just as U.S.-controlled Columbia Cellulose Company Limited was brought under Canadian control in 1973 with the formation of Canadian Cellulose Company by the Province of British Columbia, and was later privatized under Canadian control as the B.C. Resources Investment Company.

When the four categories of corporate survivorship are applied to the thirty-one financial intermediaries in the sample, a remarkable degree of stability is found throughout the three decades under investigation. Twelve financial firms consistently rank among the Top 20, including five banks and seven life insurers. Three more—the major trust companies affiliated with the big three chartered banks—have been included in the sample in all years on qualitative grounds. Thus, a majority of dominant financial firms are *consistently* dominant, indicating a highly centralized and organizationally stable financial system.

The remaining sixteen financial intermediaries are distributed over the three other survivorship categories: seven firms are extant throughout the period but not always in the Top 20; five are newly incorporated; and four are defunct by 1976. Closer examination of the firms in these last two categories provides further evidence of stability in Canadian high finance. Three of the "new" financials are products of mergers between companies whose origins can be traced at least to the turn of the century;[12] all four defunct firms were chartered banks that merged to form the Canadian Imperial Bank of Commerce and Toronto-Dominion Bank.

Since all the investment companies that qualified for the sample were included in all the years they existed as investment companies, the five firms that were extant throughout the period—Argus Corporation Limited, Power Corporation Limited, The Investors Group, Canadian General Investments Limited, and Anglo-Canadian Telephone Company—were, by fiat, in the sample in all years. Of the four that formed after 1946, three did so under foreign control (Bowater Canadian Limited, International Utilities Corporation,[13] and Canadian Chemical and Cellulose Company Limited). Only the first of these was still extant as a Canadian corporation in 1976. The other new investment company, Canadian Pacific Investments Limited, created in 1962 to manage the resource, manufacturing, and real-estate assets of Canadian Pacific Limited, grew to become a pivotal indigenous holding company in the mid-1970's.

In the commercial sector, the three big department store chains, Eaton's, Hudson's Bay Company, and Simpsons Limited (now a subsidiary of the Bay), were included in the sample in all years. Eight retail chains, mainly food-merchandisers, were extant throughout but of large size only in the more recent years, and three merchandisers formed, including Simpsons-Sears Limited, a joint venture of Simpsons Limited and Sears Roebuck Incorporated of Chicago. The concentration of capital employed in food merchandising—the decline of corner grocetarias and growth of supermarket chains—is especially apparent in the sample, which by 1976 includes four food-merchandisers among the 10 dominant commercial firms.

Just as commercial capital has concentrated in the food-merchandising sector quite markedly since the Second World War, so has capital applied to urban property development. Monopolization of land is not a new phenomenon in Canada; its history dates to the granting of charters to the fur-trading monopolies of the seventeenth century and includes, more recently, the vast landholdings ceded by the federal government in the building of the Canadian Pacific Railway. But the holding and development of large tracts of urban land is rather recent, and the composition of the sample of big property developers reflects this. With the exception of Eaton's wholly owned subsidiary—T. Eaton Realty Company Limited, extant throughout the study period—all these firms formed after 1946. In the 1960's and early 1970's, as the Canadian economy experienced a long stretch of largely uninterrupted growth, the development of urban property quickly became a highly lucrative and concentrated industry, dominated in 1976 by five very large firms: Cadillac-Fairview Corporation Limited; Trizec Corporation Limited; Oxford Development Group Limited; Campeau Corporation; and Marathon Realty Company Limited, a subsidiary of Canadian Pacific Investments Limited.

From this analysis it is clear that the concentration and centralization of capital in the era of the postwar boom served to reproduce a *stable core* of consistently dominant companies, while effecting a substantial *restructuring* of the corporate elite's accumulation base and an expansion of state capital. Within this motif of continuity in change, it is the financial intermediaries that exhibit the most stability, while the industrial and property-development companies were most subject to changes as capital flowed into and out of specific firms and industries.

CAPITAL ACCUMULATION AND CAPITALIST FRACTIONS

Against the background provided by the analysis of general tendencies in the accumulation of large-scale capital, we may now begin to assess this study's principal thesis. In its weakest form, the proposition that Canada's capitalist class is headed by an indigenous and independent monopoly fraction may be phrased as a expectation that a substantial amount of big industrial and financial capital has been controlled in Canada throughout the 1946–76 period. Tables 4.6 and 4.7 give cros-stabulations of dominant corporations and their assets, by seven economic sectors and four countries of control. Four successive. "Top 100s" are included in the tables: those of 1946, 1956, 1966, and 1976. The economic sectors are those employed in the selection of the sample: industrials (further broken into: mining, including oil and gas production, manufacturing, and utilities), financial intermediaries, investment companies, merchandizers, and property development. Country in which controlling interest is held has been categorized into three nations of key historical importance—Canadian, American, and British—plus a fourth category that includes all other countries, namely Holland, France, Belgium, West Germany and South Africa.

In the bottom panel of the tables we can note that the majority of dominant firms and assets was controlled in Canada throughout the period. In 1946, seventy firms representing 87 per cent of all assets were controlled in Canada. By 1956, Canadian control had fallen to sixty-four firms representing 77 per cent cf all assets, but by 1976 the bloc of large-scale capital under indigenous control had revived to 85 per cent of all assets, although the number of firms in which this capital is organized totalled only seventy-one. U.S.-controlled capital shows an interesting pattern of rapid growth in the first postwar decade followed by relative decline to 1976. By 1976, the proportion of large-scale capital under U.S. control had fallen to 12 per cent, only slightly above the level in 1946. This was evident in spite of the fact that the assets of several U.S.-controlled industrials are *included* in the 1976 figures but excluded from earlier tabulations, since unavailable. The only fraction of capital experiencing consistent growth relative to the others is that controlled in Europe and South Africa, which increases from one firm representing 0.6 per cent of all assets in 1946 to seven firms accounting for 2 per cent of assets in 1976.[14]

The distributions of industrial firms and their assets show a relative decline of the transportation-communications-utilities sector and an increase in the number of mining firms and the portion of big industrial capital they represent. In 1946, seventeen of the seventy dominant industrials were utilities, accounting for 45 per cent of the total assets of the Top 70. By 1976, eleven dominant utilities accounted for 24 per cent of dominant industrial assets. Much of this relative decline was a result of the slow growth of Canadian Pacific in the early years and the nationalization of electric utilities in Quebec, Manitoba, and British Columbia. For example, six utilities in the 1946 Top 70 had been nationalized by 1962, five of them to form Hydro Quebec. Conversely, the number of mining firms (and their share of industrial assets) grew from nine (17 per cent) in 1946 to nineteen (28 per cent) in 1976, pointing out this sector's importance in the postwar accumulation of large-scale capital. Finally, in the 1946–76 years, the number of dominant manufacturing firms decreased slightly, while the proportion of industrial assets in manufacturing increased from 38 per cent to 48 per cent, indicating particularly rapid concentration of capital in this sector.

It is, of course, the joint distribution, across both industrial sector and country of control, that is most important in these tabulations. In this regard the tables show the anticipated pattern of strong Canadian control of big financial capital: virtually all the assets of financial intermediaries were controlled in Canada in all years. There is also evidence of an increased Canadian presence among the investment companies, which increased their share of the total assets of financial firms from 0.7 per cent in 1946 to 6 per cent in 1976. Commercial capital remained predominantly under Canadian control throughout, although there was substantial American penetration of this sector as British control waned with the Canadianization of Hudson's Bay Company. In the emerging property development sector, the largest companies were all under Canadian control by 1976.

Large-scale industrial capital shows a somewhat different pattern of development. In 1946, 62 per cent of this capital (organized in forty-one firms) was controlled in Canada, 32 per cent (twenty-four firms) in the U.S., and 4 per cent (four firms) in the U.K. By 1976, the Canadian and British shares had declined slightly, and the American share was

Table 4.6 Distributions of Top 100 Firms by Country of Control for Seven Economic Sectors, 1946–1976

Industry	Year	Country of Control				
		Canada	U.S.	U.K.	Other	Total
Mining	1946	5	4	0	0	9
	1956	2	9	0	0	11
	1966	3	8	1	1	13
	1976	7	7	2	3	19
Manufacturing	1946	24	16	4	0	44
	1956	23	15	6	1	45
	1966	17	17	6	3	43
	1976	17	17	2	4	40
Utilities	1946	12	4	0	1	17
	1956	6	8	0	0	14
	1966	10	4	0	0	14
	1976	7	4	0	0	11
Subtotal: Industrials	1946	41	24	4	1	70
	1956	31	32	6	1	70
	1966	30	29	7	4	70
	1976	31	28	4	7	70
Financial Intermediaries	1946	23	0	0	0	23
	1956	22	1	0	0	23
	1966	22	1	0	0	23
	1976	22	1	0	0	23

Table 4.6 Distributions of Top 100 Firms by Country of Control for Seven Economic Sectors, 1946–1976

Industry	Year	Country of Control				
		Canada	U.S.	U.K.	Other	Total
Investment Companies	1946	3	3	0	0	6
	1956	3	4	1	1	9
	1966	5	2	2	0	9
	1976	6	1	1	0	8
Subtotal: Financials	1946	26	3	0	0	29
	1956	25	5	1	1	32
	1966	27	3	2	0	32
	1976	28	2	1	0	31
Commercials	1946	2	0	1	0	3
	1956	7	2	1	0	10
	1966	6	3	1	0	10
	1976	7	3	0	0	10
Property Development	1946	1	0	0	0	1
	1956	1	0	0	0	1
	1966	0	0	1	0	1
	1976	5	0	0	0	5
Grand Total	1946	70	27	5	1	103
	1956	64	39	8	2	113
	1966	63	35	11	4	113
	1976	71	33	5	7	116

Table 4.7 Percentage Distribution of Top 100 Assets by Country of Control for Seven Economic Sectors, 1946–1976

Sector	Year	Country of Control					
		Canada	U.S.	U.K.	Other	Subtotal	Total
Mining	1946	24	76	0	0	17	
	1956	13	87	0	0	18	
	1966	18	63	4	15	18	
	1976	46	35	6	13	28	
Manufacturing	1946	58	31	11	0	38	
	1956	49	39	9	2	49	
	1966	46	39	9	5	54	
	1976	53	37	3	8	48	
Utilities	1946	80	16	0	4	45	
	1956	63	37	0	0	33	
	1966	84	16	0	0	28	
	1976	79	21	0	0	24	
Subtotal: Industrials	1946	62	32	4	2	100	100
	1956	47	47	5	1	100	100
	1966	52	37	6	5	100	100
	1976	57	33	3	7	100	100
Financial Intermediaries	1946	100	0	0	0	99	
	1956	99	1	0	0	97	
	1966	99	1	0	0	93	
	1976	99	1	0	0	94	

Table 4.7 Percentage Distribution of Top 100 Assets by Country of Control for Seven Economic Sectors, 1946–1976

Sector	Year	Country of Control					
		Canada	U.S.	U.K.	Other	Subtotal	Total
Investment Companies	1946	59	41	0	0	1	
	1956	22	42	33	3	3	
	1966	40	29	31	0	7	
	1976	81	18	2	0	6	
Subtotal: Financials	1946	100	0	0	0	100	100
	1956	96	3	1	0	100	100
	1966	94	3	2	0	100	100
	1976	98	2	0	0	100	100
Commercials	1946	51	0	49	0		100
	1956	66	19	15	0		100
	1966	61	27	13	0		100
	1976	62	38	0	0		100
Property Development	1946	100	0	0	0		100
	1956	100	0	0	0		100
	1966	0	0	100	0		100
	1976	100	0	0	0		100
Grand Total	1946	87	11	2	1		100
	1956	77	20	3	1		100
	1966	78	16	4	2		100
	1976	85	12	1	2		100

very slightly larger. The portion of large-scale industry controlled by European and South African capitalists had jumped from 2 per cent (one firm) to 7 per cent (seven firms). This relative expansion of big capital controlled in Europe and South Africa is the most significant net change over the three decades: in terms of asset share, it exactly counterbalances the relative decrease in capital under Canadian control.

In the decades between 1946 and 1976, however, there was considerable shifting of national control of dominant industrial corporations. Canadian control of big industry underwent a marked decline between 1946 and 1956—coincidental with the slow growth of Canadian Pacific in these years—but resurged after 1956. U.S. control shows the opposite pattern. However, even at its lowest ebb, in 1956, the indigenous fraction of the corporate elite controlled a large portion of the industrial capital represented by the dominant industrials.

The same trends can be seen in each of the three sectors of industrial capital in Table 4.7. The decline in Canadian control between 1946 and 1956 was most pronounced in the mining and utilities sectors, where nine dominant positions were vacated and indigenous assets fell from 24 per cent and 80 per cent to 13 per cent and 63 per cent respectively. In the same decade, the number and asset share of U.S.-held mining and utilities firms increased just as dramatically. The 1956–66 period indicates much less marked changes: the number of firms and per cent of assets in mining and manufacturing under Canadian control stayed fairly constant, while Canadian control of utilities increased by four firms and 21 per cent. U.S. control of mining companies dropped in this period as British and other interests penetrated large-scale Canadian mining. In the third decade, there was a resurgence of domestic control over the manufacturing and mining sectors. In terms of numbers of firms, Canadian control of big industry declined from 1946 to 1976. However, the dramatic growth of American-controlled capital was largely confined to the first postwar decade, while industrial capital controlled in other foreign countries gained a presence among the dominant corporations in the later decades. The most recent period indicates a trend in the direction of a net repatriation of industrial capital. In fact, the only consistent trend is that of increased but relatively insignificant control of big industry by capitalist interests in Europe and South Africa.

Yet, while Tables 4.6 and 4.7 offer serviceable descriptions of gross trends in the control of large-scale capital in Canada, they leave unexamined the exact means by which each national fraction's bloc of capital has been proportionately enlarged or reduced over time. There are in fact several possibilities in this regard. (1) Most dramatically, capitalists belonging to one national fraction may take over firms controlled by another fraction. In the Canadian context this situation corresponds to the image of Canadians "selling out" to Americans and applying the proceeds to nonproductive pursuits, as in portfolio investments. (2) Firms controlled by one fraction may fail to accumulate at a competitive pace, because of low productivity or location in less profitable industries, and may therefore come to represent a declining proportion of capital. We have already noted an important instance of this phenomenon in the sluggish growth of Canadian Pacific between 1946 and 1966. Conversely, firms controlled by a national fraction may grow especially quickly, increasing the proportion of capital under that fraction's control. (3) Companies that go defunct through bankruptcy or nationalization may decrease the amount of large-scale capital controlled by a given fraction, particularly if the income received in winding up the firm is not reinvested in some other big enterprise. By the same token, new companies that form and grow under the control of a given fraction may gradually come to represent a substantial bloc of big capital.

Proponents of the thesis of Canadian dependency stress the failure of Canada's capitalists in each of these aspects of accumulation. Levitt (1970, 39–40) speaks of the Canadian entrepreneurs of yesterday "selling out the country" to become *rentiers* and branch-plant managers. Industries remaining under Canadian control are "characterized either by small production units, such as sawmills, construction concerns or certain food-processing industries or, as in the case of textiles, by thoroughly dim prospects" (ibid. 121–23). Naylor (1975b) emphasizes the strategy of "industrialization by invitation" pursued by Canadian capitalists themselves reluctant or unable to accumulate within industrial circuits. Hutcheson (1978, 95) points out that much of the early direct investments of U.S. multinationals into Canadian industries was closely associated with the second industrial revolution and therefore with excellent longterm growth prospects. Clement (1977, 88–89) maintains that both U.S. takeovers of existing Canadian corporations (centralization) and fast growth of existing U.S.-controlled firms (concentration) have contributed to the rapid increase in the American share of Canadian industry.

The analysis that follows attempts to determine how the shifts observed in Tables 4.6 and 4.7 occurred. It centres on the control of big industrial capital, since little change is indicated in the national control of financial and commercial capital, while property development presents a clear example of a sector of big business emerging under indigenous control. In Tables 4.8 and 4.9, the seventy dominant industrials of 1946 and 1976 and their assets are crosstabulated by country of control, corporate survivorship, and industrial sector. By comparing the 1946 and 1976 distributions for each country we can gain an indication of

Table 4.8 Percentage Distributions of Dominant Industrial Firms by Country of Control and Corporate Survivorship, 1946 and 1976

A. 1946 Top 70

Industry	Corporate Survivorship	Country of Control				
		Canada	U.S.	U.K.	Other	Total
Mining	Consistently dominant	5	8	—	—	6
	Extant throughout	5	4	—	—	4
	Defunct by 1976	2	4	—	—	4
Manufacturing	Consistently dominant	22	33	25	—	26
	Extant throughout	22	21	75	—	24
	Defunct by 1976	15	12	—	—	11
Utilities	Consistently dominant	7	8	—	—	7
	Extant throughout	10	0	—	—	4
	Defunct by 1976	12	8	—	100	13
Total (N)		100(41)	100(24)	100(4)	100(1)	100(70)

Table 4.8 Percentage Distributions of Dominant Industrial Firms by Country of Control and Corporate Survivorship, 1946 and 1976

B. 1976 Top 70

Industry	Corporate Survivorship	Country of Control				
		Canada	U.S.	U.K.	Other	Total
Mining	Consistently dominant	10	4	—	—	6
	Extant throughout	3	11	—	29	9
	Incorporated after 1946	10	11	50	14	13
Manufacturing	Consistently dominant	32	25	—	14	26
	Extant throughout	16	32	—	—	20
	Incorporated after 1946	6	4	50	43	11
Utilities	Consistently dominant	10	4	—	—	6
	Extant throughout	6	4	—	—	4
	Incorporated after 1946	6	7	—	—	6
Total (N)		100(31)	100(28)	100(4)	100(7)	100(70)

Table 4.9 Percentage Distributions of Dominant Industrial Assets by Country of Control and Corporate Survivorship, 1946 and 1976

A. 1946 Top 70

Industry	Corporate Survivorship	Country of Control				
		Canada	U.S.	U.K.	Other	Total
Mining	Consistently dominant	4	29(26)*	—	—	12
	Extant throughout	2	3(2)	—	—	2
	Defunct by 1976	1	9(8)	—	—	4
Manufacturing	Consistently dominant	21	26(30)	26	—	22
	Extant throughout	8	4(4)	74	—	9
	Defunct by 1976	7	7(7)	—	—	7
Utilities	Consistently dominant	44	13(11)	—	—	28
	Extant throughout	4	—	—	—	2
	Defunct by 1976	10	10(9)	—	100	11
Total		100	100(100)	100	100	100

Table 4.9 Percentage Distributions of Dominant Industrial Assets by Country of Control and Corporate Survivorship, 1946 and 1976

B. 1976 Top 70

Industry	Corporate Survivorship	Country of Control				
		Canada	U.S.	U.K.	Other	Total
Mining	Consistently dominant	16	13	–	–	13
	Extant throughout	1	8	–	42	6
	Incorporated after 1946	6	9	57	8	8
Manufacturing	Consistently dominant	32	33	–	10	30
	Extant throughout	8	20	–	–	11
	Incorporated after 1946	5	2	43	41	8
Utilities	Consistently dominant	23	6	–	–	15
	Extant throughout	3	3	–	–	3
	Incorporated after 1946	6	7	–	–	6
Total		100	100	100	100	100

*Includes Benchmark estimates for five top 70 firms missing data in 1946.

how each fraction's industrial accumulation base has changed over the three decades.

In the right-hand column of Tables 4.8 and 4.9 the overall movements of big industry across the survivorship and industrial categories are observable. Table 4.8 shows very little change in the distribution of firms, except for the trivial replacement of "defunct" firms with "new" ones, and the increase in big mining firms and decline of "utilities." The marginal distributions of Table 4.9 are more interesting: they show the great extent to which big industrial capital was tied up in the transportation and utilities sector in 1946. The relative decline of utilities—as a result of slow growth, the transformation of Brascan Limited into a *bona fide* investment company, and nationalizations—is offset to a degree by the formation of new capital in this sector, with the pipeline boom of the 1950's. By 1976 6 per cent of top industrial assets is claimed by four new utilities: TransCanada Pipe-Lines Limited, Alberta Gas Trunk Line Company Limited, Interprovincial Pipe Line Limited, and Westcoast Transmission Company Limited. On the other hand, the increases in the share of industrial assets claimed by mining and manufacturing firms are only partly attributable to the growth of newly incorporated firms. Much of the increased proportion of assets in the mining sector comes from the growth of firms extant throughout the period, such as U.S.-controlled Falconbridge Nickel Mines Limited, which moves from a ranking below 70th in 1946 to the 32nd position in 1976.

For the Canadian fraction of monopoly capital, Table 4.9 chronicles a definite bias toward investments in the broad "utilities sector" in 1946, when 58 per cent of big industrial capital controlled in Canada took this form. Even in 1946, however, a substantial proportion of large-scale indigenous industry was located in the manufacturing sector, particularly in firms that would later be consistently positioned at the higher echelons of the economy. On the other hand, only 7 per cent of indigenously-held industrial assets was tied up in the five dominant Canadian-controlled mining firms of 1946. By 1976, the indigenous bloc of large-scale industry had undergone substantial restructuring. Utilities claimed only 32 per cent of assets, while manufacturing and mining companies accounted for 45 per cent and 23 per cent respectively. A large part of these gains occurred within the category of consistently dominant firms. In mining in 1946, the assets of new firms exceed those claimed by "defunct" firms by 5 per cent, contributing further to the increased prominence of indigenous mining capital. But by far the largest portion of indigenously held industry in 1976 was made up of firms that occupied a consistently dominant position throughout the 1946–76 period. Canadian capitalists in these three decades appear to have consolidated control over some of the most concentrated industrial capitals in Canada. Concomitantly, 17 per cent of dominant industrial assets under Canadian control in 1976 was located in newly formed companies. Both these trends suggest that, on balance, the period was one of successful accumulation of large-scale industrial capital by Canadian capitalists.

There are two distinct processes related to the increased proportions of indigenously held assets among dominant industrials. One is the very favourable growth record of several large firms that were controlled in Canada in 1946 and in 1976. For instance, Noranda Mines Limited moved from 34th to 8th position, Massey-Ferguson Limited from 27th to 6th, Stelco from 17th to 10th, Algoma Steel Corporation Limited from 45th to 26th, and Moore Corporation Limited from 59th to 34th. Secondly, a great amount of industrial capital was transferred from American to Canadian control as U.S. interests divested themselves of key holdings and Canadian investors gradually acquired shares of Bell Canada, Inco Limited, and Alcan Aluminum Limited. These three industrial monopolies, under definite U.S. control in 1946, became controlled by their Canadian managements as traditional blocs of controlling interest were broken up. By implication, Bell's manufacturing subsidiary, Northern Telecom Limited, also a dominant industrial in all years, became Canadianized by 1976. Another consistently dominant manufacturer, the Price Company Limited, moved from British to indigenous control, further increasing the proportion of Canadian-controlled manufacturing assets.

Closer examination of the dominant firms incorporated after 1946 and controlled in Canada in 1976 reveals that the two manufacturing concerns, MacMillan Bloedel Limited and Consolidated-Bathurst Limited, are mergers of earlier firms. However, the three newly incorporated mining firms, Dome Petroleum Limited, Pan Canadian Petroleum Limited and Norcen Energy Resources Limited, constitute postwar start-ups, as do the two new utilities, Alberta Gas Trunk Line Company Limited and TransCanada PipeLines Limited. Incidently, both Dome Petroleum and TransCanada PipeLines were formed under U.S. control and later patriated into the hands of Canadian capitalists.

It is difficult to find evidence in these data of a cumulative tendency toward the decline of indigenous industry. By 1976, Canadian capitalists controlled only a slightly smaller proportion of dominant industrial capital than they did in 1946. In both years, their holdings were concentrated in firms consistently positioned at the higher reaches of the economy, but in the later year indigenous investments were more evenly apportioned among the main branches of industry, characteristic of a mature bourgeoisie. Between 1946 and 1976, Canadian control of industry was maintained and diversified through the formation of new capitals, the growth of existing firms, and the patriation of several foreign-controlled companies.

U.S.-controlled industrials manifest rather different changes over the period of study. Table 4.9, which gives the 1946 distribution of assets (both with and without "benchmark" estimates for firms missing financial data),[15] shows a decline of the share of assets attributable to consistently dominant firms, as Bell, Northern Tel, Inco, and Alcan are brought under Canadian control. There is also a clear tendency for mining and manufacturing firms too small to rank as dominant in 1946 to account for a substantial proportion of industrial assets by 1976. The same trend is indicated for newly-formed mining and utilities firms, which claim 9 per cent and 7 per cent of U.S.-controlled industrial assets in 1976. Therefore, we find, in the U.S. fraction a loss of several giant industrials to Canadian control, combined with considerable concentration of capital through expansion both of *smaller* industrials in mining and manufacturing and of *new* mining and utilities firms. The net effect of these changes, as already noted in Table 4.7, is a slight increase in the proportion of top industrial assets under American control.

A number of U.S.-controlled firms occupy relatively prominent positions in the 1976 Top 70 but were excluded from the rankings in 1946 because of unavailability of data. These include Hudson's Bay Oil and Gas Company Limited (ranked 58 in 1956 and 41 in 1976), Mobil Oil Canada Limited (ranked 50 in 1966 and 53 in 1976), Dow Chemical of Canada Limited (ranked 56 in 1976), Sun Oil Company Limited (ranked 57 in 1976), IBM Canada Limited (ranked 55 in 1966 and 59 in 1976), and ITT Canada Limited (ranked 61 in 1976, the first year of available data). Several of these firms seem to have favourable postwar growth records, though the lack of data in the earlier years makes this judgement tentative. The new manufacturing firm under U.S. control in 1976 is Dupont of Canada Limited, a reorganized version of Canadian Industries Limited. However, the new U.S. firms in mining and utilities do represent newly formed capitals: Iron Ore Company of Canada (ranked 31 in 1976), Amoco Canada Petroleum Limited (ranked 42), Husky Oil Limited (ranked 52), Interprovincial Pipe Line Limited (ranked 30), and Westcoast Transmission Company Limited (ranked 40).

Although the issue of foreign takeovers will be discussed in detail later, it is appropriate to note here that such transfers of control do not figure importantly in the postwar histories of the twenty-eight dominant industrials under American control in 1976. Besides Irving Oil Limited (itself an ambiguous case),[16] there are only two industrials in the 1976 Top 100 that were lost by Canadian capitalists to American interests in the 1946–76 period, namely Gulf Canada Ltd., (formerly British-American Petroleum Co. Ltd.) and British Columbia Forest Products Limited.[17] Instead of taking over large indigenous firms and constituting a direct predatory threat to the monopoly fraction of the Canadian bourgeoisie, U.S. capitalists have maintained their level of Canadian investments largely through competitive growth rates, the establishment of several new and successful firms, and the takeover of smaller Canadian firms.[18]

The history of British and other foreign-held big industrial capital may be described as a complete restructuring of investments, inasmuch as no firm survived until 1976 as a dominant corporation under the same control. The Price Company Limited became controlled in Canada by 1975; the other three dominant British-controlled manufacturers in the 1946 Top 70—Bowater's Newfoundland Pulp and Paper Mills Limited, Imasco Limited, and Anglo-Newfoundland Development Company Limited—grew too slowly to rank as dominant in the later year.[19] The British bloc of big industry in 1976 was composed of four new companies in the mining and manufacturing sectors, but only one of these (Rio Algom Limited) was truly a postwar start-up. The others were actually reorganizations of extant capital. For example, Reed Paper Limited, formed in 1961 as a holding company, eventually consolidated its subsidiary, Anglo-Canadian Pulp and Paper Mills Limited (established in 1924), to become a new industrial.

Large-scale industrials controlled in other countries exhibit the most dramatic gains over the period, with seven mining and manufacturing firms taking the place of the single utility on the 1946 list. Three of these corporations were extant in 1946: French-held Canada Cement LaFarge, consistently dominant and formerly under Canadian control; Hudson Bay Mining and Smelting Company Limited, controlled in the U.S. until 1962, when the South African giant Anglo-American Corp. acquired control; and Dutch-controlled Shell Canada Limited. The four newly incorporated companies were all genuine "start-ups" and show mixed patterns of relative growth. Aquitaine Company of Canada Limited (established in 1963 and controlled in France) was ranked 69 in 1976; Genstar Limited (established in 1951, controlled in Belgium) lept to 18th place; and Rothmans of Pall Mall Canada Limited (established in 1956, controlled in South Africa) to 64th in 1976. However Petrofina Canada Limited (established in 1953, controlled in Belgium) fell from the 24th position in 1956 to 58th in 1976.

The study of corporate survivorship in Tables 4.8 and 4.9 helps clarify the means by which fractions of big industry maintained and restructured themselves over the 1946–76 period. A complementary analysis, provided in Tables 4.10–4.12, crosstabulates firms' dispositions at two periods. These "turnover tables" permit systematic examination of shifts in industrial capital's national locus of control. In Table 4.10, initial and final dispositions are compared for industrial firms dominant in either 1946 or 1976. For each of these years, the seventy dominant firms are categorized by country of control, and companies not ranking in the Top 70 are classified as to whether or not they were incorporated at the given time. We are particularly interested in the off-diagonal entries in the table: the firms undergoing changes in country of control. Yet, most of the twenty-nine industrials ranking in the Top 70 in both years did not undergo such shifts. Eleven dominant firms controlled in Canada in 1946 were also dominant and under Canadian control in 1976. These companies make up a stable core of industry under the control of domestic capitalists.[20] Ten firms were controlled in the U.S. in both years. The remaining eight dominant corporations of 1946 and 1976 changed control during the period, and five of these changes were advantageous to the Canadian fraction. Inco Limited, Alcan Aluminum Limited, Bell Canada, and Northern Telecom Limited moved from U.S. to indigenous control; Canadian control of The Price Company was acquired in 1975 from British interests. One of the Canadian-controlled dominant industrials of 1946, Gulf Canada, continued to be dominant in 1976 but had fallen under U.S. control by the later year, while Canada Cement LaFarge Limited shifted from Canadian to French control. Finally, one formerly U.S.-held firm, Hudson Bay Mining and Smelting Company, Limited, became controlled in South Africa by 1976. These findings confirm the earlier suggestion that the decreased number of Canadian-controlled dominant industrials is not principally a result of foreign takeovers. Instead, we find that a large number of the forty indigenous industrials of 1946 went defunct ($n =12$), or grew too slowly to rank as dominant in 1976 ($n =15$), while a smaller number of the indigenous industrials of 1976 were newly dominant ($n =15$). By the same token, the increased numbers of foreign controlled industrials results not so much from takeovers of the dominant Canadian-controlled companies but from the concentration of capital within firms not dominant in 1946.

Our main concern, however, is not with the sheer numbers of large firms under Canadian or foreign control in 1946 and 1976 but with the changing industrial accumulation bases of national monopoly fractions. To this end, Tables 4.11 and 4.12 take into account firm size by

Table 4.10 Turnover Analysis of Dominant Industrial Firms by Country of Control in 1946 and 1976*

Status in 1946	Status in 1976						
Top 70 Controlled in:	Top 70 Controlled in				Not in Top 70		Total
	Canada	U.S.	U.K.	Other	Extant	Defunct	
Canada	11	1	0	1	15	12	40
United States	4	10	0	1	4	5	24
United Kingdom	1	0	0	0	3	0	4
Other	0	0	0	0	0	1	1
Not in Top 70							
Extant in 1946	8	11	0	1	—	—	20
Incorporated after 1946	7	6	4	4	—	—	21
Total	31	28	4	7	22	18	110

*Excludes Brascan Limited, classified as a diversified investment company from 1971 on.

weighting the cases in Table 4.10 by their 1946 and 1976 assets. All told, 37 per cent of 1946 industrial assets were preserved under Canadian control (Table 4.11). By 1976 this block comprised only 22 per cent of dominant assets (Table 4.12)—reflecting to some extent the slow growth of Canadian Pacific Limited. A further 1 per cent of 1946 assets (The Price Company) moved from British to Canadian control. A large proportion of 1946 industrial assets—16 per cent—was transferred from U.S. to Canadian control, and by 1976 these four firms made up 18 per cent of top industrial assets.

Canadian control of dominant industrial assets was also maintained over time through a kind of capital restructuring, in which capital formerly located in firms that went defunct or grew at slower rates was "replaced" by the assets of new firms or firms formerly too small to rank among the dominant industrials. While 21 per cent of assets in 1946 were in Canadian controlled companies that would no longer be dominant by 1976, 17 per cent of assets in 1976 were in newly dominant, Canadian-controlled firms. Still, the difference between these proportions does indicate that for the indigenous bloc of industrial capital, the rise of new capital did not fully compensate for the "disappearance" of capital in major restructurings.

In contrast, U.S.-controlled industry registers a net *gain* through capital restructuring, partially offsetting the loss of several large industrials to Canadian control. In 1946, 11 per cent of top industrial assets were in U.S.-controlled firms that would not survive until 1976 as dominant corporations. By 1976, 15 per cent of assets were in newly dominant U.S.-controlled companies. A second source of growth for the U.S. bloc is the concentration of capital within the eleven corporations under U.S. control in both 1946 and 1976. Together these firms constituted 8 per cent of assets in 1946 and 19 per cent in 1976. This difference is somewhat exaggerated because of missing data in 1946 for privately-held companies such as General Motors of Canada Limited. Even when we add "benchmark" estimates of the firms' 1946 assets, however, the percentage for that year rises only to 11 per cent, still substantially less than the 19 per cent of top assets represented by the same eleven corporations in 1976.

In this regard, we find evidence of an indigenous disadvantage in the accumulation of big industrial capital, compared with the U.S.-controlled fraction. The slow growth of the CPR contributes to a relative *decline* of industrial assets in Canadian firms dominant in both 1946 and 1976. Consistent with Hutcheson's (1978) interpretation, dominant U.S. firms appear to have occupied more advantageous positions in the economy, particularly in the expanding automobile and petroleum in-

Table 4.11 Percentage Distribution of 1946 Industrial Assets by Country of Control in 1946 and 1976*

Status in 1946	Status in 1976						
	Top 70 Controlled in				Not in Top 70		
Top 70 Controlled in:	Canada	U.S.	U.K.	Other	Extant	Defunct	Total
Canada	37	1	0	1	9	12	59
United States	16	7	0	1	5	6	35
United Kingdom	1	0	0	0	1	0	4
Other	0	0	0	0	0	2	2
Total	52	8	0	2	17	20	100

*Excludes Brascan Limited, classified as a diversified investment company from 1971 forward.

Table 4.12 Percentage Distribution of 1976 Industrial Assets by Country of Control in 1946 and 1976

Status in 1946	Status in 1976				
	Top 70 Controlled in				
Top 70 Controlled in:	Canada	U.S.	U.K.	Other	Total
Canada	22	3	0	1	25
United States	18	16	0	1	34
United Kingdom	1	0	0	0	1
Other	0	0	0	0	0
Not in Top 70					
Extant in 1946	7	9	0	2	18
Incorporated after 1946	10	6	3	4	22
Total	57	33	3	7	100

dustries. Hence, they record impressive growth, most notably in the first postwar decade. Moreover, a large proportion of Canadian assets in 1946 was tied up in firms that would no longer dominate the economy in 1976, including five utilities that were nationalized in the 1950's and 1960's. The U.S. bloc suffered smaller losses in this regard. Both fractions, however (along with industry controlled in Europe and South Africa), evidence strong growth in the form of new companies not yet dominant in 1946.

From the analysis of stability and change in each national fraction's industrial accumulation base, we can conclude that the 1946–56 decade witnessed very substantial American penetration, but that on balance the period from the 1940's to 1970's was not fundamentally one of major Canadian capitalists capitulating to U.S. interests. After the mid-1950's, U.S. control of large-scale Canadian industry declined while both indigenous and Euro-South African capitalists showed dramatic gains. This pattern of accumulation is more consistent with the generalized *internationalization* of industrial capital than with the notion of Canada's growing dependence on the American metropole. In any case, throughout the period, growth of foreign-controlled big industry was primarily *not* a consequence of the international *centralization* of capital, but of capitalist *concentration* within a booming Canadian economy. This conclusion is given further credence by the findings of Reuber and Roseman from an analysis of takeovers in the first sixteen postwar years:

> The acquisition of Canadian firms by non-residents from 1945 to 1961 contributed to the increase that occurred in foreign control during this period. It is important to recognize, however, that most of the increase in the share of Canadian industry controlled abroad reflects mainly: (i) the growth of firms that non-residents controlled prior to 1945; (ii) the growth of firms *after* they were acquired by non-residents during the period from 1945–1961; and (iii) the growth of new enterprises established by non-residents. By comparison, foreign acquisitions at the time they were acquired are relatively unimportant (1969, 7).

Meanwhile, the Canadian fraction retained under its control a number of the country's largest industrial capitals; it also gained control of several giant firms from American interests. Also, indigenous capital shifted out of the slow-growth "utilities" sector and concentrated in the expanding mining and manufacturing sectors. Facilitating this shift were (1) actions by states in freeing up capital by nationalizing electric and other utilities, and (2) the flowering in the 1960's of three diversified investment companies—Power Corporation, Brascan and Canadian Pacific Investments—each applying capital accumulated in the transportation-utilities sector to a diverse range of industrial and commercial investments in Canada and abroad. Indeed, of the sixteen Canadian multinational corporations accounting for 65 per cent of Canadian direct investment in foreign countries in 1976 (Niosi 1985, 50), thirteen appear in our Top 100. All but two of these were Canadian-controlled at that time.[21] Add to this the well-established strength of Canadian capitalists in the financial sector and it becomes clear that a definite basis for an indigenous fraction of finance capital was maintained from the 1940's into the 1970's.

5

PATTERNS OF CORPORATE INTERLOCKING
1946–1976

FINANCE CAPITAL AND INTERLOCKING DIRECTORATES

As a phenomenon within the political economy of advanced capitalism, finance capital implies not simply the control of large concentrations of industrial and financial capital, but also the functional *articulation* of these capitals in a definite structure of accumulation. To study the structure of finance capital in a given economy one would ideally want to analyze the "interconnections between capitals within related circuits of capital" (Overbeek 1980, 103), including the financial, institutional, service, and informal relations in which these interconnections are expressed. Although it is possible to piece together information on these various ties and, on that basis, to assign corporations to financial groups (see for example Sweezy 1939; Perlo 1957; Menshikov 1969; Knowles 1973), in general "systematic information about relations between companies is available only on interlocking directorships" (Overbeek 1980, 102). This limitation becomes more forceful as one delves further into the past.

Moreover, while the great quantity of information on relations between companies no doubt yields a very rich analysis, the problem arises of what to do with all the data. Fennama and Schijf point out that use of data describing different types of corporate relations may actually undermine the precise designation of financial groups, if "for one firm its belonging to a group is proven by the existence of interlocking directorates, for a second firm the financial linkages are taken as evidence, whereas a third firm is regarded as part of the group because of family relations" (1979, 305). They point to recent studies that employ well-defined concepts from network analysis in systematic examinations of the structure of interlocking directorates (ibid., 320–325). This chapter and the next one present a network analysis of corporate interlocking from 1946 to 1976. The general availability of interlock data and the rigorous nature of social network analysis allow us to make systematic comparisons across sectors of monopoly capital and over time. There is, however, a disadvantage to this methodology. The central problem with relying on interlocking directorates in the study of monopoly capital is not an embarrassment of riches but a poverty of substantive clarity. Any given interlock may signify quite a variety of intercorporate relations, ranging in importance from virtual accident (as with prominent "outsiders" who serve several firms as corporate window-dressing) through some sort of common co-optative interest (as in relations between ostensibly competing firms or between suppliers and buyers [see especially Burt 1983; Carrington 1981b]), to relations of control (as in the intertwining of share capital).

Social scientists who have analyzed corporate interlocks from a Marxist perspective have emphasized two ways in which these relations help sustain capitalist domination over the economy, civil society, and state. According to these class-based interpretations, interlocks may serve expressive and/or instrumental functions for the capitalist class (Sonquist and Koenig 1975). On one level, all interlocks create channels of interpersonal communication and acquaintanceship among directors of different corporations. The *class hegemony* view emphasizes the unintended consequences of such ties, as they promote capitalist class consciousness and consensus around important social issues. In this way, interlocking contributes to the reproduction of capitalist domination by enhancing the capacity of leading capitalists and their organic intellectuals to exercise cultural leadership and political power (see Glasberg and Schwartz 1983, 314–16; Useem 1984). On another level, certain interlocks may serve as what Michael Ornstein (1980) has termed "planned liaisons": purposeful relations that promote intercorporate accumulation of capital, often coinciding with and reinforcing financial or other relations between the same firms (see, for example, Fennema 1974; Berkowitz et al. 1976; Kotz 1978, 81). According to this perspective, certain interlocks are traces of the class power that resides in the *accumulation process itself,* as in the operational power to control corporate decisionmaking through intercorporate ownership or the allocative power to channel loan capital to corporate clients. By facilitating the production and circulation of surplus value, such planned liaisons contribute to the reproduction of capitalist domination at an economic level.

This distinction between expressive and instrumental functions of interlocks is of some theoretical help. However, it is difficult to draw in practice without resorting to other kinds of data beyond the interlocks themselves. These data can be hard to obtain. One promising approach to identifying purposeful interlocks employs longitudinal analysis of "broken ties," that is, interlocks that are dissolved by a director's retirement or death (Koenig, Sonquist, and Gogel 1978; Palmer 1983; Ornstein 1980, 1984). Broken ties that are subsequently reconstituted with the establishment of a new interlock may be indicative of instrumental relations between the interlocked firms. In his comprehensive study of broken ties, Ornstein (1984), uses the data base employed in this study; he reports that over 30 per cent of all broken interlocks between large Canadian corporations in the period from 1946 through 1975 were reconstituted within two years of the loss. What is more, when the analysis is restricted to interlocks involving two or more shared directors, the likelihood of replacement increases even further. These findings suggest that much of the observed interlock structure reflects purposeful intercorporate relations.

A second and simpler way of addressing the substantive meaning of interlocks is to forgo determining whether specific ties are "accidental" or "purposeful" and to focus instead on an aggregated pattern of interlocks. This approach grants that

> one man may hold the post of director, owing to an accidental combination of circumstances, but all directors of the biggest corporations and banks taken together are not an "accidental" group of persons and the interlocking of their posts in its entirety also speaks about certain rules and laws which personal union follows in our days (Menshikov 1969, 184–85).

This chapter examines the *aggregated pattern* of Canadian corporate interlocking in order to evaluate the general thesis that the dominant fraction of the bourgeoisie in Canada makes up a financial-industrial elite controlling a bloc of finance capital. The *specific relations* that have comprised the network of strong intercorporate ties in the 1946–76 period will be the topic of the next chapter. Using different modes of representing the network, it is possible to effect a certain "methodological triangulation," affording us numerous vantage points on the structure of corporate power.

DENSITY OF CORPORATE INTERLOCKING

Several indicators of structure may be derived from a network analysis of the aggregated pattern of interlocking. Using the pair of firms as the unit of analysis, levels of interlocking can be measured in terms of *density,* the proportion of all pairs of firms that are interlocked (Niemeijer 1973). These proportions can be broken down by the number of shared directors, giving us, for instance, the density of multiple-director interlocks and density of single-director interlocks. As Fennema (1982) points out, such a distinction is valuable in identifying the most systematically connected directorates. The density of interlocking can also be examined within and between *subnetworks* of companies to determine whether interlocks are concentrated among certain kinds of firms.

The following tables help to illustrate the overall level of corporate interlocking over time and the manner in which interlocking has been distributed across categories of corporate survivorship. This latter analysis breaks the set of dominant firms into subnetworks, a disaggregation that continues through the remainder of the chapter, as we investigate the pattern of interlocking within and between monopoly fractions of capital in Canada. For now, we are merely interested in finding whether most of the interlocks link consistently dominant corporations, and how newly dominant firms become integrated into the network over time, if at all. Is there an articulation between patterns of accumulation (for example, the concentrated structure of capital in a very few large industrial and financial corporations), and the structure of interlocking directorships? At the close of this analysis we should be able to offer a tentative answer to this question.

Table 5.1 shows the percentage distributions of the number of shared directors for all pairs of the fifty firms included in the Top 100 in all selection years. These consistently dominant corporations are of particular interest since they comprise the most stable component of monopoly capital. This stability at the level of individual firms means that there might be a concomitant tendency for certain pairs or sets of these companies to maintain stable intercorporate relations. The persistent dominance of these fifty firms renders them of potential importance in the larger intercorporate network. They may provide a stable ''core'' of institutional relations, to which other companies become attached in various ways and degrees as they grow to rank among the largest corporations.

The interlock percentage distributions in Table 5.1 are given at five-year intervals beginning in 1946. For each year, density of interlocking is simply the cumulative percentage of interlocked pairs of firms. In 1946, 16.7 per cent of pairs of consistently dominant firms shared at least one director. The density of interlocking rises to 21.5 per cent in 1956, 21 per cent in 1966, and 22.4 per cent in 1976. Between 1946 and 1966 both single and multiple-director interlocks proliferate. In 1946 10.5 per cent of pairs were tied by one director, and another 6.1 per cent were united by two or more; in 1966, the figures were 13.3 per cent and 7.7 per cent. Between 1966 and 1971 the densities of single and multiple interlocking fell to 12.6 per cent and 6.4 per cent, but by

Table 5.1 Percentage Distributions of Number of Shared Directors for Pairs of Consistently Dominant Corporations, 1946–1976

Number of Shared Directors	Percentage Distribution For:							Cumulative Percentages For:						
	1946	1951	1956	1961	1966	1971	1976	1946	1951	1956	1961	1966	1971	1976
5 or more	0.8	1.0	1.3	1.0	1.0	0.6	0.8	0.8	1.0	1.3	1.0	1.0	0.6	0.8
4	0.8	0.8	1.1	1.0	0.7	0.4	0.6	1.7	1.8	2.4	2.0	1.7	1.0	1.5
3	1.0	1.3	0.8	1.6	1.9	1.2	1.3	2.7	3.1	3.2	3.5	3.6	2.2	2.8
2	3.4	3.3	3.7	3.7	4.1	4.2	4.6	6.1	6.4	7.0	7.2	7.7	6.4	7.4
1	10.5	12.4	14.5	14.4	13.3	12.6	14.9	16.7	18.8	21.5	21.6	21.0	18.9	22.4
0	83.3	81.2	78.5	78.4	79.0	81.1	77.6	100.0	100.0	100.0	100.0	100.0	100.0	100.0
N of Firms	50	50	50	50	50	50	50	50	50	50	50	50	50	50

Table 5.2 Percentage Distributions of Number of Shared Directors for Successive Top Industrials and Financials, 1946–1976*

Number of Shared Directors	Percentage Distribution For:							Cumulative Percentages For:						
	1946	1951	1956	1961	1966	1971	1976	1946	1951	1956	1961	1966	1971	1976
5 or more	0.3	0.4	0.3	0.4	0.4	0.2	0.2	0.3	0.4	0.3	0.4	0.4	0.2	0.2
4	0.4	0.3	0.5	0.5	0.5	0.2	0.3	0.7	0.7	0.9	0.9	0.9	0.4	0.5
3	0.6	0.6	0.6	0.8	0.9	0.8	0.7	1.3	1.3	1.4	1.7	1.8	1.2	1.2
2	1.6	1.7	2.2	1.9	2.3	2.0	2.3	2.9	3.1	3.7	3.6	4.1	3.2	3.4
1	6.8	7.4	8.3	8.4	8.7	8.1	9.3	9.6	10.5	12.0	12.0	12.8	11.3	12.7
0	90.4	89.5	88.0	88.0	87.2	88.7	87.3	100.0	100.0	100.0	100.0	100.0	100.0	100.0
N of Firms	98	98	100	102	102	102	101	98	98	100	102	102	102	101

*Excluding International Harvester Company of Canada in 1946–1956 and Genstar Limited in 1951 and 1956, because of missing data.

1976 they had recovered to levels of 14.9 per cent and 7.4 per cent. However, a net decrease in density of interlocks involving the sharing of three or more directors is evidenced between 1966 and 1976.

It appears from these results that the network of firms consistently ranking at the top of the economy has been characterized over time by a fair amount of stability in the extent of interlocking. Roughly one in five pairs of firms are directly interlocked at any given time. This does not mean, however, that the same firms have been interlocked throughout the period, but it does suggest a rather close-knit network at the very top of the economy.

We can also discern some variation over time in interlocking. The first two decades show fairly steady increases, while the third decade witnesses a decrease during the first half and increase during the second. Comparing the 1946 and 1976 densities, we may note net *increases* in single-director interlocking, and double-interlocking, and stability over time in the sharing of three or more directors.

How does this description of overall interlocking change when we add companies that did not enjoy uninterrupted dominance in the post-war economy? In Table 5.2 the same analysis of densities is applied to dominant industrial and financial firms at five-year intervals. Only these firms are examined to keep the size of the network essentially constant at about one hundred firms; the sectors of big capital whose numbers grow (commercial and property development) are excluded. This procedure is advisable because densities are affected by variations in network size (Niemeijer 1973). By holding the total number of firms constant, we eliminate the effects of changes in network size on observed density, while including in the analysis the major centres of large-scale capital in Canada. Each Top 100 in Table 5.2 includes forty-seven of the fifty firms from Table 5.1[1] and adds to these the corporations ranked among the dominant industrial and financial firms for the specific year under examination.

The pattern of densities for these successive Top 100s is quite similar to that for the fifty consistently dominant firms. In 1946, 9.6 per cent of pairs were interlocked. This density rises to 12.0 per cent in 1956 and 12.8 per cent in 1966, but then falls slightly, to 12.7 percent in 1976. The increase from 1946 to 1966 is distributed among both single and multiple-director interlocks; the decrease after 1966 results from a lowered density of multiple-director ties. The net change from 1946 to 1976 may be described as an *increase* of 37 per cent in the density or likelihood of single-director interlocking and of 54 per cent in the likelihood of multiple-director ties.

Both Tables 5.1 and 5.2 indicate consistent and increasing levels of interlocking over time, rather than a sporadic pattern of heavy interlocking in some years and sparse interlocking in others. Although most interlocked firms are connected by single shared directors, a substantial portion of intercorporate ties involves the exchange of multiple directors. Finally, the probability of interlocking (the density) is generally higher among the consistently dominant firms depicted in Table 5.1. Moreover, the disparity between corresponding densities in the two tables seems directly related to the *strength* of the interlock. In 1976, for instance, 0.8 per cent of consistently dominant companies shared five or more directors while only 0.2 per cent of all top-ranked industrial and financial firms were interlocked at the same strength. Consistently dominant corporations are thus four times more likely to maintain such strong ties among themselves. In the same year, however, 14.9 per cent of consistently dominant firms and 9.3 per cent of top industrials and financials shared single directors, for a ratio of only 1.6. So, the tendency for consistently dominant corporations to interlock is especially pronounced in the case of multiple-director ties—relations that Ornstein (1984) has found most durable. The companies consistently at the top of the corporate world—the institutionally stable component of monopoly capital—are the firms with the strongest intercorporate ties. This suggests that consistently dominant companies may provide a stable core of strong ties at the centre of a broader structure of intercorporate alliances. The concentration of corporate interlocking seems in this sense to mirror the concentration of capital within the largest firms.

Table 5.3 considers this hypothesis more directly by breaking the network of interlocks among all dominant firms in 1946, 1956, 1966, and 1976 into subnetworks that correspond to the categories of corporate survivorship introduced in Chapter 4. This analysis allows us to examine the density of interlocking *within* each subnetwork of companies and *between* each pair of subnetworks. The densities are expressed as proportions rather than percentages. For instance, the table shows that in 1946, 16 per cent of all pairs of firms consistently in the Top 100 were interlocked, and 5.9 per cent of the same pairs shared multiple directors. That is, the probability of two consistently dominant firms sharing one director was 0.160, and the likelihood of sharing two or more directors was 0.059. Also in 1946, 7.1 per cent of pairs consisting of one consistently dominant firm and one firm in the "extant throughout" category were interlocked, 1.9 per cent by virtue of two or more directors.[2] By comparing the densities within and between the different subnetworks of firms we can determine whether certain of these serve as loci of intensive interlocking.

The table indicates that firms consistently ranking among the largest capitals interlock more densely with each other than do members of any

Table 5.3 Densities of Interlocks Within and Between Categories of Corporate Survivorship, Successive Top 100s, 1946–1976

SURVIVORSHIP STATUS	Year	SURVIVORSHIP STATUS							
		Consistently Dominant		Extant Throughout Sometimes Dominant		Incorporated After 1946		Defunct By 1976	
		All Ties	Multiple Ties	All Ties	Multiple Ties	All Ties	Multiple Ties	All Ties	Multiple Ties
Consistently in Top 100	1946	.160	.059	.071	.019	–	–	.120	.036
	1956	.207	.067	.088	.026	.126	.024	.178	.052
	1966	.210	.077	.109	.033	.154	.050	.227	.087
	1976	.224	.074	.113	.022	.142	.045	–	–
Extant Throughout, Sometimes in Top 100	1946			.034	.005	–	–	.071	.006
	1956			.043	.015	.048	.007	.081	.028
	1966			.084	.020	.081	.016	.105	.029
	1976			.089	.018	.077	.015	–	–
Incorporated After 1946	1946					–	–	–	–
	1956					.110	.033	.116	.013
	1966					.100	.030	.187	.040
	1976					.116	.027	–	–
Defunct By 1976	1946							.080	.029
	1956							.150	.025
	1966							0	0
	1976							–	–

Table 5.4 Percentage Distributions of Interlocks by Corporate Survivorship, Successive Top 100s, 1946–1976

SURVIVORSHIP STATUS	Year	SURVIVORSHIP STATUS							
		Consistently Dominant		Extant Throughout Sometimes Dominant		Incorporated After 1946		Defunct By 1976	
		All Ties	Multiple Ties	All Ties	Multiple Ties	All Ties	Multiple Ties	All Ties	Multiple Ties
Consistently in Top 100	1946	37.5	46.2	19.1	17.3	–	–	27.5	27.6
	1956	33.6	38.1	18.0	19.1	11.7	7.9	18.8	19.5
	1966	30.2	35.2	22.4	21.4	22.7	23.2	4.0	4.9
	1976	30.8	37.3	20.3	14.8	27.2	31.6	–	–
Extant Throughout, Sometimes in Top 100	1946			2.5	1.3	–	–	9.2	2.6
	1956			2.6	3.3	2.8	1.4	5.3	6.5
	1966			5.9	4.5	8.4	5.2	1.3	1.1
	1976			4.9	3.7	9.4	6.6	–	–
Incorporated After 1946	1946					–	–	–	–
	1956					1.3	1.4	3.4	1.4
	1966					3.5	3.4	1.6	1.1
	1976					7.3	6.2	–	–
Defunct By 1976	1946							4.2	5.1
	1956							2.4	1.4
	1966							0	0
	1976							–	–
Total	1946	84.1	91.0	30.8	21.1	–	–	40.9	35.3
	1956	82.1	84.6	28.7	30.3	19.2	12.1	30.0	28.8
	1966	79.3	84.6	37.9	32.3	36.2	32.9	6.9	7.1
	1976	78.3	83.6	34.7	25.0	43.9	44.3	–	–

of the other subnetworks. This difference is quite marked in all years. By 1976, 7.4 per cent of all pairs of consistently dominant firms shared multiple directors, but only 2.7 per cent of all pairs of new firms and 1.8 per cent of all pairs of extant firms were multiply interlocked. The social integration of big capital is most evident among firms that comprise the most institutionally stable and concentrated bloc.

Further, the next-highest densities in all years are those between consistently dominant companies and firms in the other three survivorship categories. Companies that exist throughout the period but are not consistently dominant tend to maintain more interlocks with firms always in the Top 100 than with each other, although a great increase in single-director interlocking is indicated within this subnetwork. Newly incorporated firms tend to establish interlocks with consistently dominant companies more than with each other or with extant corporations (although the difference in the former case is not very large). The picture of the interlock network that emerges is of a densely connected core comprised of the largest, institutionally stable capitals, linked to smaller or less stable capitals, which tend to occupy more peripheral positions in the network.

Similar conclusions may be drawn from Table 5.4, in which the percentage distribution of interlocks in each year is shown for the same survivorship categories. Each cell in the table displays the percentage of all interlocks occurring within (or between) the indicated subnetworks. The entire set of percentages for each year totals 100 per cent. Two distributions at four points are included: (1) the percentage distribution of all interlocks and (2) the percentage distribution of multiple interlocks. Obviously, the percentage distribution of interlocks, unlike the density of interlocks, is insensitive to changes in the total amount of interlocking, since it always totals 100 per cent. On the other hand, this indicator is sensitive to differences in the number of firms comprising each subnetwork. Small subnetworks that are densely interlocked will not necessarily account for a large percentage of all interlocks, since the number of possible ties is strictly limited by the number of firms involved. The percentage distribution of interlocks is most useful as a descriptive indicator of "how much" of the network is made up of connections between different kinds of firms.

The bottom panel of Table 5.4 supplies "Totals" for each survivorship category. These report what percentage of all interlocks involve firms belonging to the given category. Each total includes the percentage of all ties attributable to relations within the subnetwork and to relations between the subnetwork and the rest of the network. Consequently, the totals for a given year do not add to 100 per cent. We can see in the totals that most interlocks include firms securely positioned in the Top 100 throughout the study period. In 1946, 84.1 per cent of all interlocks, and an astonishing 91 per cent of all multiple-director interlocks included at least one firm that would consistently rank at the top of the economy over the next three decades. By 1976, these percentages had fallen only slightly. Of all the interlocks occurring among the Top 100 in that year, 78.3 per cent included at least one consistently dominant firm. Of all the multiple-director interlocks, 83.6 per cent included at least one such firm.

The differences between these four percentages illustrate two tendencies. First, it is clear that the structural prominence of consistently dominant firms is especially marked when only multiple interlocks are analyzed. Second, there is a trend over time for the network to become slightly less focused around corporations that have been consistently dominant.

The main diagonal of the table shows the percentages of interlocks attributed to relations *within* each corporate subnetwork (that is, ties between firms of like survivorship status). Considering again the consistently top-ranked companies, we see that multiple interlocks between these firms make up 46.2 per cent of all multiple interlocks in 1946 and 37.3 per cent in 1976. A large proportion of all the strong ties in the network are multiple interlocks between consistently dominant·corporations. Clearly, the firms consistently occupying dominant positions in the postwar Canadian economy have also occupied dominant positions in the structure of corporate interlocks: so much so that interlocks between other firms are rare.

But what of these other firms? The percentages in Table 5.4 illustrate the disappearance of firms that go defunct, as well as the progressive integration of new firms into the network. In both cases, most ties extend to consistently dominant companies, reproducing a rather centralized structure of interlocks even as its specific composition changes. As for corporations that exist through the entire period but do not consistently rank in the Top 100, there is a definite increase in their network prominence. By 1976, they participated in a third of all interlocks and a quarter of all multiple-director ties. Moreover, these gains were registered not through relatively greater interlocking with the core set of top firms, but by means of increased ties with other extant or new firms.

There is some evidence, then, of a relative weakening in the extent to which interlocks are dominated by the core set of top-ranked firms. Still the structural prominence of this sector in 1976 is impressive. Bearing in mind the tremendous accumulation of capital under control of the largest firms, and the generalized increases in interlock density, the major implication of this pattern would appear to be a greater effective centralization of capital, as the directorates of the largest and most stable corporations interpenetrate more while overlapping with the boards of newly dominant firms.

CORPORATE INTERLOCKING AND CAPITALIST FRACTIONS

Having described general features of the network of corporate inter-locks, we are now in a position to consider the manner in which national fractions of large-scale capital appear within this social structure. Our analysis of accumulation trends led us to reject the thesis that Canadian capitalists are confined in their investments to the "sphere of circula-tion" and to suggest that the most recent tendency at the higher reaches of the economy is toward greater indigenous control of industry. Still, it could be that the Canadian bourgeoisie manifests "institutional biases" in the direction of dependency. The pattern of interlocking directorates provides a means of systematically assessing the predominant kinds of intercorporate alliances in Canada. As Moore and Wells suggest, "a careful study of inter-locking directorates is needed to determine the rel-ationships between Canadian and foreign owned industrial capital on the one hand and finance capital in Canada on the other" (1975, 60–61). There are several possible scenarios.

We could find a tendency over time toward "continentalism," as indigenously controlled firms interlock more with U.S.-controlled com-panies and less with each other. This situation would correspond to Cle-ment's thesis that "the indigenous elite has entered into an alliance with the dominant comprador elite" (1977, 94, see also pp.181, 287). Fur-ther, if we were to find that most of these interlocks link Canadian financial capital with U.S. industrial capital we would have compelling evidence that "the financial-industrial axis is continental for Canada" (ibid., 179, see also Naylor 1972, 31), especially if we also found a rel-ative lack of financial-industrial ties within the indigenous fraction. Un-der such circumstances, the structural basis for capital accumulation under control of indigenous capitalists would be questionable, and an interpretation of "compradorization" would be tenable. This scenario can be most closely identified with what we have called the thesis of Canadian dependency.

The Parks's analysis of finance capital in Canada also posits a tendency toward dependent "continentalism." However, the Parks em-phasize the maintenance of a network of ties uniting indigenous indus-trial and financial companies:

the major U.S. financial groups...and other smaller groups and some big companies...have extended their operations to Canada on the basis of a certain capital invested and the re-investment of profits, and have formed alliances with Canadian banks and Canadian financial groups (1973, 32).

On the basis of this interpretation we would expect to find a good deal of interlocking *within* the indigenous fraction, along with increased interlocking *between* indigenous financial capital and American-controlled industrial capital.

We could alternatively find no strong tendencies toward continentalism but an incremental *atrophy* within the indigenous fraction. There may well have been an integrated structure of interlocks around the CPR, Bank of Montreal, Sun Life, Stelco and the like in 1946, but this network could have dissolved over the years, leaving in its place no coherent basis—at least in interlocks—for indigenous finance capital. Rather, by the 1970's, we might find an assortment of corporate interlocks having no apparent logic. This scenario lacks credibility, given what we know about the network of interlocks in the postwar period (ibid; Carroll, Fox and Ornstein 1982; Sweeny 1980). However, a less extreme version embodying the same basic metaphor of "atrophy" could be plausibly advanced. Perhaps, for instance, many of the ties uniting indigenous financial and industrial capital have been broken, leaving a network dominated by a highly integrated bloc of financial capital, relatively detached from Canadian-controlled industry. To the extent that such a trend toward "disarticulation" of interlocks reflected a weakening or severing of circuits of finance capital, the growth prospects for indigenous industry could be impaired.

A fourth possibility, corresponding to the argument advanced in Chapter 3, is that a structured set of intercorporate relations has been maintained among large Canadian firms, preserving and in some respects consolidating an indigenous bloc of finance capital. In the context of an economy undergoing rapid growth, we should expect to find that companies that rise to dominance under indigenous control are integrated into the structure: that the intercorporate network is restructured as part of the process of capitalist concentration and centralization. Similarly, the emergence of new forms of indigenous finance capital in the growth of diversified investment companies should be reflected in the development of interlocks between these firms and industrial and financial companies under Canadian control. Finally, if the network represents an indigenous *bloc of finance capital*, we should find that the preponderance of interlocks—especially the more stable, multiple-

director associations—serve to link indigenous industrial with indigenous financial capital, and that ties to foreign-controlled firms tend to be
weaker and less common.

The validity of these various scenarios cannot be determined from a
single tabulation but must be judged in the light of a whole set of considerations. In the analyses that follow the fourth interpretation is demonstrated to be the most credible.

An essential question is how the intercorporate network has been
structured in terms of its "indigenous" and "comprador" fractions. It
is helpful to address this question against the backdrop of what we have
learned so far about corporate survivorship in the 1946–76 period. On
the one hand, we observed in Chapter 4 that each category of survivorship—from consistently dominant companies to firms that go defunct by
1976—includes corporations controlled by Canadian capitalists as well
as corporations under foreign control. On the other hand, we have
found in the most recent series of analyses that the consistently dominant firms form the core of the intercorporate network at any given time
and that new companies become integrated to the network mainly by
interlocking with the firms in the core. We may now ask how the indigenous and comprador fractions of monopoly capital appear within this
social structure. Is the core network composed of both Canadian and
foreign-controlled firms, with a plethora of ties between consistently
dominant companies under indigenous and foreign control? Such a pattern of interlocking would suggest that at the centre of monopoly capital
in Canada is an alliance of indigenous and comprador fractions. By the
same token, do new firms show a tendency toward "compradorization"
in their interlocking; do indigenously controlled corporations establish
relations with companies under foreign control; do foreign-controlled
firms link up with the indigenous fraction? To answer these questions
we must analyze the interlock network with respect to two variables: a
firm's survivorship record, and its country of control.

Table 5.5 decomposes the multiple-interlock network of dominant
corporations at four times into subnetworks defined by these two variables.[3] By observing the percentage distribution of ties within and between these subnetworks, we can assess whether the strongest, most
stable relationships—multidirector interlocks—unite indigenous firms
or connect these companies to foreign-controlled capital.

At the bottom of Table 5.5, the marginal percentages point up quite
clearly that it is Canadian-controlled corporations consistently at the top
of the economy that have formed a stable core for the network. In all
years, these companies are involved in over 75 per cent of all multiple-
director ties. Among themselves they account for between 24.2 per cent

Table 5.5 Percentage Distribution of Multiple Interlocks by Country of Control and Corporate Survivorship, Successive Top 100s, 1946–1976

Country	Survivorship	Year	CANADA				U. S.				U.K.	OTHER
			Top	Extant	New	Defunct	Top	Extant	New	Defunct	All	All
C A N A D A	Consistently Dominant	1946	24.4	14.7	–	22.4	17.3	0	–	0.6	3.2	0
		1956	24.2	16.3	2.3	16.7	11.6	0.5	2.8	0.5	1.9	0.5
		1966	25.1	14.2	12.0	3.4	6.4	3.0	3.8	0.8	4.9	4.9
		1976	31.6	11.5	22.1	–	4.5	2.9	2.0	–	1.6	2.9
	Extant Throughout, Sometimes Dominant	1946		0.6	–	2.6	1.9	0	–	0	1.3	0
		1956		3.3	0.5	5.6	1.9	0	0.5	0	0	0
		1966		3.0	3.0	0	0	1.5	0	0	1.5	0
		1976		3.7	3.7	–	0.4	0	0.4	–	0	0.8
	Incorporated After 1946	1946			–	–	–	–	–	–	–	–
		1956			0	0	0.5	0	0.9	0	0	0
		1966			0.4	0.4	1.9	1.1	1.5	0	1.5	0.8
		1976			4.5	–	2.5	0.8	1.2	–	0.4	0.8
	Defunct by 1976	1946				3.2	3.8	0	–	1.9	0	0
		1956				1.4	2.3	0.5	0.5	0	0	0.9
		1966				0	0	0	0	0.4	0	0
		1976				–	–	–	–	–	–	–
U. S.	Consistently Dominant	1946					1.3	0	–	0.6	0	0
		1956					0.9	0	–	0.9	0.5	0
		1966					0.4	0	–	0.8	0	0.4
		1976					0	0	–	0.4	0	0
	Extant Throughout, Sometimes Dominant	1946					0	–	–	0	0	0
		1956					0	0	0.5	0.5	0	0
		1966					0	0.4	0	0.4	0	0
		1976					0	0.4	–	0	0	0
	Incorporated After 1946	1946							–	–	–	–
		1956							0.5	0	0	0.8
		1966							0	0.4	0	0.8
		1976							0	–	0	0.8
	Defunct by 1976	1946								0	0	0
		1956								0	0	0
		1966								0	0	0
		1976								–	–	–
U. K.	All Firms	1946									0	0
		1956									0.5	0
		1966									0.8	0.4
		1976									0	0
O T H	All Firms	1946										0
		1956										0
		1966										0.4
		1976										0
	TOTAL	1946	82.6	21.1	–	34.0	25.0	0	–	3.2	4.5	0
		1956	77.3	28.1	4.2	27.9	18.6	1.8	6.0	0.9	3.3	1.4
		1966	78.5	23.2	22.5	4.1	9.7	6.4	7.8	1.1	9.4	7.5
		1976	79.1	20.5	36.0	–	7.8	4.1	5.3	–	2.0	5.3

and 31.6 per cent. These percentages increase over time. Indigenous firms that exist throughout the period but are not consistently dominant have been much less involved in multiple interlocking. They were included in 21.1 per cent in 1946, 28.1 per cent in 1956, and 20.5 per cent in 1976. Most of these ties linked the extant firms to indigenously controlled, consistently dominant companies. Canadian-controlled corporations that were incorporated after 1946 show a strong propensity to establish relations with other dominant firms. New Canadian firms are participants in only 4.2 per cent of multiple-director links in 1956, but by 1976 their involvement has mushroomed to 36 per cent of all interlocks, tying them in most cases to Canadian-controlled firms that are consistently top-ranked.

A radically different pattern of interlocking is manifested by the U.S.-controlled companies. Among these, multiple-director interlocking is mainly a pursuit of consistently dominant firms; rarely do "extant," "new," or "defunct" corporations engage in such institutional relations. Moreover, among the consistently dominant, U.S.-controlled firms, the percentage of multiple interlocking drops from 25 per cent in 1946 to 18.6 per cent in 1956, 9.7 per cent in 1966 and 7.8 per cent in 1976. In the first row of the table we can note that this decrease occurs mainly in interlocks between consistently top-ranked Canadian firms and their U.S.-controlled counterparts. In 1946, 17.3 per cent of all multiple-director ties joined these kinds of corporations, only 7.1 per cent less than the percentage occurring among consistently dominant Canadian firms. But by 1976 the former percentage had fallen to 4.5 per cent and the latter had risen to 31.6 percent. Far from any tendency toward continentalism or compradorization, we find a shifting in the interlocks *away from* the American presence and toward a more integrated network among the largest indigenous capitals.

Nor is this trend mitigated with the formation and growth of new (or reorganized) U.S.-controlled capital. Although several dominant companies under U.S. control were incorporated during the period and several other U.S. firms grew to number among the Top 100 in the later years, these did not become more tied to Canadian capital over time. In fact, in the third postwar decade the percentage of interlocks involving "extant" or "new" U.S. companies decreased (in the latter case from 7.8 per cent to 5.3 per cent), and the percentage tying "new" U.S. firms to consistently dominant Canadian firms likewise declined from 3.8 per cent to 2 per cent.

The other subnetworks shown in Table 5.5 account for very few multiple-director ties. In 1946, 1.3 percent of all such interlocks linked consistently top-ranked U.S. companies, but by 1976 no pair of these firms was multiply-interlocked. In general over the entire period, very few ties existed among American-controlled corporations. The same is true of firms controlled outside of North America. Most of the interlocks that include such firms connect their boards with the boards of consistently dominant, Canadian-controlled companies.

The percentage distributions of multiple interlocks by country of control can be summarized as follows. Over the three decades, the percentage of ties uniting Canadian-controlled firms shows a net increase from 68 per cent to 77.1 per cent, while the share of interlocks between Canadian and U.S. companies is nearly halved, dropping to 14.8 per cent by 1976. This trend is even more compelling if we recall that in the same period the actual number of dominant corporations under Canadian control increases by only one (from seventy to seventy-one), while the number of U.S.-controlled firms increases by six (from twenty-seven to thirty-three). Even though there are by 1976 more opportunities in the Top 100 for comprador linkage, interlocks of this sort become much less evident over time. Furthermore, even in 1946, when the U.S. presence in the network was strongest, the preponderance of multiple-director ties occurred among indigenous firms. The only evidence of an increased foreign presence, in 1966, involved interlocks between Canadian and British or other foreign-held firms. By 1976 these ties no longer made up a substantial proportion of all linkages. Indeed, between 1966 and 1976, a kind of structural consolidation seems to have taken place, as interlocks between Canadian corporations came to comprise over three-quarters of all ties.

Table 5.6 explores the same set of intra- and intersectoral linkages, but it employs density as a measure of the extent to which firms share

Table 5.6 Densities of Multiple Interlocks by Country of Control and
Corporate Survivorship, Successive Top 100s, 1946–1976

Country	Survivorship	Year	CANADA Top	CANADA Extant	CANADA New	CANADA Defunct	U. S. Top	U. S. Extant	U. S. New	U. S. Defunct	U.K. All	OTHER All
C A N A D A	Consistently Dominant	1946	.068	.034	–	.064	.057	0	–	.004	.029	0
		1956	.098	.056	.076	.109	.050	.003	.020	.006	.015	.030
		1966	.119	.059	.105	.265	.042	.020	.029	.059	.035	.096
		1976	.104	.048	.081	–	.028	.012	.016	–	.021	.026
	Extant Through-out, Sometimes Dominant	1946		.005	–	.012	.011	0	–	0	.020	0
		1956		.041	.026	.063	.014	0	.006	0	0	0
		1966		.047	.047	0	0	.018	0	0	.019	0
		1976		.086	.035	–	.007	0	.008	–	0	.020
	Incorporated After 1946	1946			–	–	–	–	–	–	–	–
		1956			0	0	.033	0	.111	0	0	0
		1966			.028	.111	.046	.028	.044	0	.040	.056
		1976			.081	–	.035	.028	.022	–	.012	.017
	Defunct by 1976	1946				.042	.027	0	–	.027	0	0
		1956				.067	.033	.011	.011	0	0	.050
		1966				0	0	0	.100	0	0	0
		1976				–	–	–	–	–	–	–
U. S.	Consistently Dominant	1946					.022	0	–	.010	0	0
		1956					.019	0	.015	0	.008	0
		1966					.015	0	.017	0	0	.021
		1976					0	0	.012	–	0	0
	Extant Through-out, Sometimes Dominant	1946						0	–	0	0	0
		1956						0	0	.022	.014	0
		1966						0	.008	0	.008	0
		1976						0	.008	–	0	0
	Incorporated after 1946	1946						–	–	–	–	–
		1956						.028	0	0	0	0
		1966						0	.100	0	0	.050
		1976						0	–	–	0	.036
	Defunct by 1976	1946							0		0	0
		1956							0		0	0
		1966							0		0	0
		1976							–		–	–
U. K.	All Firms	1946									0	0
		1956									.036	0
		1966									.036	.023
		1976									0	0
O T H	All Firms	1946										0
		1956										0
		1966										.167
		1976										0

multiple directors. Here, controlling for size differences among the sub-networks, we find much the same patterns as in Table 5.5. The only stable series of high densities describes ties *among* consistently top-ranked indigenous firms, which by 1976 were multiply interlocked in 10.4 per cent of cases. After 1946, there were also many interlocks between consistently dominant Canadian firms and newly incorporated companies under Canadian control, indicating the network's adaptation to changes in the structure of indigenous capital.

U.S.-controlled companies—regardless of survivorship status—are very rarely interlocked with each other and tend to be decreasingly tied to Canadian-controlled corporations. The density of multiple interlocks between Canadian and U.S. firms consistently included in the Top 100 declined from .057 in 1946 to .028 in 1976. That is to say, by 1976 the chances of these firms sharing multiple directors were only half what they were in 1946, and less than a third of the chances in the same year of pairs of consistently dominant Canadian firms being interlocked.

The density of connections between consistently dominant Canadian firms and British-controlled companies ranges from 0.015 to 0.035, showing no clear trend. Similarly, there is no simple pattern between the same indigenous firms and other foreign-controlled corporations. Interestingly, in 1966 the density of these ties was quite high (.096, indicating thirteen multiple-director interlocks), as were densities between other foreign and newly incorporated indigenous firms (.056, indicating two multiple ties). Similar peaks are discernable in 1966 for connections between U.S.-controlled companies and new Canadian firms, and between British-controlled corporations and the same Canadian firms. Thus, in 1966, at the height of the foreign presence in the Top 100, there is evidence of greater structural integration between foreign and domestic capital. But the strongest densities of this kind linked indigenous firms not to U.S. but to an assortment of foreign interests. Many of these "cosmopolitan" associations had disappeared by 1976, leaving a network of mostly indigenous interlocks.

Within the indigenous bloc, however, we may note some interesting changes in the third decade. The densities of interlocks between consistently top-ranked firms and "new" or "extant" companies declined in this period, to .081 and .048 respectively, yet the density *within* the set of "new" firms nearly tripled to .081 and the density within the set of "extant" firms increased to .086. As a consequence, the structure became somewhat less focused around firms continually ranking at the top of the hierarchy of capitals; indigenous interlocks became more evenly distributed over the various survivorship categories.

In summary, over the three decades we find increased multiple interlocking among indigenous companies and a decreased American presence in the network. Within the indigenous fraction, the increase is attributable both to the maintenance of very high levels of interlocking among consistently dominant firms and to the integration of new companies into the network. The declining U.S. presence stems partly from a longterm decrease in interlocks between consistently top-ranked U.S. firms and their Canadian counterparts, and partly from the failure of newly incorporated U.S. firms to establish multiple-director ties with many Canadian-controlled companies. In 1966, there is evidence of more "cosmopolitan" connections, particularly involving consistently top-ranked indigenous firms and companies controlled outside of North America. However, many of these ties had disappeared by 1976. Finally, in the most recent decade, there was a levelling out of differences in interlock densities within the indigenous bloc of capital, as more ties were extended to newly dominant firms. These findings are extremely difficult to reconcile with interpretations of continentalism or atrophy in the interlock network. They are suggestive of a network of mainly indigenous corporations that has been preserved and adapted to changing economic circumstances over a lengthy period. But if these findings are indicative, they are also incomplete, since we have not yet considered the manner in which interlocks unite (or keep separate) different *types* of capital: industrial, financial and so on. This issue is broached in Table 5.7, with an analysis of the density of multiple-director interlocks for subnetworks of firms distinguished by both country with controlling interest and by economic sector.[4] Once again, the networks are composed of successive Top 100s for the years 1946, 1956, 1966, and 1976. We are especially interested in how indigenous interlocks are allocated by industry, or, more precisely, whether there exists structural evidence of the coalescence of large-scale industrial and financial capital within the Canadian bourgeoisie.

On the surface, the densities in 1946 provide only weak evidence of such a merger. In that year, the density of all multiple-director interlocks was .030. Densities of ties between indigenous financial institutions ("banking" firms) and indigenous mining (.043), manufacturing (.047), and utilities (.065) companies were all above this figure, but only in the third case was the difference very pronounced. On the other hand, financial institutions were densely interlocked with each other, as were Canadian-controlled utilities and mining firms. Indigenous manufacturers were most densely connected to the three indigenous investment companies. Interlocks between Canadian and foreign-controlled firms were relatively rare in 1946, with the major exception of the financial institutions, which were associated with U.S.-controlled in-

Table 5.7 Densities of Multiple Interlocks by Country of Control
and Industry, Successive Top 100s, 1946–1976

CONTROL:		CANADIAN							U.S.	U.K.	OTHER	NON-CAN.
INDUSTRY	YEAR	Mining	Manuf.	Util.	Bank	Invest.	Commer.	Prop.	Indust.	Indust.	Indust.	Non-Indust.
Mining	1946	.100	.033	.017	.043	0	0	0	.017	0	0	.050
	1956	0	.087	.083	.114	0	0	0	.048	0	0	0
	1966	0	.039	.100	.076	.067	0	0	.023	0	.083	0
	1976	.048	.050	.082	.104	.048	.020	.057	.010	.036	.020	0
Manufacturing	1946		.029	.035	.047	.056	.042	0	.016	0	0	0
	1956		.067	.065	.097	.087	.043	0	.017	0	.087	0
	1966		.066	.035	.110	.094	.039	0	.018	.042	.029	0
	1976		.029	.084	.118	.098	.025	.047	.013	0	.017	.010
Utilities	1946			.061	.065	.056	0	0	.018	.042	0	.021
	1956			0	.121	0	0	0	.022	.028	0	0
	1966			.067	.100	.060	.017	0	.017	.014	.075	.010
	1976			.143	.110	.071	.020	.029	.005	0	0	0
Banking	1946				.067	.029	.022	0	.043	0	0	.033
	1956				.104	.091	.032	0	.040	.015	.045	.010
	1966				.156	.100	.045	0	.045	.058	.091	.032
	1976				.104	.136	.026	.055	.032	.034	.039	.008
Investment Companies	1946					0	0		.014	0	0	0
	1956					0	.048	0	0	0	0	0
	1966					.100	.067	0	.021	.029	.050	.020
	1976					.133	.024	.033	.012	0	.024	0
Commercial	1946						0	.500	0	0	0	0
	1956						0	.143	0	0	0	.016
	1966						0	0	.006	0	0	.017
	1976						0	0	.010	0	.020	.024
Property Development	1946							0	0	0	0	0
	1956							0	0	0	0	0
	1966							0	0	0	0	0
	1976							0	0	.029	0	0
U.S. Industrials	1946								.008	0	0	.011
	1956								.009	0	0	.014
	1966								.007	0	.026	.010
	1976								.005	0	.005	0
U.K. Industrials	1946									0	0	0
	1956									0	0	.019
	1966									.095	.036	0
	1976									0	0	0
O.T.H. Industrials	1946										0	0
	1956										0	0
	1966										.167	0
	1976										0	.024
N C O A N N. Non-Industrial	1946											0
	1956											0
	1966											0
	1976											0

dustrials in 4.3 per cent of cases.

Viewed in this light, the network of multiple-director interlocks shows a potential in 1946 either for the *consolidation* of an indigenous bloc of finance capital or for *continental integration* via the financial institutions. In an institutional sense, the indigenous bloc of finance capital seems to have been composed principally of utilities and financial institutions and only secondarily of manufacturing and investment companies. If we were to consider the utilities sector as a component of "commercial capital," we could infer that the most socially integrated bloc of indigenous capital in 1946 comprised a "commercial fraction." But this sort of theoretical confusion will not do. Instead, we must refer back to Tables 4.8 and 4.9, where it is obvious that, in 1946, large-scale, Canadian-controlled industry was principally centred in the "utilities" sector. It is therefore not surprising to find that the greatest concentration of interlocks occurred among the big financial institutions and utilities, and that these firms formed the locus—by virtue of their size and directorate interlocking—of indigenous finance capital in the early postwar years.

Still, there is a definite ambivalence in this structure. In 1946, indigenous financial institutions were linked nearly as densely to U.S.-controlled industrials as they were to indigenous manufacturers and mining firms. If this pattern were to be elaborated in the ensuing years, we would have difficulty speaking of "coalescence" between indigenous financial and industrial capital. Presumably, in a monopoly fraction in which once distinct financial and industrial interests have merged, we should find a correspondence between the distribution of large-scale capital and the pattern of interlocking. Hence, as big industrial capital has accumulated in indigenous mining and manufacturing firms, we should find that these companies have participated in more interlocks with financial institutions.

This is precisely what is seen in Table 5.7. From 1956 forward, about one in every ten Canadian-controlled manufacturers and financial institutions shared two or more directors. As well, multiple-director interlocks between indigenous mining firms and financial intermediaries proliferated: by 1976 the chances of a Canadian-controlled mining firm sharing multiple directors with an indigenous financial intermediary were over twice what they had been in 1946. Multiple ties between Canadian financial capital and utilities also proliferated, although financial intermediaries were slightly more densely interlocked with indigenous manufacturers than with utilities after 1956. Thus, as big indigenous industrial capital was redistributed from utilities to manufacturing and mining, the structure of interlocks focused less on financial-utilities interlocks and more on ties between commodity-producing companies and financial institutions.

In marked contrast to the high densities of interlocking between Canadian financial intermediaries and Canadian industrials, the density between Canadian financial intermediaries and U.S.-controlled industrials is roughly similar to or less than the overall network density in each year. There is no evidence that Canadian-controlled banking capital has been more integrated with U.S.-controlled industrial capital than with Canadian-controlled industry. There is, though, evidence of greater integration over time between Canadian financial institutions and industrials controlled outside of North America. By 1976, however, even these ties are much sparser than indigenous financial-industrial interlocks. Several other findings from Table 5.7 bear discussion here. There are consistently high densities between indigenous manufacturers and investment companies. These connections often indicate relationships of intercorporate ownership, affording the investment companies *operational power* over their subsidiaries and affiliates.

In 1976, for example, Canadian Pacific Investments shared six directors with Cominco Limited, four with Pan Canadian Petroleum Limited, and three with Algoma Steel Corporation Limited, all dominant corporations. As of 1975, Canadian Pacific Investments had majority control of each of these firms, owning 54 per cent of Cominco's stock, 87.1 per cent of Pan Canadian's, and 51 per cent of Algoma's. Another five directors were shared in 1976 between Canadian Pacific Investments and its subsidiary, Marathon Realty Company Limited, a dominant property developer. Two directors linked Canadian Pacific Investments to the boards of TransCanada PipeLines Limited, in which the investment company had a 14.4 per cent interest in 1975, and MacMillan Bloedel Limited, which was 13.4 per cent owned by Canadian Pacific Investments in 1975. These subsidiaries and affiliates in turn shared directors among themselves, weaving the companies into the closely knit structure shown in Figure 5.1. All told, Canadian Pacific Investments and its parent, subsidiaries and affiliates had eighteen multiple-director interlocks in 1976, accounting for 9.6 per cent of all strong indigenous ties. Thus, certain multiple-director interlocks (and the intercorporate ownership ties they signify) further centralize control of large-scale capital while facilitating its co-ordinated accumulation. It is difficult to reconcile the existence of such an integrated bloc of finance capital, ultimately controlled by one of the country's oldest and largest industrial corporations, with the thesis that the Canadian bourgeoisie is dominated by merchants and bankers.

There is also quite a striking increase over the three decades in the extent to which indigenous investment companies share multiple directors with financial institutions: the density rises from 0.029 (two interlocks) in 1946 to 0.136 (eighteen interlocks) in 1976. This has occurred while the number of major Canadian investment companies in the Top 100 has doubled (from three to six), providing twice as many opportunities for interlocking. The share of dominant financial assets claimed by indigenous investment companies has increased tenfold, from 0.49 per cent to 4.8 per cent. In both economic and social-structural terms, the 1946–76 period brought increased prominence to Canadian investment companies. This development is important because, as noted earlier, it is often through investment companies that finance capitalists

Figure 5.1
Multiple-Director Interlocks and Intercorporate Ownership Ties:
The Canadian Pacific Group in 1976 *

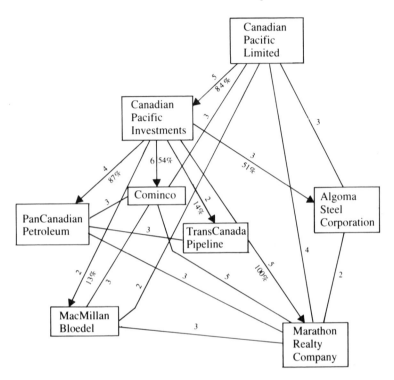

* Ownership data from *Intercorporate Ownership 1975* (Statistics Canada, 1978)
  Percentages refer to the proportion of stock owned, integers refer to the number of
  shared directors.

wield operational power over specific corporations. Certainly the stories
of financial wizardry and entrepreneurial finesse surrounding E.P.
Taylor, Paul Desmarais and the like are by now legendary. These
capitalists, who show up on so many directorates, are in one sense crea-
tures of the post-Second World War Canadian economy. Prior to the
formation of Argus Corporation in 1945, the only Canadian investment
company of any real importance was Power Corporation Limited. Its
portfolio was largely confined to a single industry (electric utilities),
rendering it more akin to a trust than a diversified investment company.
In the formative years of monopoly capital, investment banks such as
Royal Securities, Wood Gundy, and Nesbitt-Thomson served the same
function as investment companies in centralizing the ownership of stock

capital, particularly through corporate reorganizations (Stapells 1927). By the 1940's, though, investment banks had lost most of their influence as loci of finance capital (Niosi 1978, 50–63). The rise of diversified Canadian investment companies— Argus, Power, Canadian Pacific Investments and Brascan in particular—is one more indication that under the post-war conditions of propitious accumulation rates supporting a burgeoning domestic capital market, Canadian capitalists managed to consolidate a bloc of finance capital under their control. Within the network of interlocks, this is further demonstrated by the mediational status that key investment companies occupied by 1976, linking up with both industrial firms and banks. Not only did investment companies become centres of operational financial power over industrial capital, they were extensively tied to the major centres of allocative financial power: the financial institutions.

By the same token, Table 5.7 reveals that Canadian financial intermediaries were densely interlocked with each other throughout the three decades. For instance, in 1966, fully 15.6 per cent of all pairs of these firms shared multiple directors. By 1976 the density of ties had fallen somewhat to .104, which still indicates a great deal of interlocking, especially given the prohibitions against banks interlocking with other banks, life insurance companies interlocking with other life insurance companies, and (after 1967) deposit-accepting trust companies interlocking with banks. The most common ties among financial institutions connected the five biggest chartered banks with life insurance companies. Indeed, as Figure 5.2 shows, the extent of such interlocking in 1976 was nothing short of remarkable: fifteen of the twenty-four multiple-director liaisons among financial institutions were of this sort, and another four linked trust companies with life insurers. One would be hard pressed to imagine a more centralized financial apparatus. Most striking is the congenial role played by the country's largest life insurance company, Sun Life, in bringing together fourteen directors from the three largest banks: five from each of the Bank of Montreal and Royal Bank, and four more from the Canadian Imperial Bank of Commerce. Although bankers have dutifully refrained from sitting on each other's boards, their paths would seem to cross with some regularity.[5]

Table 5.7 is supplemented by the analysis in Table 5.8 of interlock percentage distributions across categories of industry and country of control. Both the distribution of multiple-director interlocks and the distribution of single-director ties are given, at four different times. Considering first the distributions of multiple-director interlocks, we can observe relative stability over the first postwar decade. About 35 per cent of all multiple ties united indigenous industrials and financials in 1946

Figure 5.2
Multiple-Director Interlocks among Canadian-Controlled
Financial Intermediaries, 1976

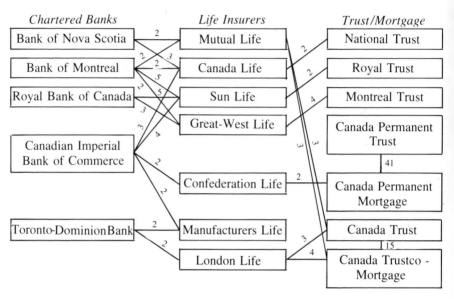

Chartered Banks   *Life Insurers*   *Trust/Mortgage*

and 1956. Another 12.2 per cent in 1946 and 14.0 per cent in 1956 linked indigenous financials with each other, and a further 17.9 per cent in 1946 and 14.4 per cent in 1956 connected indigenous industrials. The proportion of interlocks among other indigenous firms increased from 2.6 per cent to 6.5 per cent, while the proportion of multiple ties between Canadian financials and U.S. industrials declined from 15.4 per cent to 12.6 per cent.

In the second decade, the percentage of multiple interlocks among indigenous firms dropped by about 9 per cent. Relations among indigenous industrials and between indigenous financials and industrials became relatively less predominant, while proportionately more interlocks appeared between Canadian financials and industrials controlled outside of North America. However, the increased share of indigenous interlocks in the third decade reflects a redistribution in favour of indigenous financial-industrial ties and away from linkages between Canadian and foreign industrials.

What is most interesting about Table 5.8 is the comparison it affords between the distributions of single and multiple-director interlocks.

Table 5.8 Percentage Distributions of Single and Multiple Interlocks
by Country of Control and Industry, 1946–1976

SUBNETWORK	1946		1956		1966		1976	
	Single Ties	Multiple Ties	Single Ties	Multiple Ties	Single Ties	Multiple Ties	Single Ties	Multiple Ties
Within Canadian Industrial Capital	15.3	17.9	9.8	14.4	7.5	8.6	11.1	11.5
Between Canadian Industrial and Canadian Financial Capital	31.3	35.3	22.3	35.3	21.4	30.0	27.2	37.7
Within Canadian Financial Capital	11.2	12.2	9.8	14.0	9.1	18.0	6.0	18.0
Other Canadian	3.0	2.6	5.0	6.5	4.3	4.9	13.2	9.8
SUBTOTAL: Interlocks among Canadian Firms	60.8	68.0	46.9	70.2	42.3	61.5	57.5	77.0
Between Canadian Financial and U.S. Industrial Captial	11.4	15.4	15.6	12.6	14.4	12.0	10.2	9.0
Between Canadian Financial and Other Industrial Capital	1.1	0	3.7	1.4	6.7	7.1	6.8	4.1
Between Canadian Industrial and Foreign Industrial	19.3	11.5	16.0	10.2	16.0	10.5	15.9	5.3
Between Canadian Other and Foreign Industrial	0.3	0	0.9	0	1.9	0.4	2.5	1.6
SUBTOTAL: Interlocks between Canadian Firms and Foreign Industrial Firms	32.1	26.9	36.2	24.2	39.0	30.0	35.4	20.0
Within Foreign Industrial Capital	3.5	1.3	4.3	1.9	9.3	3.7	4.5	1.2
Other Interlocks	3.5	3.8	12.6	3.7	9.4	4.9	2.5	1.6
TOTAL	100.0	100.0	100.0	100.0	100.0	100.0	100.0	100.0
NUMBER OF INTERLOCKS	367	156	539	215	583	267	646	244

Although both kinds of ties manifest the same general patterns, the predominance of indigenous interlocking is less marked when the analysis is confined to single-director ties. For example, in 1976, only 57.5 per cent of all single interlocks united indigenous companies, yet 77 per cent of multiple interlocks integrated domestically-controlled capital. Conversely, in the same year, 35.4 per cent of single interlocks linked indigenous firms to foreign industrials, compared with 20 per cent of multiple interlocks. Many single interlocks linked Canadian-controlled industrials with industrials under foreign control. A growing proportion tied indigenous financials to industrials controlled outside of North America. Yet, significantly, the proportion of single interlocks uniting indigenous financials with U.S.-controlled industrials was at no time much greater than the corresponding proportion of multiple interlocks. By 1976, the proportion had declined to 10.2 per cent. Single-director interlocks, then, have been somewhat less concentrated among Canadian-controlled firms than multiple interlocks, but they do not appear to have comprised a "continental axis" of Canadian bankers and U.S. industrial interests.

More probably, single interlocks are established for a variety of purposes; they therefore show less systematic structural biases. Some may exist purely by virtue of the perceived importance of key outsiders—the C. D. Howes, John Turners, Donald MacDonalds, J. D. Torys and the like—and not represent a purposefully established intercorporate relation. Others may exist in order to facilitate the circulation of commodity capital but may stop short of any deeper co-ordination of the accumulation process. For instance, Algoma Steel shared single directors in 1976 with Domtar, Inc., Texaco Canada Ltd., Algoma Central Railway, Hollinger Mines Limited, Comstock International, and Genstar Limited. Certain of these connections may have been instrumental in providing reliable buyers (and transporters) of steel and suppliers of raw material for Algoma, but the three directors shared with Canadian Pacific Investments (Algoma's parent) were surely more influential in the determination of broader investment strategies (see also Chodos 1973, 137). The same kind of interpretation can be advanced for many dominant firms and thus for quite a few of the directorate interlocks.

Pursuing this line of argument a step further, it may be that the network of firms has assumed a two-tiered structure, increasingly focused on indigenously controlled industrials and financials on the level of multiple-director liaisons but retaining a broader base of single interlocks, which often connect domestic and foreign interests and which generally reduce the potential for conflicts between bourgeois fractions. Were this the case, the network could be said to provide a structure for both the efficient accumulation of large-scale (and largely indigenous) capital and the maintenance of national (and international) capitalist class solidarity, with multiple ties weighted toward the former function and single interlocks toward the latter (Fennema 1982, 201). But though the patterns of interlocks in Table 5.8 seem to support this interpretation, they by no means require or sustain it.

Let us summarize these findings. Looking at the central issue of indigenous versus foreign control of large-scale capital, we find that the highest interlock densities—the majority of all interlocks—have occurred among Canadian-controlled firms. This indigenous interlocking has been especially characteristic of multiple-director ties, which are more likely indicative of purposeful intercorporate relations. Indigenous interlocking has also been predominant among the consistently dominant companies that appear to have formed the core of the network. Finally, we observe very dense indigenous interlocking *between* industrials and financials and *among* financial companies.

Over time, densities among Canadian-controlled firms have increased, especially in the first postwar decade, when many new financial-industrial relations emerged. However, *fewer* interlocks are found between Canadian and foreign capitals in 1976 compared with earlier years. There is also evidence that newly-incorporated firms under Canadian control were more integrated into the network than were new firms controlled by foreign interests. Finally, the indigenous investment companies that emerged and rose to prominence by 1976 also established strong ties with indigenous industry and financial institutions.

These results contradict the thesis that an historical trend exists toward silent surrender or continental compradorization by Canadian capitalists. It seems that throughout the 1946–1976 period, and increasingly in recent years, the bulk of large-scale industrial and financial capital in Canada has assumed the form of an institutionally integrated bloc of finance capital under predominantly domestic control. The next chapter examines this bloc in more detail, noting both its stable features and its transformation since the Second World War.

6

CONTINUITY AND CHANGE
IN THE INTERLOCK NETWORK
1946–1976

In various ways, the reproduction of monopoly capital in Canada during the long postwar wave of accumulation involved elements of both continuity and change. For instance, throughout the period, most of the capital of the largest corporations was located in an institutionally stable set of consistently dominant firms, and most of the significant intercorporate relations connected these firms. Similarly, notwithstanding the rapid concentration of capital under U.S. control in the first decade, the bulk of large-scale capital remained consistently under domestic control, and most significant interlocks united indigenous firms, especially financial and industrial concerns.

On the other hand, we have taken note of a great deal of restructuring, particularly of big industry: some firms disappeared in combinations and nationalizations; others grew rapidly to take positions among the largest corporations; and as big capital shifted from the transportation, communications and utilities sector into commodity production through resource extraction and manufacturing. There were also a number of important changes in the national control of large corporations, such as Gulf Canada, Canada Cement LaFarge, Bell Canada, Hudson's Bay Company, and Inco Limited, and a great amount of change in specific alliances among dominant firms.

These general patterns of accumulation and interlocking lend credence to the general thesis advanced in Chapter 3. However, while the quantitative approach employed thus far has much to recommend it, it cannot replace a more detailed analysis of the network of intercorporate relations. To gain a deeper appreciation of the structure of corporate power and its postwar transformations, it is necessary to examine the network *qualitatively*, with attention to sources of both continuity and change.

With some noteworthy exceptions (such as Galaskiewicz and Wasserman 1981; Palmer 1983; Ornstein 1984) most longitudinal network analyses have not considered these sources. Rather, the typical approach has been to combine several cross-sectional network analyses into a time series of intercorporate relations (see Bunting and Barbour 1971; Stanworth and Giddens 1975; Piedilue 1976; Allen 1978; Sweeny 1980; Mizruchi 1982; Roy 1983; Stening and Wai 1984), much as was done in Chapter 5. Two successive "snapshots" of the interlock network in 1946 and 1976 are presented here, but these cross-sections will be supplemented with longitudinal analysis of how intercorporate relations in the intervening years were substantially transformed, yet remained in certain respects remarkably stable.

In principle, two sources of stability can be distinguished in an intercorporate network. First, as we have seen, there is considerable consistency in the composition of the monopoly fraction of the capitalist class. Consistently dominant corporations account at any given time for much of the network of strong ties; in this sense, they appear to comprise a stable intercorporate structure. More stringently, certain of these same companies may have maintained strong interlocks with each other throughout the 1946–76 period, constituting a network of stable ties around which capitalist restructuring has occurred. Likewise, we can cite two sources of structural *transformation* in the network. The first is given in the changing composition of the monopoly fraction: certain firms rise to positions of dominance in the economy; others disappear through major reorganizations, nationalizations, slow growth, and so forth. Secondly, the network may be transformed as particular intercorporate alliances are *broken* and as others *emerge*, because of changes in the control of companies, altered banking relations, or other reasons.

THE STABLE COMPONENT

For present purposes, the stable part of the network was designated as the set of multiple-director ties among consistently dominant companies that were maintained throughout 1946–76. The criteria employed in identifying stable intercorporate relationships were: (1) that the pair of corporations share two or more directors in 1946 and 1976, (2) that they share at least one director in all the intervening years, and (3) that they remain multiply interlocked in at least 75 per cent of the thirty-one years. These criteria ensured that only the interlocks that were preserved throughout and that were salient in both 1946 and 1976 were considered "stable ties," while allowing for the possibility of pauses in multiple interlocking, resulting from the retirement and replacement of particular

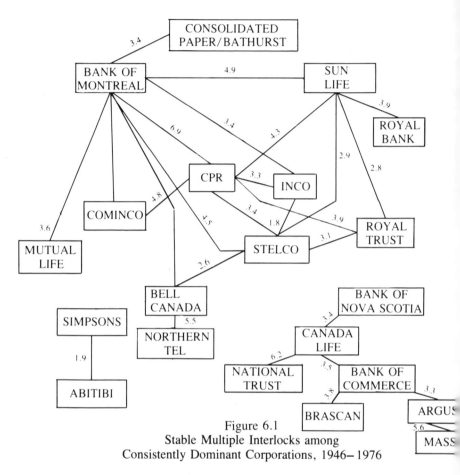

Figure 6.1
Stable Multiple Interlocks among
Consistently Dominant Corporations, 1946–1976

directors, for example (see Ornstein 1984).[1]

For this detailed firm-by-firm analysis, the criterion of consistent dominance was relaxed so that companies reorganized between 1946 and 1976 by merger with another dominant company could be included in the network of stable interlocks. Ties between these companies and consistently dominant firms were considered stable if (1) the merged company and one of its predecessors were ranked in the Top 100 in all years and (2) the three criteria for stable intercorporate relationships were met by both the merged company and the predecessor firm.[2] The result of these decisions is shown in Figure 6.1, along with the mean yearly number of shared directors for each pair of interlocked firms.

The stable ties are configured in two networks of twelve and seven firms and one dyad connecting Simpsons Limited with Abitibi Paper. The larger network may be said to form a densely connected *stable component* for the entire intercorporate structure. It includes a number of the country's largest financial and industrial firms, comprising the core of Canada's longest standing financial group (see Park and Park 1973; Piedalue 1976; Sweeny 1980). Its key members are the Bank of Montreal, Canadian Pacific Limited, Bell Canada, Steel Company of Canada, Inco Limited, Sun Life Assurance, and Royal Trust Company. More peripheral positions are occupied by subsidiaries of Canadian Pacific and Bell Canada (Cominco Limited and Northern Telecom Limited), as well as by Consolidated Paper/Consolidated Bathurst, Mutual Life Assurance, and the Royal Bank of Canada. The most central firms in this stable component are the Bank of Montreal, with seven stable interlocks to other members, Canadian Pacific Limited, with six interlocks, Stelco with five, and Sun Life with four. These four corporations are all interlocked with each other and tied to other members of the stable component. The mean number of directors that these most central firms share suggests that the interlocks are strongly institutionalized. Most notably, the Bank of Montreal shares an average of 6.9 directors per year with Canadian Pacific Limited.

It is worthwhile to compare these results with the networks diagrammed by Piedalue for the first three decades of this century. Of the twelve firms in the stable component, eight were members of the connected network of 50 leading corporations in 1930 (1976, 33–47).[3] Among the eight corporations in Piedalue's sociogram and our stable component, there are fourteen stable ties, eight of which were also present in 1930. These eight tied the Bank of Montreal to Sun Life, Cominco and Bell; Sun Life to the CPR, Royal Trust and Royal Bank; and Royal Trust and Cominco to the CPR. Much of the stable component we observe in the 1946–76 period predates the Second World War by a decade. Certain of the ties can be traced back even further. In 1910, for instance, the CPR shared five directors with the Bank of Montreal, six with Royal Trust, and three with Cominco (Piedalue 1976, 28). Thus, the stable component seems to have been at the centre of Canadian monopoly capital for most of this century.

The second stable network appears to be arranged around a set of financial relations converging on Canada Life and the Canadian (Imperial) Bank of Commerce, two financial institutions which themselves average 3.5 shared directors per year. This Toronto-based grouping can also be traced historically to the early twentieth century, when Senator George Cox assembled a financial empire based on his control of Canada Life Assurance (Drummond 1962, 211; Nelles 1974, 264). Indeed the ties between Canada Life and both National Trust and the Bank of Commerce reach back at least to 1910 (Piedalue 1976, 28). Compared with the stable component, however, this smaller network is sparsely connected and includes only a single industrial corporation: Massey-Ferguson. Stable ties to two firms that became important investment companies in the 1946–76 years, Argus and Brascan, however, suggest that the Bank of Commerce was positioned to participate in some of the major capitalist ventures and restructurings of the period.

Finally, on the issue of indigenous and foreign control, it should be noted that in 1946, three of the twenty-one firms in Figure 6.1 (Inco, Bell Canada, and Northern Telecom) were controlled by foreign capitalists (namely the Morgan and Rockefeller interests who then comprised the leading American financial groups [Perlo 1957; Park and Park 1973]). As we determined in Chapter 4, all three of these members of the stable component had been brought under Canadian control by 1976. At the highest reaches of the economy, within the densely interlocked stable component, we find further evidence of a post-Second World War consolidation of indigenous finance capital.

TRANSFORMATIONS IN THE INTERCORPORATE NETWORK:
AN ANALYSIS OF CLIQUES WITHIN THE CORPORATE INNER CIRCLE

In the light of the network of stable ties in Figure 6.1, how may we describe the morphology of the broader interlock network in 1946 and 1976 and the transformations that occurred in the intervening three decades? Researchers in corporate interlocking have devised quite an array of concepts and strategies for depicting large-scale networks to test different theoretical interpretations. In particular, the two class-based interpretations of corporate interlocking described in the previous chapter have generated complementary concepts for detailed analysis of network structure. The theory of monopoly capital, with its emphasis on the purposeful coalescence of financial and industrial capital, and the division of the monopoly fraction into competing interest groups, has suggested a methodology that examines in what pattern and to what extent particular firms cluster into *cliques*, within which the density of interlocking is especially high (see Knowles 1973; Bearden et al. 1975; Sonquist and Koenig 1975; Allen 1978; Overbeek 1980).

Alternatively, the class hegemony interpretation, which emphasizes the cultural and political functions of interlocks in integrating leading capitalists into an organized social force, has inspired a methodology that identifies the *inner circle* of the most heavily interlocked capitalists, who on account of their manifold corporate connections are in a position to represent the class-wide interests of capital in a variety of contexts (see Soref 1976; Jung et al. 1981; Useem 1984). Although some researchers have presented these approaches as mutually exclusive alternatives (Mariolis 1983), they can be more usefully viewed as complementary perspectives. They depict the relations through which capitalist class domination is expressed at two levels: the *economic*, through the accumulation of capital within various concrete circuits, and the *superstructural*, through the concerted activities of leading capitalists in civil society and the state (Urry 1981). In both respects, interlocks contribute to the reproduction of capitalist class relations, whether through the accumulation process or in the exercise of cultural leadership and political power (see Glasberg and Schwartz 1983).

The concept of finance capital does not preclude the integrative ties between capitalist interest groups that make possible the ascendance of a capitalist inner circle. Nevertheless, it *does* assert that meaningful cliques of strongly tied corporations and capitalists should be discernible in the network of interlocks. Thus, for instance, Bearden et al. conclude from their study of the changing network of U.S. corporations over the period 1962 to 1973 that

> the integration of New York, Boston, Philadelphia and California centers of business into a national and even international network of corporations has occurred simultaneously with the maintenance and further development of interest groups which continue to organize and coordinate intercorporate cooperation and control (1975, 50).

The following analysis attempts to describe the Canadian network of 1946 and 1976 in terms of its *integration* around an inner circle of corporations that participate extensively in the network (as in Mariolis 1983), and its *differentiation* into cliques of closely associated firms that may belong to distinct capitalist interest groups (as in Sonquist and Koenig 1975).

Many studies of corporate interlocking have assessed network participation using quantitative indices of relative centrality (see Carroll, Fox and Ornstein 1981, 1982; Mintz and Schwartz 1981a, 1981b; Mizruchi and Bunting 1981; Mariolis and Jones 1982). However, our goal of discerning distinct subnetworks of densely connected firms suggested a different analytic strategy that combined a qualitative concept of successive inner circles of corporations with an attempt to decompose these inner circles into cliques. The logic of this approach is depicted in Figure 6.2.

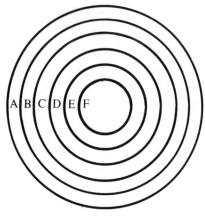

Legend:
A: Isolate from multiple-director
   interlocking
B: Interlocker, but isolate from
   dominant component
C: Member of dominant
   component
D: Clique periphery: interlocked
   with one or more clique
   members
E: Single clique member
F: Multiple clique member

Figure 6.2 Schematic Representation of Inner Circle and Clique Analyses

Furthest removed from the centre of the intercorporate network are corporations that do not participate in any multiple-director ties (category A). Companies that interlock with another dominant firm comprise a second circle, but some of them may be isolated from the largest connected set of corporations: the network's dominant component. Interlocked firms that are isolated from the dominant component (category B) participate in intercorporate relations only slightly more than noninterlocked companies, although they may form their own small networks entirely segmented from the largest connected network. Members of the dominant component make up a third inner circle, which can be further subdivided in terms of participation in intercorporate cliques: a firm may be isolated from all cliques (category C); on the periphery of the clique structure by virtue of its tie to a clique member (category D); part of the clique structure through membership in a single clique (category E); or an especially central part of the structure through membership in several cliques.

This qualitative characterization of network position assumes several factors: that the dominant component is divisible into cliques of closely associated firms; that clique membership is indicative of a company's strategic location within a functioning capitalist group; and that such groups to some extent overlap. In particular, designating clique members as a single "inner circle" assumes that the capitalist subgroupings within the dominant component are *not* highly segregated but, at a minimum, are connected through overlapping peripheries.

These assumptions require empirical assessment, but they also recommend an approach to clique detection that allows for the possibility of overlapping clique memberships. To this end, Richard Alba's graph-theoretic definition of cliques was employed in identifying subnetworks of high internal density and few external ties in 1946 and 1976 (Alba 1972, 1973; Alba and Moore 1978; see also Sonquist and Koenig 1975; Carroll 1984). This method builds each clique around a completely connected subnetwork, producing a set of cliques whose members may to some extent overlap.[4] Alba's technique also provides a statistical test to ensure that the density of interlocking within each clique is significantly greater than the overall interlock density in the dominant component. In an attempt to distinguish trivial from substantively important cliques, an additional criterion was imposed upon the clique-detection procedure: only cliques composed of *four* or more dominant corporations are considered in the subsequent analysis.[5]

The inner circles that result from the strategy described in Figure 6.2 are tabulated in Table 6.1 for both the 1946 and 1976 intercorporate networks. This turnover table depicts both change and continuity in the structure of the network and the positions of its members. In 1946, nearly one third of Canada's dominant corporations were isolated from all multiple-director interlocking. The dominant component was comprised of sixty-four firms, twenty-four of which belonged to one of two statistically significant cliques,[6] and twenty-three of which were on the periphery of the clique structure. Although no firm belonged to both cliques, there was a modest overlap of two firms between the cliques' peripheries, indicating that the intercorporate groupings were not entirely disjointed. By 1976, slightly less than one-quarter of the dominant corporations were isolated from all multiple-director interlocking, and the network's dominant component had grown to eighty-three members. Within the dominant component, thirty-three firms belonged to one of six statistically significant cliques, and seven more had memberships in two cliques. Among the former, only two clique members showed no multiple-director tie to a member of another clique. We can conclude that the inner circle became considerably more inclusive and integrated in the 1946–76 period, as the dominant component and clique structure expanded to take in most of the largest corporations, and as most members of intercorporate groups established ties to other groups. Simultaneously, the inner circle became further differentiated, as the number of distinct cliques tripled. The proliferation of linkages between cliques suggests that, by 1976, members of cliques may be described as a highly coherent inner circle, within which firms belonging to two cliques serve as potentially important "articulation points" (Harary et al. 1965), effecting strong relations between groupings that would otherwise be only tangentially connected. The precise composition of the intercorporate cliques will be discussed later; for now we pursue the

Table 6.1 Turnover of Inner Circle Status Among Dominant Corporations, 1946–1976

	Inner Circle Status in 1976							
Inner Circle Status In 1946	Not Dominant	Isolate	Inter-locker	Dominant Component	Clique Periphery	Single Clique Member	Double Clique Member	TOTAL
Not dominant	–	20	3	5	20	9	0	57
Isolate	19	3	1	2	5	2	0	32
Interlocker	2	2	0	0	3	0	0	7
Dominant Component	5	1	0	0	5	5	1	17
Clique Periphery	13	1	0	0	1	6	2	23
Single Clique Member	7	0	0	0	2	11	4	24
TOTAL	46	27	4	7	36	33	7	160

issues of structural continuity and change by examining in more depth the status of companies in the inner circles of 1946 and 1976.

As Table 6.1 shows, of the seventeen clique members of 1946 that survive the three decades as dominant firms, eleven belong to single cliques in 1976, and four have multiple clique memberships. Not surprisingly, the stable component of the network contributes most of these: eleven of its twelve companies are clique members in both 1946 and 1976 (the exception is Mutual Life, which moves from a. clique membership in 1946 to a position on the periphery of the clique structure in 1976). All seven multiple clique members in 1976 are depicted in Figure 6.1 as having maintained at least one strong tie to another consistently dominant corporation throughout 1946–76. However, only four were also clique members in 1946, namely The Royal Bank, Sun Life, Bell Canada and Inco—all members of the stable component. The other central articulation points—The Bank of Commerce, Simpsons, and Canada Life— entered the clique structure after 1946 from positions in the dominant component.

Seven other corporations show similar movement toward the network's core. The Investors' Group and Canada Trustco Mortgage were interlockers without links to the dominant component in 1946; by 1976 each belongs to a clique. Abitibi Paper, Algoma Steel, Noranda Mines, Brascan, and Gulf Canada move from positions in the dominant component but beyond the clique periphery to hold single clique memberships in 1976. Only La Banque Canadienne Nationale evidences a major shift in position over the three decades *away from* the network's inner circle, moving from the clique periphery to a completely isolated position prior to its merger in 1979 with La Banque Provinciale du Canada, another isolate. Overall, however, the positions of corporations in the inner circles remain fairly stable. For companies dominant in both 1946 and 1976, the Spearman rank-order correlation between inner-circle status in 1946 and 1976 is 0.65 (p<.001).

A sense of the changes that have occurred in the positions of foreign-controlled and indigenous companies can be gleaned from Table 6.2. Predictably, the financial institutions in the network are consistently under indigenous control, and their participation in inner circles increases. In 1946, 56.5 per cent of dominant indigenous financial institutions were in cliques or on their peripheries. By 1976, this circle took in 85 per cent of indigenous financial institutions, four of which held memberships in two cliques. Canadian-controlled industrial firms undergo essentially similar changes, but among their foreign-controlled counterparts the pattern is less straightforward. As a group, firms controlled in Europe and South Africa move closer to the core of the network,

Table 6.2 Cumulative Percentage Distributions of Inner Circle Status for Dominant Industrial Corporations and Financial Institutions by Country of Control in 1946 and 1976

Inner Circle Status	1946				1976				
	Industrials			Financial Institutions	Industrials			Financial Institutions	
	Canada	U.S.	Other	Canada	Canada	U.S.	Other	Canada	U.S.
Double clique member	0	0	0	0	6.4	0	0	20.0	0
Single clique member	29.3	16.7	0	26.1	54.8	7.1	9.1	50.0	0
Clique periphery	51.3	33.4	0	56.5	90.3	46.4	45.4	85.0	0
Dominant component	73.3	41.7	20.0	78.2	93.5	53.5	63.6	90.0	0
Interlocker	78.2	45.9	40.0	78.2	96.7	60.6	63.6	90.0	0
Isolate	100.0	100.0	100.0	100.0	100.0	100.0	100.0	100.0	100.0

although by 1976 only one company—Canada Cement Lafarge—is a clique member. American-controlled industrial corporations are relatively less likely to belong to the network's cliques in 1976 than they were in 1946 but more likely to be on the periphery or in the dominant component. As a result of these changes, by 1976 over half of indigenous industrials are clique members, and 90 per cent are situated within the periphery of the clique structure; yet less than 10 per cent of foreign-controlled industrials belong to cliques, and less than half fall within the clique periphery.

How did such a dramatic difference develop? The tabulation in Table 6.3, showing inner-circle status by corporate survivorship for seventy dominant industrials, provides some clues. In 1946, foreign-controlled firms that would be consistently dominant thereafter were, as a group, heavily involved in the network's clique structure. By 1976, however, consistently dominant firms under Canadian control (which now include Inco, Bell Canada and Northern Telecom) are far more likely to be part of the clique structure than are consistently dominant firms under foreign control. The difference between indigenous and foreign firms that rise to positions of economic dominance is especially noteworthy. Only one newly dominant industrial corporation under foreign control in 1976 belongs to a clique (namely the U.S.-controlled Iron Ore Company of Canada, an affiliate of Argus Corporation). Although 38 per cent have some connection to the clique structure, nearly half are isolated from the dominant component. Industrial corporations that grow to dominance under Canadian control show a much stronger tendency to take up positions within or on the periphery of cliques. Thus, both the Canadianization of several consistently dominant industrial companies and the rise of newly dominant Canadian-controlled corporations contribute to an inner circle that by 1976 is overwhelmingly composed of indigenous industrial and financial capital.

A graphic depiction of the network's changing structure is given in Figures 6.3–6.5, as two-dimensional plots in which corporations are represented by points and the relative proximities of pairs of firms in the network are represented by the distances between points in the space.[7] Figure 6.3 depicts the dominant component of sixty-four firms in 1946, indicating the boundaries of the network's two cliques and their peripheries.[8] Figure 6.4 shows the dominant component of eighty-three firms in 1976, with boundary lines identifying firms on the clique periphery, firms belonging to single cliques, and firms belonging to two cliques.[9] The highly integrated inner circle of corporations in 1976 is further decomposed in Figure 6.5, a plot whose boundary lines divide forty clique members into their respective intercorporate groups.[10] Finally, the

Table 6.3 Cumulative Percentage Distributions of Inner Circle Status for 70 Dominant Industrial Corporations by Country of Control and Corporate Survivorship, 1946 and 1976

Inner Circle Status	1946				1976			
	Consistently Dominant		Not Dominant in 1976		Consistently Dominant		Newly Dominant	
	Canadian	Foreign	Canadian	Foreign	Canadian	Foreign	Canadian	Foreign
Double clique member	0	0	0	0	12.5	0	0	0
Single clique member	28.6	30.8	29.6	0	68.8	20.0	40.0	3.4
Clique periphery	42.9	38.5	55.5	18.8	100.0	70.0	80.0	37.9
Dominant component	85.8	53.8	66.6	25.0	100.0	70.0	86.7	51.7
Interlocker	92.9	69.2	70.3	25.0	100.0	80.0	93.4	55.2
Isolate	100.0	100.0	100.0	100.0	100.0	100.0	100.0	100.0

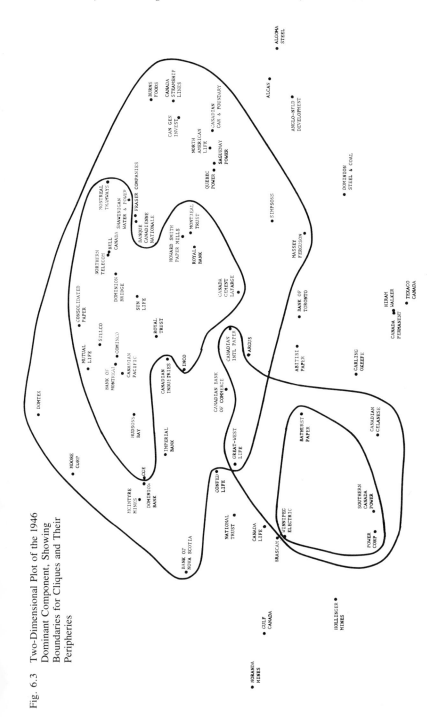

Fig. 6.3   Two-Dimensional Plot of the 1946 Dominant Component, Showing Boundaries for Cliques and Their Peripheries

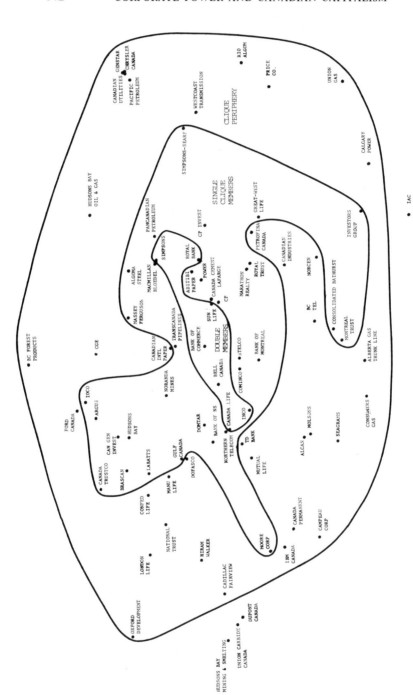

Fig. 6.4   Two-Dimensional Plot of the 1976 Dominant Component, Showing

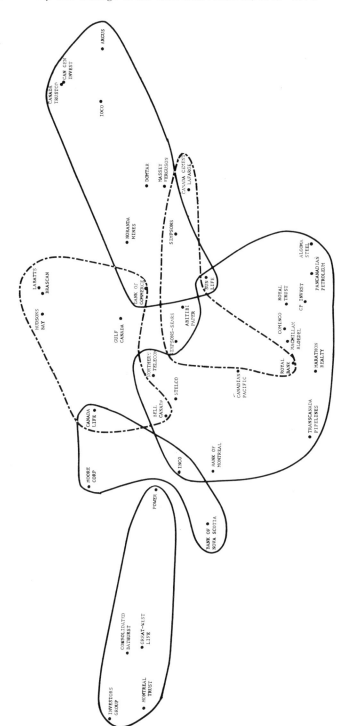

Fig. 6.5 Two-Dimensional Plot of 40 Clique Members, 1976, Showing Boundaries for Cliques

Table 6.4 Structure and Membership of Intercorporate Cliques, 1946–1976

	Largest members	STRUCTURE Clique number	Clique size	Periphery size	Clique density	Density of ties to non-members	Clique diameter
1976	Bank of Nova Scotia, Canada Life, Inco Moore, Corp.	6	4	19	1.000	0.070	1
	Royal Bank, Simpsons-Sears, Abitibi	5	5	23	0.900	0.064	2
	Brascan, Canadian Imperial Bank of Commerce, Bell Canada, Gulf Canada, Hudson's Bay	4	7	33	0.667	0.079	3
	Argus Corp., Canadian Imperial Bank of Commerce, Massey-Ferguson, Noranda, IOCO	3	10	34	0.533	0.058	4
	Power Corp., Great West Life, Consolidated-Bathurst, Montreal Trust	2	5	7	1.000	0.023	1
	Royal Bank, Bank of Montreal, Bell Canada, Inco, Canadian Pacific	1	16	46	0.417	0.065	4
1946	Power Corporation, Winnipeg Electric, Southern Canada Power	2	4	3	1.000	0.012	1
	Royal Bank, Bank of Montreal, Canadian Pacific Ltd., Inco	1	20	26	0.421	0.033	4

MEMBERSHIP (per cent)

Consistently dominant members	75	25	69	80	60	71	80	100
Foreign controlled members	25	0	0	0	10	14	50	0
Members based in Montreal	75	50	50	60	20	14	40	0
Members based in Toronto	7	0	12	0	60	57	60	50
Members linked by intercorporate ownership	20	75	63	100	60	43	40	0

structure and membership of each clique in 1946 and 1976 are described in Table 6.4. Here we can see that in all cases the density of multiple-director interlocking within each clique exceeds 0.4, yet the density of interlocking between each clique's members and non-members is comparable to or less than the overall density of interlocking in the dominant component, which was .075 in 1946 and .068 in 1976.

It is clear that in 1946 the inner circle was focused around a large group of twenty corporations based predominantly in Montreal and taking in the entire stable component. More than 70 per cent of all members of the dominant component belonged to this clique or were interlocked with its members; 75 per cent of its members would remain economically dominant over the ensuing three decades. In contrast, the second intercorporate grouping, though densely interlocked, was made up of only four firms, three of which would be reorganized or nationalized after 1946. The fourth, Power Corporation, was transformed by Paul Desmarais in the 1960's from a trust-like vehicle controlling several electric utilities into a highly diversified investment company.

The stable component of Canadian Pacific, Bank of Montreal, Bell, Inco, Stelco, Royal Bank, and so forth, continues to account for most members of the largest clique in 1976, ten of which also belonged to the larger clique in 1946. But between these years, ten companies disappear from the clique: two paper companies in reorganizations; two utilities in nationalizations; one manufacturer because of slow growth; and five companies by moving to the clique's greatly enlarged periphery. The six new clique members in 1976 are all newly dominant companies ultimately controlled by Canadian Pacific Limited: Canadian Pacific Investments plus three of its subsidiaries and two affiliates (see Figure 5.1). With these additions, the intertwining of share capital in this clique is considerable: over 60 per cent of its members are linked to other members through intercorporate ownership.

A similar intermingling of banks, industrial corporations, and investment companies is evident in the two next-largest 1976 groupings, which are comprised partly of companies affiliated with Argus Corporation (clique 3) and Brascan Limited (clique 4). These predominantly Toronto-based groups also evidence substantial intercorporate ownership ties among their members. In the smaller cliques, however, the intermingling of banks, industrial firms and investment companies is less apparent. Cliques 5 and 6 contain large banks and industrials, but not investment companies. Clique 2—the thoroughly reconstituted Power Corporation group—has no banks among its members, although it includes two financial institutions controlled by Power Corp. This group also differs from others by being relatively introverted. All its members are ultimately controlled by Power's major shareholder, Paul Desmarais, and are completely interlocked with each other. But few have ties to other companies. In contrast to all other groupings, which have peripheries far larger than their memberships, the Power clique's periphery takes in only seven firms. Moreover, this is the only clique without an overlapping membership in another clique.

The example of Power Corporation and its subsidiaries raises the more general issue of interpenetration among the six dominant corporate groupings of 1976. In Table 6.5 the proportion of overlap is reported for each pair of cliques. With the exception of the Power group, the cliques tend to be highly interconnected through overlaps on their respective peripheries, confirming our assumption that clique members comprise a socially integrated, corporate inner circle. It is not unusual for half of the total membership of two cliques to have strong ties to members of both groupings.

The largest and most stable clique (number 1) is also most linked to others. In particular, 80 per cent of the members of either of the two largest groupings (cliques 1 and 3) have at least one multiple-director tie to both cliques. Sun Life is a member of both the Canadian Pacific and Argus groups; the Bank of Commerce (a member of the Argus group) is tied to five firms in the Canadian Pacific group; the Royal Bank (a member of the Canadian Pacific group) is tied to three firms in the Argus group; and Canadian Pacific Limited and the Bank of Montreal (members of the Canadian Pacific group) are each tied to two members of the Argus group. This list does not exhaust the instances of overlaps between the two largest groups, but it does give some sense of their extent and importance.

The overlap between the Argus group and the clique that includes Brascan (clique 4) is even greater. These Toronto-based clusters share the city's major bank, the Commerce. Additionally, eight members of the Argus group are on the periphery of Brascan, six members of the Brascan group are on the periphery of the Argus group, and seventeen companies are on both cliques' peripheries. In turn, the Brascan group is extensively linked to the smallest clique (number 6), through Canada Life—a member of both—and six other corporations that are members of one clique and on the periphery of the other. Several of the key companies in these interconnected Toronto cliques belong to the smaller network of stable ties shown earlier in Figure 6.1, such as: Canada Life, the Bank of Commerce, Brascan, Argus, Massey-Ferguson, and the Bank of Nova Scotia. On the basis of these stable ties, the corporate inner circle appears to have expanded to include previously peripheral, Toronto-based capital, much of which has been reorganized under the

Table 6.5 Overlaps Between Six Intercorporate Cliques, 1976*

	Clique Number					
	1	2	3	4	5	6
1		0.286	0.800	0.636	0.650	0.474
2	0.071		0.133	0.250	0.300	0.333
3	0.326	0.114		0.938	0.643	0.429
4	0.320	0.057	0.472		0.333	0.700
5	0.326	0.227	0.167	0.182		0.000
6	0.267	0.095	0.243	0.243	0.135	

*Entries in the upper triangular are the proportion of members of either clique that have multiple-director ties to both cliques; entries in the lower triangular are the proportions of the peripheries of either clique that have multiple-director ties to both (that is, overlapping clique peripheries).

control of Argus Corporation and Brascan Limited.

Thus, by 1976, the inner circle is larger and more cohesive, yet also more clustered into capitalist subgroupings which are no longer centred predominantly in Montreal. This integration and regional differentiation of Canadian finance capital seems to parallel developments south of the border, where, since the Second World War, financial groups have become somewhat less centred in New York City yet more interconnected within a configuration that spans the eastern seaboard and takes in parts of the midwest and west coast (Bearden et al. 1975; Sonquist and Koenig 1975). In Canada in the same period, as investments flowed westward and as Toronto began to eclipse Montreal as a financial centre, the locus of finance capital shifted accordingly. By the 1970's, there was a Montreal-Toronto axis of monopoly capital which was further differentiated into particular capitalist interest groups (see Niosi 1978, 169–70).

The roles of banks and investment companies in the inner circle bear further discussion and analysis. As we have seen, the five cliques that in 1976 include banks among their members have very large peripheries, yet the Power Corporation group is more introverted. Concomitantly, in four cliques, investment companies, such as Power, are vehicles for the centralized control of several dominant corporations. The question arises whether the different roles of banks and investment companies in the circuit of finance capital have implications for the positions these corporations occupy in the interlock network. As centres of *allocative* financial power, banks may maintain ties to a wide range of companies, roughly corresponding to their credit relations with corporate clients. This would tend to produce a large periphery around any intercorporate group in which banks were members. In contrast, the concentration within an investment company of share ownership in several firms affords it (or more precisely, its controlling capitalists) *operational* financial power over a more restricted range of companies which may to some extent be managed as a unit. Such centralized control would tend to produce a dense interlock network among the investment company and its affiliated corporations, as the controlling capitalists appoint themselves to the boards of the corporations they control (see, for example, Newman 1975, 28–29).

To examine more systematically the network positions of leading banks and investment companies, an analysis was made of their respective *social circles,* that is, of the firms which shared multiple directors in 1946 or 1976. Sociologists have found the concept of social circle useful in the study of power and influence (Kadushin 1968; Alba and Moore 1978). Its importance in the analysis of financial interlocks has been emphasized by Fennema:

> An interlock between a bank and an industrial firm generally in-
> dicates the existence of a client-relation between the bank and the
> industrial firm.... [T]he set of client-relationships between a bank
> and a number of industrial firms, characterized by interlocks, is
> considered its *sphere of interests* (1982, 159; see also Pennings
> 1980, 190).

Tables 6.6 and 6.7 describe the social circles of corporations surrounding the principal loci of loan and concentrated share capital in the
Canadian economy (namely the chartered banks and investment companies that were positioned within the periphery of the clique structure
in the corporate networks of 1946 or 1976). In Table 6.6, the structure
of each social circle is analyzed using three simple indices: (1) the number of firms within the circle, (2) the density of interlocking within the
circle, and (3) the density of interlocking within the circle *excluding
the focal firm*. By comparing these two densities, we can assess the extent to which a social circle is cohesive in the sense of being tied together not merely by a single, central member but by a more general
pattern of interlocks. In the extreme case, if all members of the circle
are interlocked, then both densities will equal unity. At the other extreme, if all ties in the circle converge in starlike fashion on the focal
firm, then the second density will equal zero. Comparing social circles
over time, we can get a sense of the changing positions of key financial
centres.

Consider first the situation in 1946, when social circles in the corporate network were dominated by two large groups around the country's
Montreal-based banks, the Bank of Montreal and Royal Bank of Canada. Of these two main circles, only the Bank of Montreal manifests a
very high degree of structural integration: excluding the Bank from cal-
culation of interlock density, nearly half of all members of this circle
share multiple directors with each other.

The circle centred on the Royal Bank in 1946 is nearly as large but
less integrated as a group. It has a lower overall density, and a much
lower density when the focal bank is excluded. This is also the case for
most of the smaller circles, with the exceptions of La Banque Canadienne Nationale and Power Corporation. For instance, among the four
firms tied to the Bank of Nova Scotia, only one pair is multiply interlocked, yielding a density of 0.167 when the bank is excluded.

It appears that, in the early postwar period, the Bank of Montreal
group of corporations and capitalists was the most important locus of

Table 6.6 Social Circles Around Major Banks and Investment Companies, 1946 and 1976

1946 Network Focal Firm	Size of Social Circle*	Density of Social Circle	Density, Excluding Focal Firm
Bank of Montreal	15	.533	.462
Royal Bank of Canada	14	.374	.269
Canadian Bank of Commerce	8	.393	.174
Bank of Nova Scotia	5	.500	.167
Banque Canadienne Nationale	4	.833	.667
Imperial Bank of Canada	4	.500	0
Power Corporation of Canada	4	1.00	1.000
Argus Corporation	6	.533	.300
1976 Network Focal Firm			
Bank of Montreal	22	.186	.105
Royal Bank of Canada	21	.181	.095
Canadian Imperial Bank of Commerce	26	.182	.113
Bank of Nova Scotia	11	.291	.133
Toronto-Dominion Bank	16	.175	.057
Power Corporation of Canada	9	.472	.321
Argus Corporation	7	.667	.533
Canadian Pacific Investments	11	.582	.489
Brascan	6	.733	.600

*Excluding the focal firm.

Table 6.7 Overlapping Members of Key Social Circles, 1946 and 1976

1946 Network	Bank of Montreal	Royal Bank of Canada	Canadian Bank of Commerce	Bank of Nova Scotia	Banque Canadienne Nationale	Imperial Bank of Canada	Power Corporation	Argus Corporation
Bank of Montreal	–							
Royal Bank	4	–						
Canadian Bank of Commerce	1	1	–					
Bank of Nova Scotia	1	0	2	–				
Banque Canadienne Nationale	1	3	0	0	–			
Imperial Bank of Canada	1	0	0	0	0	–		
Power Corporation	0	0	0	0	0	0	–	
Argus Corporation	1	0	3*	0	0	0	0	–

1976 Network	Bank of Montreal	Royal Bank of Canada	Canadian Imperial Bank of Commerce	Bank of Nova Scotia	Toronto-Dominion Bank	Power Corporation	Argus Corporation	Canadian Pacific Investments	Brascan
Bank of Montreal	–								
Royal Bank of Canada	4	–							
Canadian Imperial Bank of Commerce	7	6	–						
Bank of Nova Scotia	5	1	4	–					
Toronto-Dominion Bank	4	2	4	1	–				
Power Corporation	4	3*	2*	0	1	–			
Argus Corporation	1	1	4*	0	0	0	–		
Canadian Pacific Investments	4	7*	3	1	2	0	0	–	
Brascan	1	0	4*	1	1	1	1	0	–

*Includes direct interlocks between investment companies and chartered banks

Canadian finance capital: tightly integrated, largest in size, and including a number of the country's biggest firms. The circle around the Royal Bank was much less cohesive in 1946, though larger than any of the six other minor groupings. The dominance of the Bank of Montreal group is perhaps best summarized by noting the substantial overlaps between the Bank's social circle, the network's major clique, and the stable component of consistently interlocked dominant firms. All but one of the fifteen companies within the Bank of Montreal's social circle in 1946 were also members of the large clique of twenty companies. Ten of the circle's members would belong to the stable component of twelve firms consistently at the centre of the 1946–76 network.

The stability of this largest group is not at all characteristic of the other large social circle. Only one of the thirteen firms interlocked with the Royal Bank in 1946 (Sun Life) is still within the Bank's circle in 1976. However, most of the circle does overlap with the major clique in 1946. Including the bank itself, ten members of the circle also belong to the clique. In fact, the social circles around the Bank of Montreal and Royal Bank account for the entire clique of twenty corporations, four of which are interlocked with both banks. In this sense, the main grouping of dominant corporations at the beginning of the post-war era could be described as an amalgamation of social circles surrounding the two leading Montreal-based banks.

What transformations occurred in the ensuing years? In the second panel of Table 6.6, two significant changes are notable. First, the size of social circles has increased: greater numbers of dominant firms have entered into direct contact with major indigenous centres of loan and share capital. Second, the internal cohesiveness of bank-centred circles has declined. This is apparent in the greatly decreased density within these circles, both with and without the focal bank. There has been a weakening of tendencies toward exclusivity in bank interlocking and a widening of contact between all financial centres and other corporations.

All of the 1946 circles increase in size (except for that of La Banque Canadienne Nationale, which disappears as a focal firm). The most remarkable gains are registered by the Toronto-based banks, which also merge in this period. Toronto-Dominion, formed from one bank on the 1946 periphery and one in the dominant component, is at the centre of a circle of fifteen firms. Canadian Imperial Bank of Commerce, formed from predecessors on the periphery that had circles of eight and four firms in 1946, has the largest sphere of influence, taking in twenty-six firms (nearly a third of all corporations in the 1976 dominant component). The eastern-based banks—Bank of Montreal, Royal Bank, and

Bank of Nova Scotia—all show smaller increases, the first slipping to the third largest circle in 1976. With the postwar centralization of Toronto-based bank capital and the great accumulation of industrial capital in the form of Ontario-based manufacturing and western resources, Toronto emerges as an important centre of finance capital. As Niosi has suggested, a considerable portion of this industrial capital was accumulated under foreign control (1981, 24). Not surprisingly, then, a number of the financial ties that emerge in Toronto unite the Toronto banks with foreign-controlled companies. Toronto-Dominion shares multiple directors with Dupont Canada, Union Carbide Canada, IBM Canada, Canadian International Paper, Gulf Canada (all U.S.-controlled), and Hudson Bay Mining and Smelting (controlled in South Africa). The Commerce is interlocked in 1976 with Canadian General Electric, Ford of Canada, Gulf Canada, Iron Ore Company of Canada (all U.S.-controlled), and Canada Cement Lafarge (controlled in France).

The second interesting change in Table 6.6 is a movement away from any semblance of cohesive bank-centred financial groups in the network. The change is evident in the densities of the social circles of the Bank of Montreal and Royal Bank. This tendency is *not* found among the investment companies: Argus' interlock density, for example, actually increases from the immediate postwar period (when E.P. Taylor was just beginning to assemble his corporate empire) to the mid-1970's. The density within Power Corporation's circle does decrease but is still considerable in the recent period, while Canadian Pacific Investments' and Brascan's circles also have rather high densities, whether with or without the focal firm. These continuing high levels of interlocking are consistent with the idea that investment companies serve as centres of operational financial power, through which finance capitalists exert direct, unified control over sets of firms and circuits of capital.

Compared with investment companies, banks in 1976 maintain large, loosely connected social circles. Indeed, the density of interlocking among non-focal members of the Toronto-Dominion Bank's circle is less than the overall density in the dominant component. These firms seem to have little in common apart from their bilateral relations with Toronto-Dominion, which is the only bank on the periphery of the clique structure. Members of the Toronto-Dominion circle include six foreign-controlled companies, most of them scattered around the network's periphery. Much the same may be said of the large, sparsely interlocked circle around the Royal Bank, which takes in eight industrial corporations under foreign control in 1976.

The banks' social circles tend not to resemble the intercorporate cliques to which they belong. This is partly because the circles have widened while the cliques have proliferated in number but (compared to the large clique of 1946) decreased in size. A majority of the members of each bank's circle lies on the periphery of the cliques to which the bank belongs. In contrast, social circles around the leading investment companies tend to resemble these companies' cliques. Five of nine members of Power Corporation's circle also belong to its clique; all members of Argus's, Canadian Pacific Investments', and Brascan's circles belong to their respective cliques.

Thus it seems that the operational and allocative forms of power accruing to investment companies and banks draw them toward somewhat different locations in the intercorporate structure. The centralized intertwining of corporate share capital within investment companies in 1976 provides a basis for well-defined capitalist interest groups around these firms, more or less corresponding to the inner circle's four main cliques. Within these groups, Canadian finance capitalists control and manage blocs of monopoly capital spanning several large corporations. With the rise of diversified investment companies after the Second World War, these interest groups appear to have been consolidated as supracorporate units of capital. Although the stable network of Montreal-based finance capital persists, it is no longer structured around the two large Montreal-based banks. Rather, by 1976 the five big banks have large but diffuse social circles which reach beyond the membership of any one interest group, effecting a highly integrated corporate inner circle whose periphery extends to a number of foreign-controlled companies.

The increasingly integrative role of the banks can be seen in Table 6.7, which shows the number of overlapping memberships in the social circles of leading banks and investment companies in 1946 and 1976. In 1946, there were eighteen overlapping memberships among the eight circles. Four of these, as we have seen, occurred between the Bank of Montreal and Royal Bank. Sun Life, Bell Canada, Northern Electric, and Dominion Bridge each shared multiple directors with both banks. Similarly, the Bank of Commerce shared two of its social circle members, Canada Life and National Trust, with the Bank of Nova Scotia. Bell Canada, Montreal Tramway, and Shawinigan Water and Power were interlocked with both the Royal Bank and La Banque Canadienne Nationale. The Bank of Commerce and Argus Corporation, besides being directly interlocked, shared Massey-Harris and Abitibi Paper in their social circles. But beyond these twelve cases, the number of overlapping memberships in the early period was negligible. Although the interlocks of the two main banks converged on four important companies, in general such articulations were not common in the immediate postwar years.

By 1976, there were seventy-nine overlapping memberships among the nine circles, a fourfold increase from 1946. The three largest banks each shared social circle members with nearly every major bank and investment company, and their social circles interpenetrated quite extensively. All three banks were tied to Canada's largest life insurer, Sun Life, as well as to one of the oldest industrial monopolies, Canadian Pacific Limited. The Bank of Commerce shared seven of its social-circle members with the Bank of Montreal and six with the Royal Bank. Most of the firms that interlocked with two or more banks had been consistently dominant throughout 1946–76, and many had maintained stable interlocks with other consistently dominant companies across the three decades. In addition to Sun Life and Canadian Pacific they include Stelco and Canada Cement (tied to Bank of Montreal and Bank of Commerce); Massey-Ferguson, Abitibi Paper and Simpsons (tied to Royal Bank and the Commerce); Inco (to Bank of Montreal, Bank of Nova Scotia, and Toronto-Dominion); Bell Canada (to Bank of Montreal, Bank of Commerce, and Toronto-Dominion); Canada Life (to Bank of Montreal, Bank of Commerce, and Bank of Nova Scotia); Cominco (to Bank of Montreal and Toronto-Dominion); Noranda Mines (to Bank of Commerce and Bank of Nova Scotia); and Gulf Canada and Manufacturer's Life (to Bank of Commerce and Toronto-Dominion).

Table 6.7 also reveals a *regionalized* pattern of overlaps between the social circles of the three largest banks and those of the four leading investment companies. Corporations interlocked with the Bank of Commerce are in many cases also tied to Argus Corporation or Brascan. Firms interlocked with the Royal Bank or Bank of Montreal tend also to interlock with Power Corporation or Canadian Pacific Investments. Thus, the major Toronto-based capitalist groupings link up predominantly with that city's leading bank; while Montreal-based interests seem to rely more on the banks that dominate the Montreal financial community.

The earlier clique analysis and this examination of social circles converge on an image of the intercorporate network as an increasingly integrated yet differentiated structure. In this structure, capitalist interest groups are centred primarily in investment companies, built around intercorporate ownership relations and based in Montreal *or* Toronto. Although these interest groups are structurally discernible, they are themselves extensively interconnected. Financial institutions are positioned particularly well in the network as articulation points between intercorporate groupings, suggesting that they tend to maintain multilateral credit relations with a wide range of large corporations. As such, financial institutions also serve to draw into the corporate inner circle numerous corporations that are not members of interest groups.

On the issue of foreign control, two findings stand out. The close interpenetration within the inner circle of Canadian and American interests in 1946 disappears as consistently dominant corporations such as Inco and Bell Canada fall under Canadian control, retaining their central positions in the network. By 1976, foreign-controlled companies are largely absent from capitalist interest groups and from the inner circle as a whole, as indigenous corporations that rise to economic dominance take up positions in the interlock network. Secondly, however, and in contrast to the Bank of Montreal, the extensively reconstituted social circles of the Royal Bank, Toronto-Dominion Bank, and the Bank of Commerce include a number of foreign-controlled industrial firms, drawing these companies onto the inner circle's periphery. In this way, financial institutions seem to mediate not simply *among* indigenous interest groups but *between* Canadian interest groups and the subsidiaries of foreign-based MNCs (see Carroll, Fox and Ornstein 1982, 62).

7

THE CONSOLIDATION OF
CANADIAN FINANCE CAPITAL
1946–1985

In this chapter, this study's principal findings on patterns of corporate accumulation and interlocking between 1946 and 1976 are reviewed, supplemented where possible with more recent data on the structure of Canadian corporate power in the 1980's.

THE ACCUMULATION OF CAPITAL

In Chapter 4, the changing composition of monopoly capital in Canada was analyzed by following a set of dominant corporations over three decades. The post Second World War period, through the mid-1970's, brought an unprecedented wave of capitalist accumulation in which the position of the largest Canadian firms was perpetuated through both centralization and concentration of capital. Dominant corporations merged to form even larger capitals; many smaller concerns were taken over by the largest corporations. Simultaneously, capital was concentrated in firms already dominant in the 1940's as well as in companies that grew quickly to rank among the largest corporations in more recent times.

The industrial composition of large-scale capital in Canada changed quite dramatically, especially with the full development of a domestic oil and gas industry, integrated with exploration and extraction and with transport, refining and petrochemical production. Conversely, however, financial capital remained quite stable institutionally. In part, this stability reflects the very highly centralized state in which Canadian financial capital has been organized throughout this century (Neufeld 1972). There is, however, a more general explanation for the consistent dominance of leading financial institutions, related directly to their strategic location as centres of allocative power in a changing capitalist economy. As Kotz has pointed out:

It is not surprising that the wealthiest and most powerful capitalists operate through the banks. Any particular industrial corporation may decline in the long run, under the impact of changing technologies and new products. A bank, on the other hand, is tied to no particular industry in the long run. The future of banking will become clouded only when that of capitalism itself does. Through a bank, a capitalist can shift his main sphere of investment over time (1978, 149).

The institutional stability of financial capital in Canada should not be taken as evidence of a peculiar "overdevelopment of the financial sector" (as in Clement 1977). Indeed, as a proportion of GNP, the assets of financial intermediaries in Canada have been consistently *smaller* than those in the United States since the turn of the century (Neufeld 1972, 22, 59–61; see also Richardson 1982). More likely, the financial sector's stability is a result of both the highly centralized state of bank capital in Canada and the flexible form of financial capital in general.

Granting that major changes have occurred in the composition of dominant industrial corporations, it is still the case that, from 1946 through 1976, much of the capital of the country's largest firms was tied up in companies that occupied a dominant position throughout the period, providing an institutionally stable basis for a bloc of monopoly capital. The key question this study has addressed is the character of that monopoly fraction.

Our findings indicate a sustained control of large-scale capital by Canadian capitalists. This generalization is most unequivocally true of financial intermediaries, but it also applies to industry and commerce. In the postwar era, capital also concentrated under Canadian control in investment companies. The strong position that Canadian capitalists occupied in all these sectors by the mid-1970's is evidence neither of a cumulative "silent surrender" nor of an anachronistic "commercial elite." Rather, it indicates an indigenous fraction of finance capital.

Moreover, longitudinal trends in the national control of monopoly capital defy reconciliation with the thesis of Canadian dependency. We may cite several developments in this regard, each of which is consistent with accumulation strategies based not on a "colonial mandate" to sustain a dependent alliance with dominant foreign interests, but with the capitalist rationality characteristic of a mature bourgeoisie.

(1) Although the growth of U.S.-controlled large-scale industry outstripped its Canadian counterpart in the first postwar decade, the Amer-

ican expansion was accomplished not primarily through takeovers of the largest Canadian companies.[1] Instead, it occurred principally through takeovers of smaller firms (which were also targets for big indigenous corporations) and rapid concentration of capital in the large mining and manufacturing companies already under U.S. control, in combination with the sluggish growth of big indigenous "utilities" such as Canadian Pacific. In the early postwar years, Canadian-controlled big industry was concentrated in transportation and power production. U.S.-controlled industrials were involved more in mining and manufacturing industries and were thus able to take more immediate advantage of the rising demand on the world market for resources and the increasing domestic demand for such manufactured goods as automobiles, electrical equipment, and petroleum products.[2]

The most favourable accumulation prospects embraced sections of Canadian industry that tended to be under American control. This difference led to the great increase between 1946 and 1956 in the proportion of U.S.-controlled industrial capital. But the growth of indigenous industry was not precluded. Over time, major Canadian capitalists shifted their industrial investments toward more promising sectors. In the case of Power Corporation of Canada, for example, "the real strategical reorientation occurred in 1957 when Power sold its subsidiary, Southern Canada, to Shawinigan Water and Power in exchange for Shawinigan stock and began buying shares in companies in a variety of sectors" (Niosi 1978, 44). The same kind of industrial diversification was pursued in earnest by the nation's largest industrial corporation, Canadian Pacific, from 1955 on (Chodos 1973, 78), increasingly through its investment company, Canadian Pacific Investments.

By the same token, some indigenous firms that were already well positioned in the manufacturing and resource sectors in the 1940's (such as the big three steel makers, Massey-Ferguson, and Noranda Mines) concentrated enormous amounts of capital in the ensuing years and, in the process, improved their relative standing among dominant industrial firms. As well, several new companies (for instance, Dome Petroleum, Norcen Energy Resources, and Alberta Gas Trunk Line Company, now Nova Corporation) grew up in the oil and gas boom to become major Canadian-controlled industrials by the mid-1970's.

(2) In the years since the 1950's, leading Canadian capitalists "reclaimed" the share of their home market lost in the period of rapid U.S. expansion in Canada. At the same time, there was a *redistribution* of large-scale industrial assets under Canadian control, from a bias toward the transportation-communications and utilities sectors in 1946, to a more even distribution in the 1970's. By 1976, leading Canadian capi-

talists had assumed a strong presence in both the commodity-producing and "service" sectors of industry, consolidating control over much of the economy: the production of raw materials, the manufacture of finished goods, the service industries (such as transportation and communication) essential to advanced capitalism. Of course, the level of foreign direct investment in the Canadian economy remains higher than other advanced capitalist countries (Kemp 1978, 128). We will return to this issue in the concluding chapter.

(3) Throughout the three decades there was tremendous growth in the assets of the major investment companies in Canada. After the mid-1950's, most of this accumulation occurred under indigenous control. The important companies that have emerged since the early 1940's— Argus Corporation and Canadian Pacific Investments—or that have diversified from restricted investment portfolios in the utilities sector—Power Corporation of Canada and Brascan—are themselves examples of a consolidation of indigenous finance capital. Their existence presumes a highly developed domestic capital market, while it promotes greater centralization of indigenous capital under the operational control of a few Canadian finance capitalists.

(4) Another tendency leading to the recent consolidation has been a transfer of control from foreign to Canadian interests of several of the country's oldest and largest corporations, through gradual acquisition of shares by Canadian investors. This phenomenon, evident in the cases of Bell Canada, Inco, Alcan Aluminum, and Hudson's Bay Company,[3] has again been predicated on the existence in Canada of an advanced form of capitalism, including a capital market in which the shares of these companies could find Canadian buyers. (The precise reasons for these incremental shifts are not immediately apparent and are in any case beyond the scope of this research.)[4]

(5) In the mid-1970's, a more aggressive series of repatriations began, with Canadian capitalists actively pursuing foreign-controlled firms (Perry 1979; Niosi 1981, 31–33, 143–45). These include Canadian Pacific Investment's takeover of Algoma Steel Corporation and its subsidiary, Dominion Bridge Company from German interests in 1973; Abitibi Paper Company's takeover of the Price Company from British interests in 1975; and the Bronfman's takeover of Trizec Corporation. from British interests in 1976. In the same period, provincial crown corporations purchased three dominant industrial firms from foreign capitalists, illustrating the more active role of the state in the repatriation of foreign-controlled industry.[5]

Since 1976, this repatriation of capital has proceeded apace, lending further support to the claim that the indigenous monopoly fraction has

Table 7.1 Percentage Distributions of Corporate Assets by Industry and Country of Control, 1970, 1976, and 1982

Sector	Year	All Corporations with Assets of $25,000,000 and over			All Corporations		
		Canada	Control Foreign	Total	Canada	Control Foreign	Total
Mining	1970	24.08	75.92	100	30.60	69.40	100
	1976	43.09	56.91	100	44.79	55.21	100
	1982	64.49	35.51	100	65.87	34.13	100
Manufacturing	1970	33.91	66.09	100	40.37	59.63	100
	1976	38.83	61.17	100	45.49	54.51	100
	1982	49.24	50.76	100	54.54	45.41	100
Utilities	1970	93.71	6.29	100	92.14	7.86	100
	1976	93.36	6.64	100	92.53	7.47	100
	1982	96.34	3.66	100	95.28	4.72	100
Wholesale Retail Trade	1970	66.98	33.03	100	72.75	27.25	100
	1976	65.37	34.63	100	75.81	24.19	100
	1982	72.48	27.52	100	80.81	19.19	100
Total Industrial and Commercial Capital	1970	60.09	39.91	100	62.10	37.90	100
	1976	63.34	36.66	100	67.68	32.32	100
	1982	70.54	29.46	100	74.65	25.35	100

*Industrial categories match those used in Table 4.7: mining includes petroleum and natural gas unless the company is integrated into manufacture of petroleum. Utilities include transportation, communications, storage and public utilities. Total Industrial and Commercial Capital includes the major sectors listed in detail plus Construction and Services sectors. Very small corporations (with assets less than $250,000 and sales less than $500,000) are excluded as are non-profit organizations; most crown corporations are included.

Source: Canada, Corporations and Labour Unions Returns Act, Report, Part I: Corporations. (Ottawa: Statistics Canada, various years).

| Enterprise Rank | Year | Canadian Capitalists | Control | | | Concentration Ratio |
			Canadian State	Foreign	Total	
25 leading enterprises	1975	34.33	46.89	18.53	100	29.2
	1977	29.56	51.64	18.80	100	29.4
	1979	31.72	49.18	19.11	100	30.3
	1981	51.43	30.79	17.78	100	32.1
	1982	48.67	35.01	16.32	100	34.1
100 leading enterprises	1975	35.84	33.06	31.10	100	46.5
	1977	33.50	36.19	30.31	100	47.5
	1979	35.16	35.90	28.94	100	48.5
	1981	47.15	27.54	25.31	100	49.8
	1982	48.39	28.45	23.16	100	52.1
500 leading enterprises	1975	36.35	25.92	37.73	100	64.6
	1977	34.60	29.31	36.09	100	65.2
	1979	37.03	28.86	34.11	100	65.3
	1981	47.65	22.19	30.15	100	65.6
	1982	49.06	22.73	28.21	100	67.2
All enterprises*	1975	47.86	18.37	33.78	100	95.7
	1977	47.88	20.47	31.65	100	95.9
	1979	50.36	20.11	29.54	100	96.5
	1981	58.64	15.08	26.27	100	97.0
	1982	58.90	15.75	25.35	100	97.1

*Excludes small companies not classified by CALURA, e.g., 147,993 firms in 1975, accounting for 4.3 per cent of all non-financial assets; 235,800 firms in 1981, accounting for 3.0 per cent of all non-financial assets.

Source: Canada, Corporations and Labour Unions Returns Act, *Report Part 1: Corporations* (Ottawa: Statistics Canada, various years).

consolidated its economic position. In Table 7.1, it is clear that the repatriation of mining and manufacturing capital has continued into the 1980s, while Canadian capitalists have retained control of the utilities and merchandising sectors. Between 1976 and 1982, foreign control of mining (including crude oil and gas production) fell from 55 to 34 per cent, and foreign control of manufacturing fell from 55 to 45 per cent. As Table 7.2 shows, the movement toward greater indigenous control has been particularly strong at the highest reaches of the economy.[6] Between 1975 and 1982, foreign control of the capital in the one hundred leading enterprises fell from 31 per cent to 23 per cent.

(6) In the same period, the centralization of capital already under indigenous control reached a dizzying height. The proportion of all corporate assets controlled by just twenty-five leading enterprises grew from 29 per cent to 34 per cent. Among the corporations that make up the Toronto Stock Exchange 300—the major investor-owned companies in Canada—there were 37 takeovers in 1978 totalling $2.3 billion; seventeen takeovers in 1979 totalling $2.1 billion; and fifteen in 1980 accounting for $1.6 billion (Booth 1981, 8). Consequently, from January, 1978 to the summer of 1981, fifty-one firms disappeared from the TSE 300 (Francis 1981, 56).

The principals and ultimate beneficiaries of these machinations include some of Canada's wealthiest and most powerful capitalists. Conspicuously absent from the Canadian scene in recent years, however, has been the centralization of large-scale capital under foreign control: that is, acquisitions by foreign-controlled companies of major indigenous firms. With some noteworthy exceptions (such as the merger of Canada Permanent Mortgage and Canada Trustco by the Belgium-controlled Genstar Corporation), monopoly capital has further centralized under Canadian control. Along with continuing capitalist concentration and significant repatriations, this has contributed to a further consolidation of the dominant indigenous fraction.

To assess the extent of this consolidation, methods analogous to those described earlier were employed in compiling a list of the dominant corporations of 1985, using the most recent financial data.[7] The results of this analysis in Table 7.3, when compared with the tabulations in Tables 4.6 and 4.7, show Canadian capitalists increasing their control of large-scale industrial capital from thirty-one firms representing 57 per cent of assets in 1976 to forty-six firms representing 71 per cent of assets in 1985. It also shows a commensurate decrease in American-controlled big industry. As well, the indigenous bourgeoisie maintained its dominant position in the financial, commercial and property-development sectors.

Table 7.3 Distribution of Dominant Corporations and Assets by Country of Control for Four Economic Sectors, 1985

Sector	Country of Control				
	Canada	U.S.	U.K.	Other	Total
Distribution of companies (N)					
Industrial	46	16	4	4	70
Financial	19	1	0	0	20
Commercial	8	2	0	0	10
Property Development	7	0	0	0	7
Total	80	19	4	4	107
Distribution of assets (per cent)					
Industrial	71.2	20.0	3.2	5.7	100.0
Financial	99.0	1.0	–	–	100.0
Commercial	74.0	26.0	–	–	100.0
Property Development	100.0	–	–	–	100.0
Total	90.9	6.6	0.9	1.6	100.0

The analysis in Table 7.4 and 7.5 of turnover from 1976 to 1985 in the composition and control of dominant industrial corporations indicates that both repatriation of foreign-controlled capital and concentration of capital in newly dominant firms contributed to the relative expansion of the indigenous fraction. In 1985, Canadian capitalists controlled the vast majority of industrial firms (and assets) rising to dominance after 1976. Of the fourteen newly dominant indigenous industrials, only two represented centralizations of previously dominant capital. The balance was comprised mainly of firms in the resource sector. Their rapid growth is indicative of the general profitability of investments in resource extraction and the competitiveness of Canadian capitalists in their home market (particularly in comparison with the early post-Second World War years, when U.S.-controlled capital concentrated at a more rapid rate). Moreover, all six of the changes in nationality of control shown in the tables were transfers from American to Canadian interests. The capital of another six dominant industrial firms under foreign control in 1976 had been repatriated by 1985, but these companies were not longer extant, having been wholly absorbed by indigenous companies. All told, of the thirty-nine dominant industrial corporations under foreign control in 1976, twelve had been Canadianized by August 1985, and nine of these were purchased from American interests. Again, the Canadian state—in this case through its National Energy Program and through the Federal crown corporations PetroCanada and Canada Development Corporation—played an important role in a number of these repatriations.[8]

This expanding accumulation base has not been confined within Canadian borders. Indeed, since the late 1970's the executives and directors of large and middle-sized U.S. corporations have grappled with takeover attempts by Canadian capitalists.[9] In some cases, these attempts have simply been means of forcibly repatriating control of oil and gas companies held by American firms, as in Dome's takeover of Hudson's Bay Oil and Gas in 1981.[10] This trend itself is not without importance, since it challenges the validity of a pivotal assumption within the thesis of Canadian dependency: that foreign direct investment is in essence irrevocable and therefore that a nation state such as Canada, which has allowed a great proportion of its industrial capital to accumulate under foreign control, must necessarily reap a "harvest of lengthening dependency" (Levitt 1970).

There are other cases such as: Brascan's unsuccessful bid to take over F. W. Woolworth Co. in 1979 and its subsequent acquisition of controlling interest in Scott Paper Company; Hiram Walker Resources' purchase of the assets of Davis Oil Co. in 1981; Canadian Pacific

Table 7.4 Turnover Table of Industrial Firms, 1976 and 1985

| Status 1976 | Status 1985 — Top 70 Industrials | | | | | | |
| | Top 70, controlled in | | | | Not in | Not incor- | Total |
Top 70, controlled in	Canada	U.S.	U.K.	Other	top 70	porated	(N)
Canada	26	—	—	—	1	4	31
U.S.	6	13	—	—	6	3	28
U.K.	—	—	2	—	1	1	4
Other	—	—	—	2	3	2	7
Not in top 70							
Incorporated before 1946	3	—	1	—	0	0	4
Incorporated 1946–1976	9	2	1	2	0	0	14
Incorporated after 1976	2	1	—	—	0	0	3
Total (N)	46	16	4	4	11	10	91

Table 7.5 Turnover Table of Industrial Assets, 1976 and 1985 (in per cent)

Status 1976 Top 70, controlled in	Status 1985 Top 70, controlled in				
	Canada	U.S.	U.K.	Other	Total
Canada	52	–	–	–	52
U.S.	8	18	–	–	26
U.K.	–	–	1	–	1
Other	–	–	–	4	4
Not in top 70					
Incorporated before 1946	2	–	1	–	3
Incorporated 1946–1976	6	1	1	1	9
Incorporated after 1976	3	1	–	–	4
Total	71	20	3	5	100

Enterprise's unsuccessful bid for Hobart Corporation; Seagram's attempt to acquire Conoco Inc. and its consequent ascension as the largest shareholder of E. I. DuPont de Nemours; and the Bank of Montreal's takeover of Harris Bankcorp in 1984. In these instances, the penetration of the American economy by Canadian finance capital presents a clear example of capitalist internationalization. In either case, there can be no doubt that since the early 1970's Canadian finance capitalists have successfully consolidated their economic position at home while expanding their investments abroad.

THE STRUCTURE OF MONOPOLY CAPITAL

The manner in which monopoly capital is institutionally structured provides important clues to the character of the capitalist class. The longitudinal analysis of interlocking directorates confirms Clement's (1975) claim that the Canadian corporate elite has become more integrated. The probability of a pair of dominant industrial or financial firms exchanging two or more directors increased by 54 per cent between 1946 and 1976, while the likelihood of a single director tie rose 37 per cent.

The structure of corporate interlocks changed considerably over the three decades. However, a subnetwork of multiple-director interlocks among consistently dominant firms was maintained, around which the network of dominant companies was substantially restructured. As a group, consistently dominant corporations have formed a densely interlocked core, in and around which the majority of all interlocks at any given time has been focused. The set of firms economically dominant from the 1940's through the 1970's also occupied the dominant positions in the interlock network. These longitudinal results dovetail nicely with cross-sectional findings that centrality in corporate networks is strongly correlated with firm size, a measure of economic dominance (see, for instance, Allen 1974; Ornstein 1976; Carroll, Fox and Ornstein 1981, 1982). Viewed in historical perspective, this relationship means that corporations occupying a position of sustained economic dominance tend to be located at the centre of a network of institutional relations that is likewise sustained over time, even though the precise ties composing the network—the particular shared directors and interlocked directorates—are subject to replacement and modification over the decades.

This pattern of continuity in the midst of change suggests that, to some extent, the reproduction of Canadian monopoly capital in the years since the Second World War has occurred as an accumulation within a stable bloc of capital, under the auspices of a socially integrated business establishment. By the same token, firms not dominant in the early postwar period have come to represent a larger portion of big capital. The considerable degree of restructuring over time—both in the capitals themselves and in their interrelations—should caution against a portrayal of the accumulation process as a "conspiracy of monopolists," who together possess the supreme power to insulate themselves from the strictures of the market by effectively lining each other's pockets.[11]

The fact is that, in the period since the Second World War, capitals *have* formed and concentrated to reach enormous dimensions under the control of "independent entrepreneurs" such as Olympia and York's Reichmann brothers, Campeau Corporation's Robert Campeau, and Nova Corporation's Bob Blair. The dominance of monopoly capital is not rooted in the ability of certain capitalists to erect barriers of entry and to fix prices and output, as common as such practices may be.[12] Rather, it rests on the more fundamental conditions under which large-scale capital accumulates: principally those of financial-industrial coalescence and international mobility.

By systematically examining corporate interlocks, I have attempted to show how major financial and industrial interests have articulated in postwar Canada. The network analysis of indigenous and comprador fractions has demonstrated that within the indigenous fraction the coalescence of financial and industrial capital is very far advanced.

The densest ties have linked Canadian-controlled firms, especially those consistently in economically dominant positions and those in the industrial and financial sectors. Interestingly, in the first postwar decade, the period when the relative share of indigenous capitalists in big industry actually declined, there was a marked *increase* in the density of the multiple-director interlocks within the indigenous fraction. On the other hand, although U.S. capitalists augmented their control of large-scale production in this period, the dominant U.S.-controlled firms showed no tendency to establish significant institutional relations with Canadian financial companies, either then or afterwards. The relations that do connect indigenous and foreign-controlled capital have tended to involve the sharing of single directors, compared with the multiple-director relations that predominate more among indigenous firms. Finally, although Canadian financial intermediaries in 1946 were about as densely tied to U.S. industrials as to Canadian mining and manufacturing companies, this was no longer the case by 1976. In that year, Canadian financial institutions were as densely linked to British and other foreign industrials as to U.S. industrials but were three times more likely to share multiple directors with industrial corporations controlled domestically.

This pattern does not support Clement's idea of an alliance of Canadian financial and U.S.-controlled industrial capital. It is consistent instead with our expectations that: (1) a *consolidation* has occurred within the indigenous fraction in the coalescence of financial and industrial capital, and (2) that relations between national fractions of finance capital operating in Canada increasingly reflect the general *internationalization* of productive capital that has occurred since the Second World War.

Within the indigenous fraction, there appears to have been a general interdependence between patterns of capital accumulation and corporate interlocking. In 1946, when most large-scale industrial capital under indigenous control was concentrated in the transportation-utilities sector, the density of significant interlocks between that sector and Canadian financial intermediaries was highest. By 1976, when large-scale indigenous industry had become more evenly apportioned among the major lines of production, the financial interlocks themselves were rather evenly distributed across the major industries. Roughly one in ten pairs of Canadian-controlled financial institutions and industrial corporations were directly connected by virtue of two or more shared directors. Similarly, as Canadian-controlled investment companies enlarged their share of concentrated financial capital, their interlocks with both indigenous industrial capital and banking capital proliferated.

The same may be said of the domestically controlled companies which rose to dominance after 1946. Over time, these firms established institutional relations with other large corporations under Canadian control, effecting a reproduction of the network that reflects the changing social and technical conditions of accumulation. In this way, transformations in the structure of domestically controlled monopoly capital were incorporated into the network. Within the indigenous fraction, accumulation and interlocking seem closely related. On the one hand, as capital has shifted into and concentrated in different economic sectors, these sectors have come to participate more in the network of interlocks, especially through the major financial institutions. On the other hand, as firms have grown to rank among the largest companies they have established significant institutional relations with other large Canadian corporations.

This interdependence of accumulation and interlocking seems less evident for large firms under foreign control. In the first postwar decade, U.S. control of big industry increased dramatically, but with the exception of ties between U.S.-controlled industrials and indigenous mining firms, the density of interlocking between big U.S. and Canadian firms showed no corresponding increase. Significant interlocks between Canadian financial institutions and American industrials actually declined somewhat in this period of American expansion. In the second decade, when the share of big industrial capital controlled in Europe and South Africa expanded, there were increases in interlock density. For instance, interlocking between Canadian financial institutions and these industrials doubled. But in the next decade the same kinds of interlocks became less common, even though the proportion of large-scale industrial capital controlled outside of the North Atlantic Triangle continued to grow.

Hence, not only are institutional relations among indigenous firms stronger than those linking Canadian to foreign interests, but they also seem to be more directly related to the accumulation process itself. On these grounds we may speculate that "continental" and other connections linking Canadian and foreign interests serve less as vehicles for the co-ordinated accumulation of capital than as communication ties, expressing class solidarity between national fractions of capital (see Fennema 1982). The tendency Niosi (1981, 137–42) has found for indigenous and foreign companies to use the same investment dealers and corporate law firms may also account for many of the weak ties between Canadian and comprador fractions. Apart from these points of contact, it may be that foreign subsidiaries operating in Canada, particularly wholly owned branch plants, tend to adopt a largely "co-respective" attitude toward other Canadian companies (as in Baran and Sweezy 1966). This may be because they require less external financing and are not sufficiently independent of their parents to exercise much autonomous action.[13] Indigenous firms, in contrast, are key elements of a national economy characterized by large concentrations of capital and a fully developed credit system. As such, they are more liable to participate in indigenous circuits of finance capital and in the network of dominant Canadian corporations. This interpretation, however, is in the realm of speculation.

In general, there is a need for more systematic analysis of the substantive significance of corporate interlocking. The broad promise of network analysis lies precisely in its capacity to integrate the study of social "morphology"—that is, structure *per se*—with the study of behavioural consequences of structure for dynamic interaction among network elements (Berkowitz 1982, 154–58). Thus, it is encouraging to see studies that relate interlocking to the economic and political actions of corporations and their directors (see, for example, Fennema 1974; Burt et al. 1980; Pennings 1980; Ratcliff 1980; Soref 1980; Carrington

1981; Useem 1984; Richardson 1985), or that examine the extent to which interlocks broken on retirement or death of shared directors are repaired with the appointment of another shared director (Koenig, Sonquist and Gogel 1978; Palmer 1983; Ornstein 1980, 1984). We have assumed in this study that corporate interlocks, particularly stable ties involving several shared directors, are institutional relations that often correspond to such precise economic bonds as longstanding financial ties and the intertwining of share capital. These interlocks generally serve to co-ordinate the accumulation of monopoly capital under the control of a financial-industrial elite. This assumption is probably most tenable when the interlock data are aggregated into subnetworks; it is tenuous when specific connections between pairs of firms are examined.

When the analysis moves to the latter level—considering only multiple-director ties—we find that the most institutionally fixed section of monopoly capital (firms consistently in a dominant economic position and forming a connected network of significant interlocks throughout) has been made up predominantly of core members of the country's oldest financial group, whose origins extend back to the incorporation of the Canadian Pacific Railway under the control of capitalists associated with the Bank of Montreal. Within this stable component, there has been a postwar weakening of U.S. interests, a breakup of the alliance between Canadian capitalists directing such firms as Canadian Pacific, Stelco, and Bank of Montreal and the Rockefeller and Morgan interests formerly in control of Inco and Bell Canada. The cases of Inco and Bell suggest that in the postwar period foreign-controlled companies with significant institutional ties to Canadian finance capital have been more likely to become "Canadianized." This is evidence against Park and Park's (1973) thesis that the logic of capital accumulation cumulatively draws Canadian monopoly into a dependent alliance with American capital.

Bell Canada and Inco are actually part of a larger trend, in which a greater share of indigenous big industry has become integrated into the network of significant interlocks, while the proportion of U.S.-controlled industry positioned in the network has actually declined. By the mid-1970's, there is an integrated inner circle of large-scale capital that includes within its periphery nearly all of Canadian-controlled big industry. However, it encompasses less than half of the dominant industrial corporations under foreign control. Moreover, few of the U.S.-controlled firms that participate in the 1976 network belong to any of the densely interlocked cliques in the structure. Examining the cliques in more depth, we find considerable continuity in the Montreal-based monopoly interests that in 1946 clustered around the Bank of Montreal. Otherwise, there is a great deal of restructuring into cohesive intercorporate groups, four of which each include one of the major investment companies that have arisen since the Second World War.

These developments support the idea that indigenous monopoly capital has become further differentiated into interest groups in which finance capitalists exercise operational power over supracorporate units. The major interest groups of the mid-1970's were organized around investment companies, which were vehicles for the concentrated ownership of financial capital and the consequential control of various corporations. As Aglietta (1979, 220) has argued, such intercorporate empires regroup under a single power of disposal and control circuits of capital that may, from the standpoint of commodity production and circulation, remain distinct from each other.

In Canada, these capitalist groupings have established close ties to banks and other financial institutions. These relations integrate interest groups into a wider inner circle in which many dominant corporations are linked to two or even three big banks. The increased size and interpenetration of the bank-centred social circles suggests a structural consolidation bringing greater numbers of large corporations within more articulated circuits of finance capital. The banks' "sharing" of several large industrial firms is consistent with Menshikov's observation that "the largest industrial corporations grow beyond the narrow bounds of exclusive service by one bank or one bank group" (1969, 217). Menshikov argues that, for this reason, American financial groups have formed alliances around some of the largest industrials, such as Exxon Corporation. On the basis of our results, the same could be suggested in Canada for Canadian Pacific, Bell Canada, Inco, and other large corporations with significant ties in 1976 to several chartered banks.

Compared with the 1940's, when Canada's leading financial group could be described as an amalgamation of interests around the Royal Bank and the Bank of Montreal, by the mid-1970's it is impossible to partition the network into bank-centred cliques. Although the major chartered banks do occupy central locations, their mutual interlocks with other firms do not lend support to a model of an economy dominated by separate bank-centred interest groups. What the structure does seem to indicate is an advanced form of finance capital, in which banks allocate loan capital multilaterally to large industrial corporations. This same pattern has been found not only in the contemporary American economy (see Mintz and Schwartz 1981a, 1981b; Gogel and Koenig 1981) but also in the international network of corporations studied by Fennema (1982, 161), who reports that "that majority of banks have overlapping spheres of interests at the national level."

The most probable implication of these multilateral financial-industrial relations is an increase in what has been termed *bank hegemony*, namely the allocative financial power of the leaders of a handful of co-acting financial institutions "to mold the broad contours of coordinated corporate action, to their own interests" (Glasberg and Schwartz 1983, 318). To the extent that major Canadian financial institutions exercise their allocative power collectively, Marx's description of the bankers' role in capitalist accumulation as "general managers" of the social capital seems remarkably prescient. In linking up with common corporate clients, the financial institutions at the centre of the corporate power structure tend to transcend particular capitalist interests, to express the general interests of the capitalist class in allocating surplus value to the most promising sites of accumulation. Again, it must be emphasized that this form of financial power is quite distinct from the operational power that accrues to major corporate shareholders. As Glasberg and Schwartz point out:

> bank and insurance company decisions regarding the most promising locale for capital investment lead to the nurturance of some industries or firms and the decline of others. Since most companies are dependent upon outside funds, they will adapt to conditions placed upon available funding, thus allowing financial suppliers to influence and coordinate the activities of industrial companies without necessarily intruding on their decision-making process or tampering with executive authority (ibid.).

Not all the multiple-director bank interlocks we have analyzed are necessarily traces of allocative financial power, but there is good reason to suppose that many are. In 1980, for instance, longterm debt was the single most important source of funds for large Canadian corporations. In 1973, nearly a quarter of Canadian bank assets were in the form of industrial loans and securities: a greater proportion than that found among American banks (Carroll 1984, 265). Although Canada's banks do not disclose the proportion of their loan capital that they allocate to their own directors, the Royal Commission on Banking and Finance reported in 1962 that approximately 30 per cent of all authorized credit lines in excess of $100,000 were "to directors, their firms or corporations of which they were officers or directors" (quoted in Newman 1975, 120).

Jack Richardson's recent analysis of replacement patterns for corporate interlocks broken because of retirement or death is especially important in this regard. Using the same data base as employed in this study, Richardson reports a significant relationship between the profitability of nonfinancial corporations in 1963 and the presence of replaced interlocks five years later (1985, 112). He describes the connection between financial-nonfinancial interlocks and nonfinancial profitability as a "circular and self-sustaining process." Profitability appears to be a causal factor in the formation of interlocks which, in turn, seem to provide advantages that reinforce the original profit position (ibid., 115). Richardson's general finding that the largest and most profitable corporations are most likely to be purposefully interlocked with financial institutions "is consistent with the finance capital theory's proposition that modern economies are dominated by a highly profitable financial-industrial complex which comprises a fusion of financial and industrial capital" (ibid.).

In Canada, the integrated corporate inner circle that has resulted from the proliferation of multilateral financial-industrial relations also provides a structural basis for enhanced *class* hegemony. Although various capitalist interests continue to compete for shares of surplus value, their dense ties to common banks present opportunities for behind-the-scenes co-ordination and conflict resolution and for the development of a unified corporate orientation toward government policy (Gogel and Koenig 1981, 25). Thus, corporate interlocks have a practical importance beyond the accumulation of capital and the reinforcement of an upper-class culture. They create a social network which can be instrumental in mobilizing leading capitalists for political purposes.

In the 1970's and 1980's, the political importance of corporate interlocks became more apparent, as economic crisis brought intensified class conflict to the advanced capitalist societies. According to Michael Useem, the general challenge of declining overall profits, and the specific political problems of Labour Party socialism in Britain and state interventionism in the United States, inspired a collective capitalist response, a corporate activism which in both countries was significantly facilitated by the pre-existing networks of the corporate inner circle:

> The simultaneous rise of corporate enemies and fall of company profits suggest the immediate genesis of the rising corporate activism. The rise would not have been as rapid, however, nor its thrust as effective were it not for the presence of the transcorporate networks of the inner circle, the classwide social organization that had gradually developed over the years, largely for reasons unrelated to political mobilization but highly facilitative of it. The preexistence of this transcorporate organization, itself strengthened by the forces threatening business during the 1970's, allowed for more rapid mobilization, quicker identification of the common cause, and stronger expression of the right policies (1984, 171)

The inner circle thus played a strategic role in helping to mobilize the political forces that would bring to power neo-conservative regimes in Britain and the United States. The precise political consequences of corporate interlocking in Canada have yet to be explored, but the highly integrated inner circle surely carries the same general strategic value for the capitalist class here as it does elsewhere.

One further structural feature of the 1976 network deserves discussion. At that time, the major chartered banks were positioned not just as articulation points between indigenous groups; three banks were similarly located between Canadian and foreign interests. Although the density of interlocking between Canadian financial institutions and foreign-controlled industrial companies was relatively low, the social circles of the Royal Bank, Toronto-Dominion Bank and Bank of Commerce did include a number of industrial corporations controlled outside of Canada, drawing these firms onto the periphery of the corporate inner circle. It is relations of this sort that Clement (1977) and others have pointed to as evidence of the dependent nature of Canada's corporate elite. However, of the sixteen foreign-controlled industrials within the clique periphery in 1976 that were interlocked with a chartered bank, seven had been repatriated by 1985. This record does not establish a credible case for the incipient coalescence of Canadian financial capital with foreign interests. Quite to the contrary, the relatively few strong interlocks of this type that were in place in 1976 may have facilitated the financial arrangements that enabled Canadianization of several foreign-controlled firms. In any case, such linkages cannot be attributed to any cumulative process of compradorization in which Canadian bankers finance the foreign takeover of domestic industry (as in Drache 1977, 23; Marchak 1979, 126–28).

Canadian Interest Groups in the 1980's

Increased indigenous control is not the only change that has occurred in the structure of Canadian monopoly capital since the mid-1970's. Against a backdrop of deepening world economic crisis, Canadian interest groups have recently undergone dramatic restructuring, supporting Overbeek's hypothesis that "the network of relations in finance capital will change considerably in density and/or structure, when the continued accumulation of capital comes under pressure" (1980, 116).

By 1985, each of the four groups centred around leading investment companies in 1976 had been restructured through massive exchanges of corporate shares. In 1978, Canadian Pacific Investments (now Canadian Pacific Enterprises) formed Canadian Pacific Enterprises (International)

B. V., to hold its foreign investments, chiefly in American manufacturing and mining. In the ensuing two years, it sold its shares in Trans-Canada PipeLines and MacMillan Bloedel to other Canadian interest groups. In 1981, it repatriated Canadian International Paper from American control.[14]

Paul Desmarais's Power Corporation sold its interest in Canada Steamship Lines in 1981 and in 1984 consolidated its financial subsidiaries, Montreal Trust, Great West Life and The Investors Group, into Power Financial Corporation, a financial conglomerate with interests in the Geneva-based investment company Parsega Holding S. A. Power also acquired a 6.4 per cent share in Canadian Pacific Limited (which gave Desmarais a seat on its board of directors) and, through its subsidiary Consolidated-Bathurst, took dominant positions in several oil and gas firms.[15]

With the death of the second chairman, John A. (Bud) McDougald, in 1978, a struggle for control of Argus Corporation began, from which Conrad Black emerged as victor. Through his holding company Revelston Corporation, Black and his allies control a corporate empire that has gone through three major reorganizations since 1978. Financially troubled subsidiaries such as Massey-Ferguson and Dominion Stores have been cast off in favour of new acquisitions in the resource sector such as Norcen Energy Resources. An attempt to take over Hanna Mining Co., an American firm with interests in the Argus affiliate Iron Ore Company of Canada (IOCO), left Black with 28 per cent ownership of Hanna through Norcen, establishing his presence in the American economy and strengthening his influence in IOCO. Finally, Argus's long-standing interest in the mass media was enhanced in 1985 with the acquisition of the London *Daily Telegraph*. Through deft shuffling of corporate assets Black has managed nearly to triple the value of his holding company since gaining control in 1978.[16]

But the most remarkable restructuring of the major Canadian interest groups of the mid-1970's has occurred around Brascan Limited, control of which was wrested from Jake Moore by Peter and Edward Bronfman in 1979. While retaining control of Brascan's longtime subsidiary, John Labatt (itself a diversified manufacturer), the Bronfmans have consolidated an empire which gives them an active say in companies whose collective assets approach $70 billion.[17] Through their private holding company, Edper Investments, this wing of the Bronfman family controls Canada's largest forestry company (MacMillan Bloedel), largest mining company (Noranda), largest trust company (Royal Trustco), and second largest property developer (Trizec Corp.)[18] Since 1980, Brascan has also held controlling interest in the Philadelphia-based Scott Paper Company, and in 1982 the Bronfmans consolidated many of their financial intermediary assets into the financial conglomerate, Trilon Financial Corporation. They have also been forging a major merchant bank and investment management company out of Hees International, the principal shareholder of the Continental Bank of Canada.[19]

Meanwhile, new centres of corporate power have been emerging, as established Canadian capitalists have diversified their investments through takeovers and mergers. Four important capitalist groupings have been consolidated since the mid-1970s from longstanding Canadian interests, primarily through the centralization of capital. Bell Canada reorganized itself as an investment company, Bell Canada Enterprises, in 1983. It has recently added controlling interest in two major corporations, TransCanada PipeLines and Daon Development Corp. to its longtime subsidiaries, Northern Telecom, Maritime Telegraph and Telephone and New Brunswick Telephone Co.[20]

The other wing of the Bronfman family, Charles and Edgar, has pursued a strategy of international expansion and diversification through its investment company, Cemp Investments, which currently gives them control of nearly $40 billion in assets, including the world's largest distillery (Seagram) and one of North America's largest property developers (Cadillac-Fairview). Their attempt in 1981 to take over American oil giant Conoco left them with the largest single bloc of shares (21 per cent) in E. I. DuPont de Nemours & Co., the American chemical conglomerate which now owns Conoco, raising the question of whether DuPont's Canadian subsidiary can still be considered an American-controlled branch plant.[21]

The empires of the Thomson and Weston families, both with extensive investments—and second residences—in Britain, have also undergone further diversification in recent years. Through private holding companies on both sides of the Atlantic, the Westons control the largest complex of bakeries and the second largest grocery chain in the world, but they have also established extensive interests in the Canadian fisheries and forest products sectors.[22] Galen Weston's attempt in 1979, however, to take over the Hudson's Bay Company, formerly a Brascan affiliate, met with failure. Kenneth Thomson, having succeeded his late father, Roy, as chairman of the family's private holding company, the Woodbridge Co., outbid Weston in capturing control of the Bay and its recently acquired subsidiaries, Simpsons and Zellers. The Thomsons' traditional accumulation base in newspaper publishing was further consolidated in 1980 with the purchase of FP Publications, owner of the *Globe and Mail,* against a competing bid by a consortium led by Argus's Conrad Black. Concomitantly, Thomson has been shifting capital through his investment company, International Thomson Organization, to the lucrative oil and gas sector, particularly in the North Sea, where the company's annual share of the generated revenue amounts to $1.2 billion.[23]

Other diversified capitalist interest groups have been consolidated since the mid-1970's on the basis of less established wealth. By far the most significant of these is the Reichmann family's holdings through Olympia and York Developments. Canada's largest property development company and North America's biggest landlord, Olympia owns or has developed properties in Canada, the United States, Belgium, Britain, and France.[24] Largely a product of the Toronto real estate boom of the 1960's, Olympia and York realized hundreds of millions in profit after its speculative purchase of a large piece of Manhattan in 1976. This capital was then parlayed into a series of acquisitions that have placed the Reichmanns at the centre of a formidable corporate empire. Besides having minority stakes in three of Olympia and York's major competitors in property development (Cadillac-Fairview, Trizec, and Bramelea), the Reichmanns own the world's largest producer of newsprint, Abitibi-Price (a 1979 merger of two dominant firms), which they took over in 1981 against a counter bid by a consortium led by Kenneth Thomson. They also control Hiram Walker Resources (a 1980 amalgamation of Home Oil Company, Consumers' Gas and Hiram Walker-Gooderham & Worts—all dominant companies in 1976), and have a 13 per cent stake in Peter and Edward Bronfman's financial conglomerate, Trilon.[25] Most recently, in August 1985, the Reichmanns paid $2.8 billion to purchase majority control of Gulf Canada from Chevron Corp. of San Francisco in a complicated deal which was to result in the reorganization of Olympia and York as a pure holding company.[26]

A rather less spectacular empire of middle-sized companies in finance, resources, and manufacturing has emerged in Vancouver around the Belzberg brothers' First City Financial Corp., which in 1984 acquired the Canadian and British packaging operations of American Can Corp., whose annual sales total $475 million.[27] The Belzbergs followed this up in early 1985 when First City bought Scoville, Inc., an American manufacturer of various consumer products, for $520 million.

An example of a private-sector interest group forming through privatization of a state-capitalist investment company is the Canada Development Corporation (CDC), capitalized with $322 million of seed money in 1971 by a Liberal government intent on strengthening the Canadian economy with a melding of public and private capital. CDC's investments are centred in petrochemical production, with lesser holdings in mining, computer hardware and software, and biotechnology. It controls Polysar Ltd., a major Canadian multinational, and Canterra Energy Ltd., most of whose assets were repatriated in 1981 from the French state-capitalist multinational Elf Aquitaine. The Mulroney government is in the process of selling the federal government's controlling interest in CDC to private investors. Control of the privatized CDC is to be safeguarded in the hands of Canadian capitalists, with individual foreign shareholdings limited to 10 per cent and total foreign shareholding held to 25 per cent.[28]

A government-owned investment company that may endure the current drive to privatize is Le Caisse de Depot et Placement du Quebec. Incorporated in 1966 with capital from the Quebec Pension Fund, the Caisse was a passive investor in Hydro-Quebec bonds for years. In the 1980's, it was transformed by finance minister Jean Campeau to an active centre of finance capital, ostensibly in the service of provincial economic development. The Caisse's assets compare with those of Canada's sixth largest bank. It holds large blocs of shares in quite a number of major Canadian companies: Domtar Inc., Gaz Metropolitain Inc., Dominion Textile, Canron Inc., Provigo Inc., the Canadian Commercial Bank, Brascade Resources (a joint venture with Brascan), and Canadian Pacific Limited. Reportedly, the expansion of this state-capitalist empire has been met with some consternation by private-sector capitalists, as the Caisse has demanded proportional representation on the boards and executive committees of corporations in which it has invested.[29]

The only clearly defined interest group to emerge in recent years under foreign control is headed by Genstar Corporation. This Belgian-controlled company holds interests throughout North America in manufacturing, construction, real estate and finance. Its acquisitions of Canada Permanent Mortgage Corporation in 1981 and Canada Trustco Mortgage Company in 1985 created an important financial-industrial complex while centralizing capital in the mortgage and trust sector. Genstar's emergence as a financial group was further confirmed in 1985 when it purchased a ten per cent interest in Gordon Capital Corporation (a major Canadian investment bank) and agreed with Gordon to establish a jointly owned investment corporation to operate on a continental basis. Genstar presents a case of highly internationalized finance capital. It integrates the North American interests of a major Belgian-based capitalist grouping. At the same time, Canadian investors have participated extensively in its share offerings: sixty per cent of its shareholders are Canadians. With head office in Vancouver and executive offices in San Francisco, Genstar's managers are able to pursue a highly diversified, continental investment strategy, with 61 per cent of 1983 revenues originating in the U.S. and 39 per cent originating in Canada.

Notwithstanding the example of Genstar, the recent consolidation of interest groups in Canada has, of course, brought a further centralization of capital under indigenous control. Indeed, the financial empires of the Bronfmans, Thomsons, Desmaraises, Westons, Blacks, Reichmanns and others have grown so large that the Canadian Bankers Association was recently moved to publish a study which attempted to quell fears about the power of chartered banks by pointing to the leading Canadian interest groups, which now rival the banks in size. Such a comparison may do little to allay concern about the concentrated power of monopoly capital in Canada. However, the finding that nine Canadian families control 46 per cent of the value of the three hundred most important companies on the Toronto Stock Exchange is a succinct comment on the extent to which the major interest groups at the heart of Canada's economy have consolidated themselves in recent years.[30]

Among these groups, both of the patterns of operational control identified by Aglietta (1979, 270) are evident. In some cases, corporate ownership and control are concentrated in a single dominant interest—typically a family—and the boards of directors of the associated companies reflect a homogeneous recruitment from the controlling group. The empires of the Reichmanns and Westons show this pattern of ''inside boards,'' rendering them relatively detached from the inner circle of corporate interlocking, although they maintain ties to Canadian financial institutions. For example, Paul, Albert and Ralph Reichmann own 92 per cent of Olympia and York, with the remainder believed to be divided among three siblings who reside outside of Canada. Albert is Olympia's president, Paul is executive vice-president, and its board of directors is comprised of mother Renée (the chairperson) and wives Lea, Ada, and Egasah. Olympia and York's directors and executives generally do not hold positions in companies not controlled by the Reichmann family.[31]

Alternatively, the controlling groups in the Argus, Brascan, and Canadian Pacific empires have tended to be looser, with share ownership somewhat more dispersed and the board of directors more mixed in composition. In the case of Canadian Pacific, for example, we have seen how a coalition of financial institutions has formed a ''community of interests'' for many years. From its inception, Argus Corporation has been controlled by a fraternity of allied capitalists led initially by E. P. Taylor and most recently by Conrad Black. Although Black has majority control of Argus through Western Dominion Investment Co., he is ''surrounded by a galaxy of stars'' that include Fredrik Eaton and Douglas Bassett, each with a minority interest in Argus and majority interests in other firms.[32] Eaton and Bassett have been friends of Black since university days; their own relationship goes back even further, to when their fathers co-founded Baton Broadcasting. Argus's principal shareholders often sit on each other's boards, as well as on the boards of several banks and trust companies,[33] thus situating the Argus group near the centre of Canada's corporate inner circle.

A similar pattern holds for the Brascan group, whose major share-holders Peter and Edward Bronfman have encouraged top managers to become minority shareholders by offering them remuneration in the form of stock options. As Brascan's president Trevor Eyton, formerly a prominent corporate lawyer, indicates, the fifteen managers in the Brascan interest group "work as partners and each of us has a relatively big piece of our investments." Eyton alone owns about $7 million of Brascan stock, plus shares in Trizec Corp.[34] Besides the Bronfmans and their hired executives, the Brascan group includes minority shareholder Jaime Ortiz-Patino, a Dutch-based capitalist whose family has had extensive investments in South America.[35]

Whether they are tightly bound around a single family interest or loosely knit into a more heterogeneous community of interests, the capitalist groups dominating Canada's economy do not act in isolation from each other. In several cases, interest groups appear to have entered into alliances in which they exercise joint control over certain capitals. Until July 1985, the Caisse de Depot and Paul Desmarais's Power Corporation were both major shareholders in Canadian Pacific Limited, weaving three groups into a Montreal-centred complex. Although Desmarais subsequently sold his shares, the Caisse has retained its dominant position in CP and is also the leading minority shareholder in Power's subsidiary, Power Financial Corporation.[36] Moreover, the Caisse holds a large bloc of shares in Bell Enterprise's TransCanada PipeLines and is partner to Edward and Peter Bronfman in Brascade Resources (the holding company through which Brascan controls Noranda Mines, MacMillan-Bloedel, and other firms). For his part, Paul Desmarais has for several years served as a director of Seagram Corp., Charles and Edgar Bronfman's major industrial enterprise. Since 1983, Charles Bronfman has repaid the favour by serving on the board of Power Corporation.

In turn, there are several points of contact between the Brascan Bronfmans and the Reichmanns. The families have almost equal equity in Trizec Corp., although the Bronfmans control a majority of voting shares.[37] After their joint takeover in 1981 of Royal Trustco, the Bronfmans and Reichmanns each held three positions on Royal's board which complemented their longstanding banking relations with the Bank of Montreal, another shareholder in Royal Trustco.[38] More recently, Brascan's subsidiary Trilon Financial Corp. acquired London Life from the Jeffery family. It then purchased control of Royal Trustco in a share deal with the Reichmanns and Toronto-Dominion Bank. The resulting financial conglomerate was 40 per cent owned by Brascan, 11 per cent by Olympia and York, 8 per cent by Toronto-Dominion, and 5 per cent by the Jeffery family.[39] For his part, Conrad Black insinuated himself into the Reichmann's takeover of Gulf Canada in August 1985, with a $300 million cash deal in which Argus subsidiary Norcen Energy Resources would become a partner to Gulf in "certain exploration and production assets."[40]

These and other alliances between interest groups contribute to a greater effective centralization of capital and a further "socialization of capital" within a cohesive financial-industrial elite.[41] But this consolidation does not signal a transcendence of competition within the monopoly fraction. Apart from their day-to-day struggles for the good graces of investors on the money markets and for shares of commodity markets, capitalists' desire for higher rates of return are periodically seen in takeover battles. Indeed, the interest groups of the mid-1980's and the alliances between them are in good part the provisional consequence of ongoing struggles for control of capital. In keeping with its traditional orientation toward monopoly capital (Young 1974; Goff and Reasons 1978), the Canadian state has "responded" to these developments with a policy best described as benign neglect. The most celebrated takeover battle of the 1970's—Power Corporation's bid for control of Argus Corp.—provoked the federal government to establish a Royal Commission on Corporate Concentration, whose major recommendation ironically gave a green light to further centralization of capital in the 1980's by emphasizing the need for a Canadian economy organized around large, internationally competitive enterprises (Canada 1978, 407; Clement 1983, 107–33).

The financial sector, however, has played a more active and direct role in these amalgamations and reorganizations. Canada's chartered banks have extended hundreds of millions in credit facilities to corporate predators and have given advice to reluctant takeover targets (Evans 1980, S4). The banks have also worked together in creating elaborate rescue schemes for corporations on the edge of bankruptcy, such as Dome Canada, the Canadian Commercial Bank, Chrysler Canada, and Massey-Ferguson. In the last case, the Canadian Imperial Bank of Commerce amicably took over operational control in 1980 from Argus Corp., increasing its representation on the Massey board to four directors, who oversaw Massey's international restructuring.[42]

Meanwhile, Canada's leading capitalists have been creating their own financial conglomerates: enormous fusions of capital that may become strategically central nodes in the network of finance capital, as federal deregulation of the carefully delineated "four pillars" (banking, trust companies, insurance, investment dealers) creates the possibility of diversified financial holding companies. The two most visible financial conglomerates to date are Paul Desmarais' Power Financial Corporation and Trilon Financial Corporation, though other ventures are also jostling for position.[43] Such companies carry the potential through their financial intermediation and investment management activities to wield both allocative and operational power, a combination unseen since the formative period of Canadian finance capital, when investment bankers often gained control of the firms whose shares they underwrote (Niosi 1978, 47–63). The latest creation of Peter and Edward Bronfman, Great Lakes Group Inc., suggests that this possibility is well on the way to being realized. Formed in 1984 with owners' equity four times larger than the leading investment dealers, this subsidiary of Brascan is slated to deal in corporate shares, sell advice on mergers, and manage large stock holdings in various companies. Brascan's partners in the venture—the Bank of Commerce, investment dealer Merrill Lynch Canada, and several leading trust companies—illustrate the keen interest that financial institutions are taking in the ongoing restructuring of Canadian finance capital.[44] Just as the founders of the CPR in the late 1800's showed considerable resourcefulness in using the most modern methods of mobilizing large pools of capital on an international basis (Anderson 1985), a century later Canada's business leaders continue to search for the most effective organizational forms for accumulating capital.

It is equally important to emphasize the highly *internationalized* character of this capital in the 1980's. Many of the corporations within the sphere of Canadian interest groups are major multinational investors, accumulating much of their capital in the United States, Europe, South Africa, Australia, and a host of less developed countries. Considering just the sixteen largest Canadian MNCs described by Niosi (1985a),[45] Peter and Edward Bronfman control Brascan, Noranda, and MacMillan-Bloedel; their cousins Charles and Edgar control Seagrams; the Reichmanns control Hiram Walker Resources; the Canadian Pacific group controls Cominco; Bell Canada Enterprises controls Northern Telecom; and the Canada Development Corporation controls Polysar. This international reach of Canadian interest groups has been matched by Canadian banks, whose subsidiaries operate in scores of industrialized and less developed countries and contribute large proportions of the banks' total profit (Kaufman 1985; Mittelstaedt 1985). The issues raised by this internationalization of capital will be taken up in the final chapter.

8

CONCLUSION: CANADIAN CAPITAL
IN THE ERA OF IMPERIALISM

Our examination of the changing structure of Canadian corporate power has questioned several claims within the thesis of Canadian dependency. Instead of an alliance between Canadian commercial interests and U.S.-based industrial interests, the network of corporations is increasingly focused around indigenous financial-industrial alliances. Instead of a cumulative drift to foreign control of Canada's industrial sector, the past decade and a half have been marked by a dramatic reclamation of capital from foreign interests and an expansion of Canadian investments abroad. These findings challenge the contention that Canada's capitalist class has followed an exceptional course of dependent development. Other purported symptoms of dependency, however, have not been considered in this study. These include the continental trade of Canadian raw materials for U.S. end-products, the relative dearth of indigenous research and development, and the pervasive influence of American culture.

How can the consolidation and international expansion of Canadian finance capital be reconciled with these aspects of Canadian society? The notion that Canada occupies a contradictory location in the world system, as a dependency of the United States and as an advanced capitalist power in its own right, seems appealing at first, and in recent years political economists have reached important insights about Canadian society by concretely analyzing capitalist social relations while retaining certain *dependentist* concepts[1]. Ultimately, however, the serious conceptual and empirical problems of the dependency theory that we reviewed in Chapter 2 recommend a different approach.

If dependency theory falls short of scientific adequacy, the moral premise of its Canadian variant—that the machinations of international capitalism conflict with the needs and aspirations of most Canadians—has been both valid and inspirational. The problem lies not in criticizing international capitalism but in theorizing the connection between the dynamics of international capitalism and the lives of ordinary Canadians as a monolithic relation between American metropole and Canadian satellite.

A comprehensive reformulation of the nature of this connection is well beyond the scope of this study. Still, the broad theory of monopoly capitalism and imperialism and the particular findings from our examination of the changing structure of Canadian monopoly capital invite overtures toward such renovation. Two considerations seem indispensible in this regard. First, what dependency theorists mistook to be a universal process of "underdevelopment" in the Third World needs to be theorized as a *conjunctural* phenomenon in the history of imperialism. In this light, much of what Canadian dependency theorists described in the 1960's and early 1970's as a cumulative regression toward hinterland status, permeating the economic, political and cultural spheres, can be viewed as part of a world-wide process of capitalist internationalization. Secondly, however, the *specificity* of Canadian capitalism—particularly its striking tendency toward what Lumsden (1970) and others called "Americanization"—needs to be accounted for and distinguished from the more general features that Canada has shared with most other imperialist powers. In this concluding chapter, I offer some notes toward a reinterpretation of the connection between American capitalism and Canadian society in the era of imperialism. This is done first with an examination of general trends toward capitalist internationalization operating at the level of the world system, then with a brief discussion of the specific regime of accumulation within which Canadian capitalism has developed.

CANADA AND THE INTERNATIONALIZATION OF CAPITAL

The era of modern imperialism can be separated into two phases. In the *early* phase financial capital exported to the periphery spurred the limited production of infrastructure and of raw materials for export to advanced capitalist economies; in the *late* phase, after the long crisis of 1914–45, transnational corporations brought a broad range of industrial production and a predominance of capitalist production relations to a growing number of less developed countries (LDCs) (Howe 1981; see also Brewer 1980; Szymanski 1981; Weeks 1986).

Throughout the early period, capitalist development of the periphery occurred at a slow pace, a result of a conjunction of conditions both internal to peripheral social formations and integral to the imperialist powers' own regimes of accumulation.[2] The period since the Second World

War and especially from about 1960 may be characterized as one of un-relenting capitalist internationalization. Having attained political inde-pendence, a number of LDCs have successfully encouraged industrial development through state capitalism, subsidies, tariffs, and interna-tional cartels, as industrial capital has flowed from advanced capitalist countries to take advantage of cheaper labour and expanding Third World markets (Cypher 1979a, 39; Szymanski 1981; Petras 1984b). Transnational production, now made feasible by a new wave of tech-nology—such as air cargo, containerized shipping, and commercial satellites (Cypher 1979b, 521)—and engendering in its turn a suprana-tional banking system, has brought a qualitatively new level of interna-tional interdependence, a world economy characterized by global corpo-rations and banks (Hawley 1979, 80–81).

This postwar movement toward internationalized production carries several important implications for our understanding of Canadian capi-talism and the Canadian bourgeoisie. If "underdevelopment" was not primarily a *cumulative* process organically rooted in the metropolis-satellite relation but was, rather, a *conjunctural* phenomenon in an era of monopolization and capitalist internationalization, it follows that re-lations between countries cannot be adequately understood by the theory of dependency. To appreciate the position of Canadian capital within an *interdependent* imperialist system, we must begin not from a bilateral relation (the metropolis-hinterland metaphor), nor even with a single agency, (the multinational corporation), but from the totality of interna-tional capitalism and its dynamic tendencies. In particular, four pro-cesses at work on a world scale provide a context in which we may un-derstand the evolving position of Canadian monopoly capital: (1) the tendency toward capitalist cross-penetration, (2) the changing forms of capitalist internationalization, (3) the shifting relations between im-perialist powers, and (4) the increasingly internationalized formation of the bourgeoisie.

The Tendency Toward Capitalist Cross-Penetration

Initiated by the massive American expansion into Canada and Eur-ope, the postwar internationalization of capital has engendered a multi-lateral cross-penetration: circuits of finance capital quite often cross po-litical boundaries, whether as merchant capital (trade), financial capital (loans, interest, dividends) or industrial capital (transnational produc-tion). From 1960 to 1972, the average annual growth rate of total for-eign direct investment among OECD countries was nearly 12 per cent

—one and a half times the same countries' average growth in GDP. In recent years, about three-quarters of world foreign direct investment has been concentrated in the advanced capitalist countries, compared with two-thirds in the 1960's (Portes and Walton 1981, 142; Marcussen and Torp 1982, 25).

The result of all this interpenetration has been a general tendency toward *increased foreign control* in the advanced economies. In Britain, U.S. subsidiaries' sales alone accounted for 22 per cent of the GDP in 1976, up from 13.5 per cent nine years earlier. In France, more than 50 per cent of sales in the petroleum, agricultural equipment, electronics and chemical industries are currently attributable to foreign-controlled firms. In West Germany, foreign investment predominates over German capital in oil refining, glass, cement and brick production, food, electrical machinery and iron and metals. As in Canada, foreign investment in Europe tends to concentrate in large companies, reflecting its character as internationalized monopoly capital. For example, "among West Germany's 30 largest corporations are nine foreign subsidiaries, including Exxon, GM, Ford, IBM, Texaco, and Mobil Oil" (Szymanski 1981, 502). By way of comparison, in a recent listing of the largest corporations in Canada ten foreign subsidiaries appear in the top 30, among them GM, Exxon, Ford, IBM, and Texaco (*Financial Post 500,* June 1985).

Although the overall levels of foreign (particularly American) investment in Canada are definitely higher than those in other imperialist countries, this example does put what has often been depicted as a unique Canadian situation into a proper international perspective. Moreover, since most capital has flowed between monopoly capitalist countries, it is doubtful that the *importation* of capital—abstracted from the totality of intercapitalist relations—can provide an unambiguous indication of any country's position in the world system. Indeed, the leading host countries for both MNCs and transnational banks read like a list of the imperialist powers, with the addition of a few newly industrializing countries (NICs):

> The U.K. is the leading country in the world for the location of foreign industrial *and* banking capital. Further, eight countries are among the first ten host countries *both* for TNBs *and* MNCs: the U.K., U.S.A., West Germany, France, Switzerland, Belgium, Holland, Australia. Among the next in order are Brazil, South Africa, Singapore, Canada, Mexico, Hong Kong, Italy, Japan, Lebanon, S. Korea, Indonesia: all either developed countries, or NICs (Andreff 1984, 62).

In this respect, we can begin to understand the problems in Levitt's (1970, 25) depiction of Canada's post-war importation of U.S. capital as a regression to dependence and underdevelopment at the hands of the American transnational corporation.

Forms of Capitalist Internationalization

Analysis of the dynamics of foreign direct investment does not tell the whole story of post-Second World War accumulation, however. Too often in studies of world capitalism, exclusive focus on transnationals results in an oversimplified analysis in which large, international, and apparently uncontrollable companies are identified as "the objective enemy of the people" (Barkin 1981, 159).

However, transnational corporations represent only one form of internationalized finance capital (Nabudere 1979, 50; Portes and Walton 1981, 140; Andreff 1984). Depending on the internal character of the host society, this form need not be the most pernicious. A central element in Canadian dependency analysis has been the contrast, first drawn by Levitt (1970), between the beneficial developmental effects of portfolio investment and the regressive ramifications of foreign direct investment. The latter is claimed to destroy indigenous entrepreneurship, to close off opportunities for accumulation by the national bourgeoisie, and to culminate in the "appropriation in perpetuity of the economy's surplus" (Watkins 1970, xii). To the contrary, several recent analyses of international capitalism stress the similar effects of *both* these forms of foreign investment in social formations where capitalist production relations are, or are becoming, predominant. Both direct and portfolio investment bring a local accumulation of capital and a return flow of wealth to the capital-exporting country. Although direct investment implies a form of multinational control and a flow of repatriated profit, a share of the profit must be kept in the country, if the investment is to be maintained. In the final analysis, the rate of reproduction of this capital "depends on conditions of accumulation in the receiving country relative to the returns on capital that might be obtained by redeployment" (Friedman 1978, 143). Warren has pursued the larger implications of this rather basic fact of modern capitalist accumulation:

> To the extent that political independence is real, private foreign investment must normally be regarded not as a cause of dependence but rather as a means of fortification and diversification of the economies of the host countries. It thereby reduces "dependence," in the long run (1980, 176).

Warren's point is especially well taken *vis-a-vis* the Canadian case, where we have witnessed the capacity not simply to *transpose* foreign investment into indigenous circuits of accumulation, but also to *reclaim* much of the foreign-controlled capital that contributed to Canada's economic growth during the postwar boom. The existence in Canada of an advanced capitalist economy with an extensive and integrated domestic market has allowed domestic industries to reap multiplier effects as foreign investments have crossed circuits of domestic capital in associated economic sectors (see Amin 1974; Palloix 1975, 76; Williams 1983, 4). The excellent postwar growth record of the Canadian steel industry, for example, is related in part to the expansion or emergence of such major steel consumers as the U.S.-controlled automobile makers and pipeline companies. Similarly, the full development of an oil and gas sector under predominantly American control supplied industrial and residential consumers with an abundant source of fuel at comparatively low prices. And, during the postwar boom, increases in the size of the work force, resulting from capital accumulation under both foreign and domestic control, augmented demand for various articles of consumption, many produced by Canadian capitalists (see Warren 1980, 142).

The fact that large foreign-controlled firms predominated in certain of these industries no doubt deterred accumulation by smaller indigenous companies, as Levitt (1970) argued. But this "closing off" of investment opportunities in some industries should not be mistaken for a general stifling of indigenous industrial accumulation. If it were stifled, how might one explain the growth of industries under predominantly Canadian control, such as steel, forest products, and food and beverages?

More recently, as we have seen in this study, the advanced form of Canadian capitalism has reduced the permanency of foreign direct investment in the manufacturing, mining, oil and gas, and pipeline sectors. Because they possess the independent financial power that accrues to an advanced economy, capitalists in Canada (as well as crown corporations) have been able to repatriate foreign-controlled companies through share purchases, just as they have been able to expand their investments abroad.

It is instructive in this respect to compare the Canadian experience with that of LDCs, where the bulk of foreign investments has shifted in recent years from equity participation (portfolio and direct investment) to the use of loans and credits (Marcussen and Torp 1982, 26–27). As the global economic crisis has deepened, international banking capital has shifted its emphasis from supplying multinational corporations with working capital to providing enormous amounts of long term credit to countries strickened with balance of payments deficits (Hawley 1979, 86; Andreff 1984). Unlike portfolio and direct investment, such internationalized loan capital does not necessarily entail local investment, at least not at a rate adequate for repayment of the principle. Rather, as the historical example of British imperialism in Egypt shows (Luxemburg 1951, 429–39), "the debt-service implied by massive loans can greatly outweigh the local accumulation of capital" (Friedman 1978, 142). This is especially true when growth is trade-related and when protectionism is on the rise in the advanced capitalist countries, as is presently the case (Hawley 1979, 88).

In a growing number of countries, the desperate need for lenders has led to the re-establishment of an extreme form of neocolonialism. Institutions such as the IMF require debtor governments to submit their economic policies to surveillance by international finance capital (Kolko 1977, 14–15; Phillips 1980, 1983; Szymanski 1981, 250–52). The proud participation of Canadian bankers with other monopoly capitalist powers in these relations of imperialist domination is well known. But in sorting out the *specificity* of Canadian capitalism we should be no less cognizant of the crucial difference between the generally stimulative and increasingly cosmopolitan form of foreign investment that predominates in Canada and the highly centralized economic relation that has been imposed upon many LDCs.

Inter-imperialist Relations in the Post-Second World Era

To appreciate this difference, it is necessary to examine the character of relations not simply between centre and periphery but *among imperialist powers themselves*. In particular, U.S.-Canada ties need to be viewed against the backdrop of American hegemony, which provided essential direction in reconstituting world capitalism in the wake of the Second World War. In this period, inter-imperialist relations were marked not by the sorts of rivalry which had spawned both world wars, but by the hegemony of one power acting to enhance and preserve the unity of the entire capitalist system in the face of internal and external threats (Camilleri 1981, 141; see also Arrighi 1978, 96–103; Cardoso and Faletto 1979, 182; Castells 1980, 104–9; Szymanski 1981, 492).

After the Second World War, the potential for socialist revolutions in Western Europe and in South East Asia gave the financially and technologically advanced United States a compelling interest in reconstructing European capitalism and converting Japan from a defeated nation to a junior partner in containing communism in the East (Nabudere 1977, 156–58). These objectives were achieved under the formal aegis of the Bretton Woods Agreement and Marshall Plan (Arrighi 1978, 96) with the willing consent of the old prewar bourgeoisies of Europe and Japan, who were for the most part restored to their positions as ruling classes (Dann 1979, 70).

America's role as a state above states had appeal not merely because of its contribution to the viability of world capitalism as a whole. With the reconstruction of Europe, U.S. capitalists secured an increasing demand for American goods, without which the U.S. economy probably would have stagnated (Marcussen and Torp 1982, 18). At the same time, through its Open Door strategy, the U.S. effectively dismembered many of the colonial relations that had benefited its rivals, replacing them by a system of open trade and investment more congenial to American interests. The dominant international position of the U.S. economy, accounting for over 60 per cent of total OECD output in the early 1950's thus

> placed the other advanced capitalist countries in a position of significant dependence on the USA (though this was realised only slowly by the strongest such country, Britain). The USA was able to use this power (together with the political influence deriving from its wartime role), to secure a general commitment to the principal of openness and freedom in trading relations among advanced capitalist countries (Currie 1983, 83).

The new regime of imperialism that grew up under the hegemony of the United States would witness the eclipse of particular "spheres of influence," as formal colonial ties of classical imperialism were replaced by informal multilateral relations with "client states" (Nabudere 1977, 145–46).

In this period of American hegemony, most world capital exports emanated from the booming U.S. economy, to be placed internationally on the basis of longterm comparative profit prospects. During the Korean War years, for example, the U.S. feared a shortage of strategic raw materials, and Canada received half of all U.S. foreign direct investment (Levitt 1970, 163). We have seen the effects of this in a great expansion of U.S. control of large-scale Canadian industry between 1946. and 1956. Despite the exhortations and incentives of the U.S. government, American capital remained skeptical of the economic and political viability of western Europe and reluctant to expand across the Atlantic (Tugendhat 1973, 50). Confirmation of Europe's recovery as a reliable and lucrative locus for U.S. capital came with the creation of the Common Market in 1957. Thereafter, Europe attracted an enormous flow of U.S. direct investment (Nabudere 1977, 156; Castells 1980, 105–6).

The legacy of American world hegemony in the 1950's and 1960's was, in the 1970's, an ironic constellation of concern in other imperialist countries about the "American Challenge," coupled with an eroding basis for that concern. The period of unrivalled American dominance was drawing to a close. Canadian expressions of consternation about Americanization need to be reviewed against the broader pattern of inter-imperialist relations. In Europe, U.S. direct investments, concentrated in basic industries, brought the same sorts of dominance relations in the areas of technology and marketing as have been observed in postwar Canada (Poulantzas 1974, 162; Dann 1979, 72; Marcussen and Torp 1982, 21). The tremendous amount of U.S. direct investment was perceived by some fractions of European national capital as a definite threat. However, "in the longer perspective this view was probably an exaggeration, and the importance today of U.S. investments is partly that of an external pressure contributing to a fast concentration and centralization process among the national capital groups in Western Europe" (Marcussen and Torp 1982, 22). This insight was not lost on Canada's Royal Commission on Corporate Concentration. The commission concluded that "the growth of domestic firms, even at the cost of an increase in concentration, will offset, in part, both the proportion of the economy under foreign control and some of the undesirable consequences of foreign investment" (Canada 1978, 408). The enormous centralization of Canadian finance capital and the declining levels of U.S. direct investment in the past decade seem to confirm this prediction.

Moreover, the very relations of international dominance that grew up under the wing of American hegemony ultimately served to erode the U.S. position in world capitalism. They fostered revitalized national economies capable of competing directly with American capital (Camilleri 1981, 141). The high wage rates and strong dollar that characterized the American imperial state presented opportunities to the high-skill but low-wage economies of Western Europe and Japan, whose postwar expansion, like Canada's, was built on a massive outflow of exports (Barnet 1980, 240). These same countries welcomed (or at least tolerated) American direct investment as a means of expanding and strengthening domestic capitalist production (Warren 1975, 139; see also Frank 1979, 121; Castells 1980, 105–6). Because the European and Japanese economies had relatively little capital tied up in ageing and obsolete equipment they were able to realize the "merits of borrowing" while the financially and technologically stronger U.S. paid the "penalty of taking the lead.'' U.S. companies often found it more costly to introduce technology since they had to take into consideration the book value of existing fixed capital (Cypher 1979b, 521). Moreover, the U.S. (as the leading economy) bore much of the costs of *developing* new technology, which could then be incorporated into the productive structures of competing economies, allowing them to grow more rapidly (Szymanski 1981, 517; see also Warren 1980, 180; Niosi 1983, 132).

The ironic effects of international accumulation under American imperialism became visible in the 1970's in two ways. First, parts of the formal structure of *Pax Americana*—such as the dollar standard—were jettisoned (Arrighi 1978, 102–3) as the competitive position of American capital visibly deteriorated. The decline of the United States from unrivalled dominance is evident across a range of indicators: from per capita wealth (Szymanski 1981, 495) and the shrinking U.S. share of the world market in such industrial goods as steel and machine tools (Barnet 1980, 273–75) to the decreasing number of the world's largest firms based in the U.S. (Franko 1978; Szymanski 1981, 496; Droucopoulas 1981), and the declining U.S. share in world capital exports (Nabudere 1977, 203; Szymanski 1981, 504). The recent resurgence of indigenous control in the Canadian economy is partly a measure of this decline.

Secondly, as a regime of multilateral capitalist internationalization emerged, several of the economic problems interpreted by dependency theory as consequences of foreign direct investment actually came to characterize the American metropole. Indeed, these problems spread to other advanced economies as the crisis of the 1970's and 1980's deepened. Massive capital exports from the U.S. led to a relative *stagnation* of internal production, as the foreign operations of U.S.-based MNCs effectively competed with domestic American establishments (Baran and Sweezy 1966, 23; Friedman 1978, 134; 138–39; Castells 1980, 109; Portes and Walton 1981, 146). Developments such as deindustrialization in the American northeast have, ironically, been linked by Portes and Walton (1981, 154–161) to U.S. direct investment *abroad* (see also Barnet 1980, 275; Seidman and O'Keefe 1980; Bluestone and Harrison 1982). Similarly, on the matter of foreign trade, Barnet and Muller have described the ''LatinAmericanization of the United States,'' as the American economy ''becomes increasingly dependent on the export of agricultural products and timber to maintain its balance of payments and increasingly dependent on imports of finished goods to maintain its standard of living'' (1974, 217).

The story, of course, does not end with an American ''regression to dependence,'' recalling Levitt's description of postwar Canada. With a devalued dollar, rising costs of production in Europe, and an ineffectual trade union movement at home, U.S. exports became somewhat more competitive in the late 1970's, and U.S. as well as foreign capital began returning to the American economy (Barnet 1980, 275; Portes and Walton 1981, 184; Halliday 1983, 183). Canadian repatriations of U.S.-controlled corporations and takeovers of American-based companies in the 1970's and 1980's form part of this broader pattern. For instance, between 1973 and 1978, 623 U.S. corporations were taken over by European, Canadian, and Japanese firms (Andreff 1984, 60). As a consequence of investment flow to the U.S., the pattern of unilateral American investments in Canada, Western Europe and Japan is in the process of being superseded by a tendency toward cross-penetration of capital. This tendency is also visible in the net change in control of large-scale Canadian industry from the 1940's to the 1970's, favouring investors in Western Europe and South Africa, and in the substantial investments Canadian capitalists have made in these same countries.

The International Formation of the Bourgeoisie

Capitalist internationalization has also had an impact on the formation of the bourgeoisie. With growth of an international capital market and cross-penetration of investments, and with development of supra-capitalist institutions such as the World Bank, the IMF, and the Trilateral Commission, the "contours of an international capitalist class are emerging" (Portes and Walton 1981, 174; Frieden 1977; Goldfrank 1977; Sklar 1980). This class is a loose grouping of internationalized finance capital conscious of the manner in which transnational capitalist production divides labour against itself while enabling the freest flow of capital (Hymer 1972, 99–103; DeCormis 1983; Andreff 1984).

This nascent class formation is evident in the international network of corporate interlocks studied by Fennema (1982). He examined interlocking directorates in 1970 and 1976 among 176 large corporations from twelve countries—including Canada—and found one large connected network of European and North American companies and a smaller network of Japanese corporations. Strongly connected capitalist interest groups were discernable at the *national* level. But within the *international* network weak ties predominated, suggesting that such interlocks serve primarily as "a communication network rather than a network of domination and control" (1982, 201). The few multiple-officer interlocks that integrated certain firms into international structures of intercorporate control in 1970 were in most cases broken by 1976. The one strong linkage between Canadian and American financial groups disappeared completely by 1976, as Inco Limited moved out of the realm of the Morgan empire (ibid., 145, 192, 194, 197). Fennema found that between 1970 and 1976, the density of international interlocks increased, indicating a growing need for international consultation as the world economic crisis set in (ibid, 201). This trend, together with the increasing centrality of banks in the network, led him to conclude that "the international network of interlocking directorates can be regarded as an indication of the internationalization of finance capital" (ibid., 199).

The existence of an international network of the largest companies in Europe and North America puts into a broader perspective Clement's notions of a Canadian economic elite that is "distorted" by the presence of foreign-affiliated compradors (1975, 117), and a continental elite that expresses the symbiotic but ultimately dependent ties of Canadian capitalists to the American metropole (1977, 179–80). Canada's bourgeois formation certainly appears distorted in comparison with an autarkic ideal type in which "the economic elite would be contained within a national economy and controlled by citizens and residents of that nation" (Clement 1975, 123). But relative to other capitalist classes experiencing internationalization, the comprador elements within the bourgeoisie in Canada are not particularly exceptional[3], especially since they tend to maintain weak ties with Canadian firms and to occupy peripheral positions in the structure of Canadian corporate power. By the same token, while there is no doubt that a "continental elite" of leading Canadian and American capitalists exists, it can perhaps be most fruitfully viewed as a segment of a larger, international network of finance capital that has developed with capitalist cross-penetration in the post-Second World War era.

The Legacy of Capitalist Internationalization

Lastly, the internationalized capitalism that has matured in the period since the Second World War has brought important changes to the relationship between capital accumulation and national states. In the first place, cross-penetration of capital has made the advanced economies more dependent upon one another (Scott 1979, 177); so much so that Radice (1984) has questioned the extent to which "national" economies may be said to exist. MacEwan (1984) has shown that among the seven major capitalist countries there has been a dramatic increase in the extent to which business cycles are synchronized. Prior to 1971, cycles were synchronized within western Europe and within North America, but much less so across the continents. In the 1970s, however, the

American economy became more closely synchronized with the economies of Japan and the European nations (MacEwan 1984, 68). MacEwan suggests that synchronized patterns of accumulation result in large part from the decisions of capitalists, consumers, and governments in a financially integrated world economy:

> As compared with the 1960's, the 1970's saw a qualitative change of interdependence through international financial integration. More and more, it seems businesses (and consumers) in different countries are faced with parallel conditions in capital markets, and one would expect them to respond in similar manners. Second, partly as an outgrowth of financial integration and more generally because the different countries have been facing similar sets of economic difficulties, it appears that there has been a greater homogeneity of governments' policies than in earlier years. A homogeniety of policy among countries would, of course, tend to effect a greater synchronization of output movements (ibid., 76).

The internationalization of capital thus carries important implications for the actions of both corporations and governments. As Barkin suggests, "increasingly the dynamics of the world capitalist economy cannot be understood with reference to a single nation or group of nations. Productive decisions are now made on a global scale" (1981, 156). Political decision making, however, continues to be the perogative of territorially bounded states. With the development of internationalized monopoly capital, then, a growing disjuncture appears between the big bourgeoisie's accumulation base and the state's national boundaries, making it hazardous at best to assign "nationalities" to capitalist interest groups. According to Friedman, "it is just as serious an error to reduce international capital to its place of origin as to assume that all capital belongs to the place where it is employed" (1978, 141). As Rowthorn's discussion of postwar British capital illustrates, there is no simple relation between the strength of a "national fraction" of monopoly capital and the vitality of a national economy or the "independence" of a national state. Indeed, in Rowthorn's view, it was the very international *strength* of British big capital in the post-Second World War era that led to a *weakening* of the domestic economy and state: "as the British economy became more integrated into a global capitalism over which the British state had no control, it became increasingly vulnerable internationally and the potential benefits to big capital of a straightforwardly aggressive nationalist development have dwindled accordingly" (1975, 174–75; see also Radice 1984).

Rowthorn's analysis of the "denationalization" of British monopoly capital and its contribution to that country's industrial decline, together with the example of diminishing American hegemony and international competitiveness, provides an important lesson in the dynamics of capitalism and nation-states in the present era. Simply put:

> the most powerful sectors of capital are no longer committed to the stability or rationalization of national societies *qua* national markets. The TNC benefits from *particular* national economic conditions—favorable labor conditions in one instance, favorable tax laws in another—rather than from the health of a domestic economy as a whole. TNCs can, in effect, skim the cream of national economies and then abandon them—and their currencies—when they falter (Hawley and Noble 1982, 116).

On these grounds, however, recalling the strength of Canada's "own" multinationals, it is misleading to attribute the problems that beset ordinary Canadians to the dominance of "foreign" capital. The national control of capital is quite secondary to the capitalist logic according to which finance capital is allocated across national borders. The central position of Canadian financial institutions in the network of Canadian corporate power and their numerous international ties and foreign subsidiaries enable them to allocate capital efficiently on the basis of just such a logic.

Notes on Canada's Regime of Accumulation

Notwithstanding the general tendencies associated with capitalist internationalization, there is a pressing need to grasp the specificity of Canadian capitalism. The great contribution of the Canadian dependency school has been to direct critical attention to that specificity and, in the process, to create the space for a resurgence of radical scholarship that has had some success opposing the received ideology of liberal continentalism. But although the dependency approach has placed the issue of specificity on the agenda of Canadian scholarship, the problematic of dependency has tended to hamper understanding in at least two ways. There has been a certain "insularity of focus" on imputed political and economic effects of Canada's relationship with the United States (Panitch 1981, 28). This has obscured the fact that many "symptoms" of Canadian dependency are, as we have seen, consequences of the internationalization of capital in the post-Second World War period, evident in all or most advanced capitalist societies. Related to this first problem has been a tendency to impose qualitative distinctions between Canadian capitalism and other advanced capitalist economies, where differences are perhaps better viewed as matters of degree.

A concept that holds promise as a means of capturing the specificity of Canadian capitalism, while avoiding the problems outlined above, is that of the *regime of accumulation*. This refers to the manner in which labour power and means of production have been concretely configured into a functioning social economy (see Aglietta 1979; Therborn 1983, 42; Lipietz 1982, 1984). The strong presence in Canada of U.S. monopoly capital, especially since the Second World War, furnishes a good initial example of how a feature of Canadian capitalism previously explained as a symptom of dependency can be fruitfully analyzed by considering Canada's specific regime of capitalist accumulation.

The issue of U.S. direct investment in Canada ultimately turns on the way in which capital became monopolized and internationalized in the early phase of modern imperialism. It is crucial to note in this connection that the difference between Canada and Europe is essentially one of the timing of American capital exports to particular countries. As Schmidt (1981, 92) points out, Canada simply presents the first case of a more general phenomenon in the internationalization of productive capital. Still, in Canada the extent of U.S. control in sectors such as automobiles, petroleum, and electrical equipment has been especially great.

The question is: What class-structured conditions made these investments more attractive to American capitalists than possible investments elsewhere, while limiting the extent to which Canadian capitalists could directly compete in the same industries? These conditions can perhaps be best seen as a conjuncture of inter-related features, several of which have been recognized by Canadian dependency writers. In the early decades of the twentieth century, for instance, surplus American capital was attracted because of Canada's proximity (in light of the technical limits on intercontinental enterprise [see Clement 1977, 6]) and because of the protected and expanding market that Canada provided as a high-growth capitalist economy, (both in its own right and as a member of the British Commonwealth [see Drache 1970; Clement 1977; Williams 1983]). By the same token, for a number of reasons which Panitch (1981) has incisively analyzed, Canada's working class developed in the late nineteenth century as a relatively high-wage proletariat. This placed constraints on the extent to which Canadian capitalists could compete with the large and technologically advanced U.S. firms that concentrated their Canadian investments in the growth industries of the second industrial revolution (McNally 1981, 55; see also Clement 1977, 59; Hutcheson 1978, 95).[4]

In conjunction with this first constraint on indigenous capitalists was the tying up of enormous amounts of finance capital in the construction and operation of a domestic transportation system. Here again, the differences between Canada and other capitalist countries should not be overdrawn. In general, the development of railways has been a fundamental aspect of capitalist industrialization (Singelmann 1978, 17), a fact well documented in the Canadian case by Pentland (1981, 145–48; see also Palmer 1983, 60–62). The importance of the transportation industry to modern regimes of accumulation has been explained by Richard Walker (1978, 31):

> A general aim of capital is to lower its time of circulation, i.e., the speed of self-expansion of capital. Geographic movement of capital is one aspect of the circulation problem as a whole. The most specifically *geographic* problem for capital is in overcoming the barriers which (absolute) space presents, and the primary way capital overcomes this barrier is by what Marx called ''the annihilation of space by time''—i.e., speeding up physical movement, especially through the development of transportation and communication systems.

In Canada, the vast expanse of space to be annihilated, relative to the size of the home market, necessarily required a proportionately large outlay of capital to the transportation sector, leaving little finance capital for the rising industries in which American capital came to predominate. Between 1901 and 1915—a period of rapid expansion of manufacturing—total rail investment accounted for 27 per cent of gross capital formation in Canada but only for 7 or 8 per cent of total gross investment in the U.S. (Williams 1983, 32, 177). By 1923, 60 per cent of the total assets of the one hundred largest non-financial corporations—and nearly 40 per cent of all industrial and merchant capital in Canada—was claimed by just two indigenous enterprises: the CPR and CNR (Canada 1937, 21–22, 330). In the meantime, subsidiaries of U.S. corporations had become well entrenched in several expansive branches of Canadian manufacturing (Hutcheson 1978; Williams 1983, 28–29).[5]

In short, we find in Canada a regime of monopoly capitalism emerging at the turn of the century, based on the dual premises of (1) international concentration and centralization (U.S. direct investment), and (2) domestic monopolization (formation of indigenous financial groups, particularly the CPR-Bank of Montreal interests). Both national fractions expanded their investments in the interwar period, as Canadian capitalists made fortunes in the hydro-electric and paper industries and American capitalists developed much of the mining sector (Niosi 1981,

27–28). During the Second World War, the strong commitment of the Canadian state to the Allied effort placed a burden of price controls and heavier taxation on Canadian capitalists. This may have undermined the ability of Canadian business in the immediate postwar period to expand without using the enormous reserves of capital under American control (Dow 1984, 61). More broadly, the period of American economic and political hegemony in the capitalist world culminated in the late 1950's in an enlarged presence of U.S.-controlled monopoly capital in Canada and an intermingling of U.S. and Canadian financial groups (Park and Park 1973, 15).

Although these have been interpreted by Levitt and others as symptoms of a cumulative regression to dependence, we have found otherwise in this study. A more meaningful issue to explore in light of post-Second World War developments in the imperialist system is the rate at which the accumulation base of the Canadian bourgeoisie has been internationalizing, compared with the rate at which other imperialist class fractions have been expanding their circuits of accumulation within Canada. As Table 8.1 shows, between 1950 and 1965—the era of unrivalled American hegemony—U.S. direct investment in Canada grew faster than Canadian direct investment in the United States.[6] But by the mid-1970's, Canadian capitalists were augmenting their U.S. investments at a rate far greater than that of U.S. direct investment in Canada. Moreover, through the late 1960's and the 1970's, there was a strong tendency for Canadian capital to internationalize beyond the economies of the United States and the British Commonwealth.

These trends are consistent with Niosi's (1985b, 63) claim that in the last fifteen years, federal economic policies and Canadian business strategies have converged on a "continental nationalism" that has strengthened indigenous firms in their home market and pushed them toward international expansion, particularly into the United States. These developments are a measure both of the competitiveness of Canadian capital (Niosi 1983) and of the political stability and high rates of return that have been attracting international capital from various sources to the United States (Halliday 1983, 183).[7] The post-Second World War pattern of accumulation makes it clear that a focus on Canadian dependency (to paraphrase Warren 1980, 114–15) ascribes increasing significance to a phenomenon that has been declining both relative to other advanced capitalist economies (as monopoly capital has further internationalized) and absolutely (as the proportion of Canadian industrial capital under U.S. control has recently dropped while capital exports from Canada have continued to expand). The resilience and recent consolidation of Canadian finance capital is particularly underscored by our

Table 8.1 Average Annual Rates of Growth of Foreign Direct Investment in Canada and Canadian Direct Investment Abroad, 1946–1984

Year	Foreign Direct Investment in Canada — Controlling Country				Canadian Direct Investment Abroad — Host Country				
	United States	United Kingdom	Other	Total	United States	United Kingdom	Other Commonwealth Countries	Other	Total
1946–1949	8.6	5.7	0.8	8.0	14.6	2.3	2.5	-12.7	7.2
1950–1953	17.1	10.7	48.4	16.9	13.8	19.1	18.8	18.2	14.9
1954–1957	15.7	22.5	41.8	17.2	7.4	16.3	19.2	19.4	10.1
1958–1961	8.3	9.7	17.5	8.9	5.1	16.9	4.8	10.3	6.6
1962–1965	6.1	6.6	12.6	6.6	4.2	16.8	15.4	15.5	8.1
1966–1969	10.5	4.8	16.0	10.2	11.5	5.9	15.0	21.2	12.6
1970–1973	7.7	7.5	18.0	8.6	7.9	8.5	15.0	27.9	12.5
1974–1977	11.0	7.9	11.4	10.7	19.8	19.2	2.8	23.1	18.0
1978–1981	9.7	10.1	15.7	10.4	52.7	18.5		30.6	35.5
1982–1984	7.6	8.7	12.3	8.3	11.9	-8.2		6.7	9.1

Sources: Calculated from Dominion Bureau of Statistics, *The Canadian Balance of International Payments 1961 and 1962* (Ottawa, 1964), p. 127; Statistics Canada, *Canada's International Investment Position* (Ottawa, various years).

findings on corporate interlocking: the network of large Canadian companies is increasingly integrated around indigenous financial-industrial interests, and it is further differentiated into capitalist groupings whose investments span various economic sectors and national boundaries.

All this is not to deny that the Canadian economy of the 1980's continues to be weak in domestic research and development and oriented to raw-material production. Nor is it to minimize the national question of cultural self-determination, particularly in English Canada. But rather than invoking the spectre of dependency to explain each departure from the mythical ideal of balanced, self-sufficient capitalist development, critical scholars would do well to consider the socially structured profit prospects that have steered capital flows in specific directions, as capitalists in Canada have struggled to realize higher than average profits, whether in the home market or in the world market. Such an analysis will require considerable theoretical and empirical work. As with the issue of U.S. direct investment in Canada, it may be useful to present some very schematic notes toward a more general reconceptualization of Canada's regime of accumulation.

On the issue of staple production in the Canadian economy, the question is not why industrialization was "truncated," "arrested," or "aborted" (see Ehrensaft and Armstrong 1981; Williams 1983; Laxer 1985). Rather, we should ask why industrial capital has accumulated at a faster rate in raw materials production than in manufacturing. The enormous investment of capital in building a transportation system provides one clue to this puzzle. Because of its high fixed-capital composition, the transport industry typically has "weak powers of surplus value production within its confines. This weakness has therefore to be offset by compensating advances in capacity for surplus value production in the sectors served by the transport industry if aggregate rates of profit are to be maintained" (Harvey 1982, 379). For several reasons, the resource sector has provided such a compensation to the Canadian capitalist class. Factors include the large element of economic rent that has accrued directly to capital in the resource sector, partly because of the richness of Canada's resource base and partly because of state policies which have generously distributed concessions to resource entrepreneurs (see, for example, Nelles 1974; Govett 1975; Ehrensaft and Armstrong 1981, 102; Niosi 1981, 27; Drache 1984, 52). In addition to this incentive of surplus profit in the form of unappropriated rent, the rising world demand for raw materials throughout the twentieth century has spurred capital acccumulation in the Canadian resource sector by supporting high rates of turnover: an integral component of profitability (Marx 1967, II, p.314; Mandel 1968, 186–88; Harvey 1982). Both the productive structure of the domestic economy and the evolving state of the world market have presented compelling motives for the kind of specialized capitalist industrialization that has occurred in Canada. As Drache (1984) has shown, this specialization in resource extraction has had profound implications for the formation of the Canadian working class and the texture of class struggle in Canada.

Canada, of course, has not been alone among the advanced economies in specializing in particular forms of capitalist activity. James Petras, in his attempt to replace the bipolar metropolis-hinterland schema with a view of the world system as a diverse network of changing social relations, points out that such specializations occur in various forms: "in the case of the metropolis, these principally take the form of advanced technological centers (U.S.), heavy industrial centers (Germany, Japan, Italy), financial centers (Switzerland, England), and agricultural or resource surplus centers (U.S., Canada, Australia, France)" (1984a, 30).

Nor has the rich resource base been the only source of surplus profits through which Canadian capitalists have sought a competitive edge. As in other capitalist economies, the introduction of technology into the production process has been a common lever for increasing labour productivity and thus bolstering profits. In discussing technology, Canadian dependency analysts have been quick to compare Canada's meagre outlay on research and development with that of the United States. But here again a more sensitive analysis of the capialist accumulation process is needed. For one thing, resource firms in general direct a relatively small percentage of revenue to research and development, hence, much of the gap between American and Canadian outlays reflects differences in industrial composition. Although research and development in Canada lag behind American rates in certain manufacturing industries where branch plants dominate (for example, in automobiles and computers), the Canadian rates are comparable in other sectors (such as aerospace, steel). In telecommunications, relative Canadian outlays exceed those of U.S. industry.[8]

Moreover, as the example of rising Japanese robotics and declining American manufacturing shows, technology developed under capitalism in one country (in this case the U.S.) does not necessarily become incorporated into its productive structure, nor is it beyond the means of capitalists to incorporate "foreign" technologies into the productive process they control domestically (Cypher 1979a; Szymanski 1981). According to Niosi (1985a) this is precisely what Canadian capitalists have done in their domestic operations and in their rapidly growing foreign investments. As "technological imitators" major Canadian corporations have acquired foreign technology in a number of ways. They have purchased patents, technical services, and equipment in foreign countries; they have taken over innovative foreign-based producers; they have used technology "inherited" from former foreign-based parent firms (as in the cases of Alcan and Inco); and they have established research centres in foreign countries (1985a, 170–72). Niosi holds that

> Canada's geographical, cultural and commercial closeness to the United States and Britain allows Canadian companies to absorb technology a short time after it is introduced in these highly advanced industrialized countries. It is hard to imagine an Argentinian or Australian company establishing its research laboratories in Boston, New York or Detroit. But for a company based in Montreal or Toronto—only a short flight away—such a move is entirely appropriate. A Montreal- or Toronto-based company is also in a good position to purchase and control dynamic, innovative American subsidiaries. In fact it can supervise an American subsidiary more easily than a subsidiary in Vancouver or Halifax. And even Britain is not that far away; for a Montreal-based firm, London and Edmonton are the same distance from head office (ibid., 166).

The regime of accumulation in Canada in this regard is the product of Canadian business strategies to take competitive advantage of Canada's cultural, commercial and spatial location within the international structure of capital. It is not the result of any congenital deficiency in entrepreneurship.

More generally, the technological innovations that have contributed to a restructuring of the labour process toward enhanced profitability must be placed in the context of broader changes in the regime of accumulation, whether in Canada or in the other advanced capitalist societies. The French regulationist school has reached important insights about these changes, with its Gramscian-inspired analysis of *Fordism*, a specific system of advanced capitalist production and consumption (see Aglietta 1979; Lipietz 1982, 1984). On the production side, Fordism comprises a regime of intensive accumulation: everincreasing productivity levels are achieved through continual upheaval of the labour process, so that workers' knowledge is incorporated into automated technological forms, such as the assembly line pioneered by Henry Ford. In the years following the Second World War, the consumption side of Fordism also became a common feature of advanced capitalism, as practices developed to adjust mass demand to increases in productivity, thus promoting a long wave of rapid accumulation.

Through the institutions of collective bargaining and the welfare state, wages were linked to productivity. At the same time, the commoditization of mass-consumption goods further integrated the lifestyle of wage-earners into circuits of capitalist accumulation (Houle 1983, 132–33; Lipietz 1984, 98).

Originating in the United States, Fordism has paralleled the internationalization of productive capital in forming a basic aspect of the regime of accumulation in most imperialist countries and in a number of newly industrializing countries such as Mexico and Brazil (ibid., 1984, 101–2). Lipietz's description of its uneven spread among capitalist powers between 1918 and 1945 shows the important role that class struggle has played in influencing the fate of specific nation-states in the international capitalist system:

> This revolution did not take place overnight. Under the leading role of the United States new norms of production, consumption and wage-regulation were invented or adopted with more or less success. The uneven spread of intensive accumulation...worked wonders in Northern Europe, Japan, Australia, Canada and New Zealand. But because of the strong resistance of its working-class and the weight of financial capital that was too heavily internationalized to be interested in this kind of internal revolution, Britain missed the Fordist train and therefore began to be excluded from the centre. Argentina, one of the richest and most developed countries in 1945, missed it too because of the resistance of its workers and the decision by its ruling-class to continue to rely on export-oriented agriculture (ibid., 98).

There is no doubt that the spread of Fordism in Canada was promoted by close trade relations with the U.S. and especially by the branch-plant structure of several lines of production. But regardless of whether the controlling capitalist interest was American or Canadian, this particular form of capitalist accumulation proved remarkably profitable, especially during the postwar boom.

The result is a national economy whose predominant norms of production and consumption seem highly derivative from the American example. Although much the same may be said of Northern Europe and Japan, where in many cases the adoption of Fordist practices was a prerequisite to postwar American aid (ibid., 107), in English Canada the American influence extends very deeply into the area of cultural reproduction.

Since their consolidation in the 1920's as cultural industries that replaced community- and class-based activities with privatized forms of leisure (Palmer 1983, 191–95), the mass media in Canada have functioned above all as capitalist enterprises, constrained by the same market forces which affect other industries, and thus "dependent on ever increasing audience shares and advertising revenue" (Belkaoui 1982, 455). Despite the efforts of the Canadian state to encourage "Canadian content" in cultural production, the general requirements for successful accumulation in this industry, combined with the close proximity of the U.S. and the common linguistic heritage, have recommended that media corporations maximize profits by importing ready-made American productions or more recently mounting nominally "Canadian" productions for the large American market. The consequent tendency has been for many Canadians to develop a preference for American mass culture, further blurring the national border between the countries (ibid., 458–60; see also Crean 1976; Smythe 1981, 98; Audley 1983).

In this case as well as in their adoption of the Fordist system of accumulation, Canadian capitalists have acted in a rational, forward-looking manner, within the parameters of their own social existence. Ultimately, the drift toward "Americanization"—whether in industrial production or cultural reproduction—finds its source not in the conflict of metropolis versus hinterland, but in the primacy that the capitalist system assigns to exchange-value over use-value:

> The capitalist's aim is to accumulate capital, to capitalise surplus value. The very nature of the circulation of money implies this aim. Industrial capital pursues this aim of accumulation even more, much more insatiably than usurer's capital or merchant capital. It produces for a free and anonymous market, *dominated by the laws of competition* (Mandel 1968, 133; emphasis in the original).

The social product's use-value is always of secondary importance to capital. In pursuing maximal exchange-value, Canada's capitalists have taken full advantage of the international circuits of capital most available to them. By implication, they have often been active promoters of Americanization, incorporating use-values into the Canadian social formation that seem barely distinguishable from the "American way."

Herein lies one source of the continuing appeal of dependency analysis in Canada. The very success of Canadian capitalists *as capitalists* in expanding the quantity of exchange-value at their disposal has brought a system of production and consumption many of whose qualities "derive" from a larger, proximate imperialist power. In the dependency formulation, the abject failure of Canadian *capitalism* to satisfy the needs and aspirations of ordinary Canadians has been seen as the failure of Canada's *bourgeoisie*: a weak colonialist anachronism. Even in the 1980's, it is held that in Canada "nothing approaching a national bourgeoisie with its own political, ideological and economic unity vis-a-vis other national capitals has emerged" (Panitch 1985, 10). On the issue of economic unity, our examination of the structure of corporate interlocking suggests otherwise. Had we looked beyond the corporate boardrooms to the political ideologies expressed by Canada's leading capitalists (Ornstein 1985), or by the copious employers' associations and policy-planning organizations that "provide effective centres for the development of consciousness and political activity within the capitalist class" (Niosi 1985b, 59), an even stronger case could have been made for the consolidation of the Canadian bourgeoisie as a ruling class.

There is, however, a deeper problem in the dependency formulation of corporate power and capitalist domination, evident in Panitch's claim quoted above. Within this perspective, the power of capitalists has been conceived in primarily voluntaristic terms, not as a social relation of class domination but as a capacity to make decisions without being constrained by external forces (Mellos 1979, 83; see also Sweezy 1972, 106–7; Angotti 1981, 127). To the extent that Canadian capitalists have not developed "their own" technology or mass cultural products, nor cultivated sufficiently multilateral trade relations, nor converted Canadian resources into end-products on the basis of internally generated capital, they are judged dependent on some stronger agency with the power to dictate conditions as it pleases: namely the American bourgeoisie. Similarly, to the extent that Canadian capitalists are not independently powerful agents, the Canadian state must also be judged dependent on—and dominated by—American capital (Clement 1983, 84). The same voluntarist conception of power thus informs an instrumentalist theory of the state, which in its boldest form asserts that "the Canadian state is now in the control of the dominant section of the ruling class in Canada—the U.S. corporations" (Hutcheson 1978, 174; see also Stevenson 1983; Ornstein 1985, 133–35).

Such a view reduces a complex international network of politico-economic relations (embracing capital/labour struggle and inter-capitalist competition) to a dichotomous relation between dominant and dependent social agents. The dependency formulation forgets that "social domination in capitalism is not simply domination by a social grouping but is the abstract domination exercised by the historically-specific structures of the labour-mediated and hence alienated social relations" (Postone 1985, 238).

In Canada, as elsewhere, the domination of capital is constantly expressed in the profit-motivated decisions of capitalists, constrained as they are by market conditions well beyond the control of any agency (see Walker 1978, 30; Brewer 1980, 276). Within this anarchic economic system, the changing opportunities for valorization have motivated Canadian capitalists to: purchase or produce "American" cultural products instead of mobilizing indigenous talent; sell raw materials in the world market instead of producing more end-products; reinvest profits in the low-wage American sunbelt or in less developed countries; introduce technological changes that eliminate far more jobs than they create; engage in financial manipulations that centralize capital without creating social use-values of any sort; and so on.

A similar analysis of power and constraint can be applied to the Canadian state. Although the commodity relations of capitalist production and circulation give the state relative autonomy to mediate capital/labour, inter-capitalist, and other conflicts, the same commodity relations ultimately constrain the state to meet the requirements of capital-in-general (Holloway and Picciotto 1978). Much as the market disciplines the entrepreneur to minimize cost-price while maximizing turnover, the forces disciplining the state are primarily financial:

> states that stray too far from organizational forms and from policies that are consistent with the circulation of capital, the preservation of the distributional arrangements of capitalism and the sustained production of surplus value soon find themselves in financial difficulty. Fiscal crisis...turns out to be the means whereby the discipline of capital can ultimately be imposed on any state apparatus that remains within the ambit of capitalist relations of production (Harvey 1982, 153).

Throughout its history, the Canadian state's form and its actions to mediate social contradictions—whether in the era of the National Policy (Craven and Traves 1979; Anderson 1985), the early era of monopoly capitalism (Traves 1979; Cuneo 1980; Russell 1984) or in the period since the Second World War (Wolfe 1983)—have been constrained by the impersonal power of increasingly concentrated and internationalized capital. In the era of imperialism, the transnational allocative power of finance capital has constituted an ever-present threat to the state: that of capital withdrawal (see Offe 1984, 244). Since the 1970's, this capitalist class power has disciplined the Canadian state (1) to solve its deepening fiscal crisis by reducing social expenditures and renouncing full-employment Keynesian policy, and (2) to improve capitalist profit prospects by restricting trade-union rights and enhancing investment incentives (Wolfe 1984; Calvert 1984; Panitch and Swartz 1985). In this respect, however, the Canadian state has hardly been exceptional. Brett has explained the underlying significance of the drift to neo-conservatism among the capitalist democracies:

> Generally presented in its "monetarist" guise, the new policy package requires the reimposition of market criteria during a period of intensified competition as well as reduction in all social services that can be classified as "non-productive" and therefore expendable in the general struggle to raise the rate of profit to acceptable levels. What is actually going on here is a struggle to determine which components of the world's productive capacity are going to be closed down to get rid of the surplus capacity which had emerged at the end of the long boom by the middle of the 1970's (1983, 244).

Indeed, the ultimate implication of finance capital's international mobility is a strong tendency for the law of value to operate more effectively than ever on a world scale. This produces in the present moment uneven patterns of economic fragmentation, truncation and deindustrialization, as well as state-imposed austerity programmes, as the international division of labour is violently restructured under the weight of global crisis (see, for example, Kolko 1977, 20–21; Walker 1978, 32; Portes and Walton 1981, 16; Harvey 1982, 154; Hawley and Noble 1982; Roddick 1984, 131).

Understandably, this study's principal finding—that in an era of rising and then declining American hegemony, the dominant fraction of Canadian capital has consolidated control over circuits of finance capital at home and abroad—will come as cold comfort to most Canadians. There is little cause for a nationalistic sigh of relief that the American Challenge of the 1940's–60's has been beaten back. For if the harvest of lengthening dependency that Levitt foresaw has not been reaped, the fruits of economic crisis are miserably plentiful. Moreover, as American decline and generalized recession have intensified international competition, the militantly nationalistic Reagan administration has attempted to recover lost economic space by projecting its political power (Petras and Morley 1982, 6, 30–31; Halliday 1983, 174–86). The Reagan Challenge may be predicated more on American economic weakness than strength, but the threat of retaliatory protectionism against competing states is real enough, particularly for Canada, whose open economy relies on access to the American market. The election in 1984 of an avowedly pro-American prime minister, whose government seemed committed to enhanced continental ties, increased the likelihood that the class politics of economic crisis in Canada would be conjoined with a struggle over "the nature of the national interest" (Clarkson 1985, 353, 367).

Thus, despite—and in some measure because of—the successes of Canadian capitalists in consolidating their economic position in the world system, the national question continues to shape the terrain of political struggle in Canada. It is likely that the themes of cultural sovereignty and economic self-determination will continue to furnish a popular discourse in terms of which international capitalist hegemony can be immediately resisted. It may even be that growing Canadian-American tensions in economic, political and cultural realms will inspire a proactive "politics of popular nationalism" among ordinary Canadians (Watkins 1983, 156). Any movement for change, however, will need to contend not with the failures of a dependent bourgeoisie, but with Canadian capitalists' considerable success in establishing a regime of accumulation well suited to the internationalized form of contemporary capitalism. In this sense, the challenge in Canada parallels the situation elsewhere in the advanced capitalist world (Radice 1984, 38): to transpose popular sentiments against the dominance of international capital into politics that confront the class character of our present political economy, while developing an internationalism of labour to confront the internationalism of capital.

APPENDIX I

SAMPLING, MEASUREMENT, AND DATA
MANAGEMENT PROCEDURES

This appendix describes the procedures employed in compiling longitudinal data on the dominant corporations in Canada. The compilation required several stages. First, a theoretical universe of units of capital was defined, and the largest units within this universe were selected, yielding a sample of 194 corporations that at some time in the 1946–76 period were economically dominant in terms of the amount of capital controlled. Two sorts of data were systematically gathered for each firm over the entire period: (1) information about the firm's directors and executives: their names and corporate positions, and (2) information describing the firm in terms of size, industry, and country in which controlling interest was held. The former data provided the basis for an analysis of corporate interlocking; the latter made possible a study of patterns of capital accumulation.

SELECTING THE DOMINANT CORPORATIONS

In its most general sense, the concept of monopoly capital applies not only in cases of "absolute" monopoly but also describes large concentrations of capital, irrespective of the particular market conditions under which each capital functions. Large corporations may operate as monopolies in the neoclassical sense (such as Bell Canada, Canadian Pacific Limited), as oligopolies (such as the major steel producers or auto makers), or even in relatively competitive markets (such as the textile industry). While the particulars of pricing policy may vary somewhat across these categories, the general social power that accrues to control of vast amounts of capital does not. It is this aspect of large corporations, the control over great concentrations of productive resources and labour, that lends significance to the concept of monopoly capital.

Identification of monopoly capitals in Canada required that two substantive problems be addressed: (1) the definition of a theoretical population of Canadian capitals from which a suitable sample could be selected, and (2) the specification of appropriate selection criteria.

The Population

Although larger units such as enterprise groups (Berkowitz et al. 1976) have sometimes been advocated, the standard unit of analysis in studies of large-scale capital and the unit employed in this research is the incorporated firm. The corporation represents the smallest legally discrete unit of capital, and, while some corporations may function virtually as operating divisions of their parent firms, it is ultimately corporations that make up larger units of capital such as interest or enterprise groups. In this sense, identification of the largest individual corporations must be recognized as a methodological prerequisite to the study of interest groups.

Beyond the general issue of the unit of analysis, several criteria were considered in specifying the universe of Canadian capitals. Only corporations with a majority of stock owned by individuals or other firms were included in the population. Crown corporations or corporations such as Canada Development Corporation that were majority-owned by the state during the study period were considered state organizations not directly controlled by members of the capitalist class. Firms that were taken over by the state during the postwar period (such as the hydro-electric utilities), were eligible for the sample only until their nationalization. On the other hand, wholly owned subsidiaries, regardless of whether their parents were domestically or foreign based, were included in the population. Although it may be argued that such firms are only nominally autonomous of their parents and do not practically represent discrete capitals, the importance to the Canadian economy of such wholly owned subsidiaries as General Motors of Canada Limited, IBM Canada Limited, Mobil Oil Canada Limited, and International Harvester Company of Canada Limited strongly advised their inclusion in the population.[1] For the sake of methodological consistency, Canadian-owned subsidiaries such as Canadian Pacific Investment's Marathon Realty Company were also included, as were firms that became wholly owned subsidiaries after being taken over by other corporations.

Mention of takeovers brings up the broader issue of corporate reorganizations and their effect on the units of analysis. A pair of firms may combine in two principal ways. One company may acquire shares in the other and ultimately convert it into a wholly owned subsidiary. The takeover of The Price Company by Abitibi Paper, described by Mathias (1976), is an example. In this situation, the parent and its subsidiary were treated as distinct capitals, so long as they continued as legally separate entities with their own boards of directors and executives. On the other hand, two or more firms may effect a merger, from which a new corporation with a new capitalization and directorate results. In these cases the predecessor corporations were considered as distinct from the merged company, which was deemed a new firm.

A final issue in the specification of the population was establishing a firm's Canadian credentials. This question, so basic to this study, arises from the knotty problem of delineating a national economy in an era of internationalized capitalism (see Radice 1984). As an advanced capitalist country, Canada maintains substantial investments in other countries, while being itself a locus for investment of foreign capital. Given this interpenetration of national capitals, the issue of when a capital is "Canadian" can be a difficult one. Our focus on economic power suggested two criteria by which the nationality of a firm could be assessed: (1) the location of the company's operations, that is, the locus of the material basis of its corporate power; and (2) the location of the firm's head office, that is, the locus of its managerial function. Canadian firms were designated as those with either a majority of assets in Canada *or* a head office in Canada. The first criterion provided for the inclusion of firms whose assets but not head offices were substantially located in Canada (such as Iron Ore Company of Canada, Hudson's Bay Company before 1970). The second allowed for Canadian-based multinationals with substantial assets outside of the country, such as Massey-Ferguson and Brascan Limited. To summarize these criteria, the population was designated as the set of incorporated firms, majority-owned by capitalist interests, and having either their head office or a majority of assets in Canada.

Selection Criteria

The most straightforward approach to identifying dominant corporations is to employ some quantitative yardstick of firm size, such as assets, revenue, or number of employees. In one form or another, this strategy has been followed in most studies of monopoly capital in Canada (see McCollum 1947; Porter 1965; Park and Park 1973; Clement 1975; Niosi 1978; Carroll, Fox and Ornstein 1982). Exclusive use of a single, quantitative criterion, however, may introduce certain biases into the selection process. Obviously, firms with very high ratios of fixed to circulating capital, such as industrials, will show greater assets than firms with smaller ratios of fixed to circulating capital, such as merchandizers. A second problem in implementing quantitative selection criteria in the present study was the differential availability of information on firm size over time. Many firms in Canada did not report sales or gross revenue until the 1960's, and most wholly owned foreign subsidiaries did not report financial information of any kind until required to by the Corporations and Labour Unions Returns Act in the early 1970's. In the light of these complications, a selection strategy was adopted that would identify, on the basis of both qualitative and quantitative criteria, the firms that at one time or another represented the largest concentrations of capital in the Canadian economy.

A judgement sample of corporations, stratified by type of capital, was selected on the basis of total assets for the years 1946, 1951, 1956, 1961, 1966, 1971, and 1976. To ensure maximum coverage, a variety of sources were consulted in compiling these ranked lists, the principal ones being the annual surveys published by the *Financial Post* (that is, *Survey of Industrials, of Mines, of Energy Resources)*, and the ranked lists of Canadian Corporations published by the *Financial Post* since 1965 and by *Canadian Business* since 1973. Additional sources included lists compiled by Porter (1965, 581–95), Park and Park (1973, 239–46), and Clement (1975, 400–48). The *Report of the Superintendent of Insurance,* which provides yearly financial information on financial institutions not covered in the Financial Post *Survey of Industrials*, was also consulted in some cases.

As a measure of corporate power, assets take on different meanings in different economic contexts, as examination of various corporate balance sheets will confirm. Financial intermediaries control vast assets, much of which comprise fictitious capital (that is, debt instruments, such as bonds, having no material referent). Industrial firms, on the other hand, have most of their assets tied up in physical plant, raw materials, and inventories. For these firms, assets have a tangible significance as indicators of direct control over productive capital. In the case of commercial capital, assets have a similar tangible significance but tend to be smaller, since fixed capital represents a deduction from possible merchant profit, not an element of productive capital. Property development firms act much like financial intermediaries in engaging in urban land speculation, but in some respects their balance sheets resemble those of industrials, with a large share of assets tied up in fixed capital and land. To avoid over-representing some categories of capital while under-representing others, a fixed number of firms for the first two of these four categories was specified in advance. For each year, the 70 largest industrials and 20 largest financial intermediaries were selected, yielding totals of 132 industrial and 28 financial firms.

Dominant Industrial Corporations and
Financial Intermediaries

Designation of the seventy dominant industrials for each selection year raised a problem in the case of certain private, foreign-owned subsidiaries, several of which have figured importantly in Canadian economic development. Until the early 1970's, such firms as General Motors of Canada, Chrysler Corporation of Canada, and Canadian International Paper Company made no public financial statements, yet they were almost certainly among the very largest industrial firms in Canada. To ensure comparability of the sample over time, a procedure was devised that would, on the basis of available information, identify those private firms likely to have been among the seventy largest industrials prior to the 1970's. Three criteria were employed in this identification. Firms in existence continuously since 1946, ranked in the fifty largest industrials at the earliest time for which financial data were available, and included in Porter's (1965) sample on the basis of being among the leading employers in the late 1940's, were assumed to have been dominant industrials throughout the earlier period. Five such companies, all American-controlled, were found: General Motors of Canada; International Harvester of Canada; Chrysler Corporation of Canada; Union Carbide of Canada; and Canadian International Paper Company. One other private firm was known to have controlled large assets from the mid-1950's, but it was established after 1946. It was assumed that this firm—Iron Ore Company of Canada—was among the leading industrials from 1956 forward, although the only unequivocal evidence of its size was an asset estimate for 1976, at which time it ranked thirtieth.[2]

In designating these six privately held firms among the dominant industrials, a number of publicly traded companies that would have otherwise qualified were displaced from the sample. This procedure, however, was clearly preferable to the alternative, which for example would have excluded two of the three major Canadian automakers from the sample until 1971. Several difficulties of a different kind were encountered in selecting the top financial corporations. As Neufeld (1972, 61–70) has shown, financial capital in Canada has been concentrated principally in chartered banks and life insurers since 1910. Yet it is also clear from Neufeld's research that other kinds of financial intermediaries—trust companies and trusteed pension funds, and investment and consumer loan companies—have gained prominence in recent years, particularly since 1950. In principle, changes in the relative size of different types of financial institutions do not raise methodological problems: a ranking of the firms by size at several times and selection of the Top ''n'' for each would provide serviceable samples. This procedure was in fact adopted: the largest twenty financial institutions, ranked by assets, were selected at five-year intervals beginning in 1946 and ending in 1976. This method, however, was not deemed adequate for the selection of trust companies and investment companies, whose own assets are often misleadingly small.

Traditionally, an important function of trust companies has been administering pension and other funds held in trust. Technically, this capital is accounted for separately from the assets of the company *per se,* under the rubric of ''assets under administration,'' but in practice the management of these vast pools of capital adds substantially to the trust company's economic power (Chevalier 1969). Until the mid-1950's, trust companies in Canada routinely reported assets under administration in yearly financial statements. In 1951, for example, Montreal Trust reported assets under administration of $1,017 million and assets of $57 million. Ranked according to the total assets owned or administered, this company was the sixth largest financial institution in Canada, but in terms of owned assets it ranked well below twentieth. After the 1950's, moreover, some trust companies stopped reporting assets under administration, introducing a problem in the analysis of their growth over time. To produce a consistent time series, only owned assets were attributed in each year to the trust companies in the sample. But these figures, gross underestimates of capital actually controlled, would have relegated both Montreal Trust and National Trust to positions consistently below the Top 20. Yet these firms, along with Royal Trust Company, have been acknowledged by researchers as Canadian financial institutions of key importance, having close and longstanding ties to the three largest chartered banks (Neufeld 1972; Park and Park 1973). With these considerations in mind, the Top 20 financials were expanded to include the twenty top-ranked financial institutions in each year, plus Montreal, Royal, and National Trust in all years.

Dominant Investment Companies

Investment companies represent a category of financial capital that, unlike others in the sample, does not engage primarily in banking. Chartered banks, life insurers, mortgage, loan and trust companies all buy and sell money capital, and reap the accrued interest as their main source of profit. They centralize the savings of individuals and firms alike and put these at the disposal of capitalists in need of major financing or means of payment. Such financial intermediation is not the main concern of investment companies. Instead, these firms buy shares in other corporations with the aim of gaining higher than average profit rates. This longterm holding of corporate shares makes investment companies of special interest in the study of monopoly capital. It is important, however, to distinguish ownership of shares in industrial corporations from ownership of industrial capital itself (as in the case of privately held companies). Niosi (1978, 98), in describing investment companies such as Power Corporation of Canada as "conglomerates," fails to draw this distinction and is led erroneously to conclude that "public holding companies are nothing more than a type of concentration; they cannot possibly be seen as examples of 'finance capital' " (ibid., 173).

In fact, corporate shares are themselves merely forms of money capital, much like bonds and debentures, except that they give title to ownership of a highly fetishized commodity: the corporation itself (Fitch and Oppenheimer 1970; Hussein 1976, 10). A capitalist who amasses a substantial bloc of shares in a given firm can thus gain operational power over that company. Investment companies facilitate and institutionalize such practices by serving as repositories of stock capital.

Two types of investment companies may be distinguished: "investment trusts," and holding companies (Neufeld 1972). The prime contemporary example of the former is Maxwell Meighen's Canadian General Investments Limited. This firm shows a portfolio of investments distributed across many companies and not affording definite control of any one corporation. Consequently, the investment trust tends to take a largely passive role with respect to the management of companies whose shares it owns. Of course, an absence of direct domination does not preclude "communities of interest" between the investment trust and the firms in which it has invested. To pursue the same example a bit further, for years Meighen shared control of Argus Corporation with several other Canadian capitalists, under the leadership of E. P. Taylor and, later, J. A. McDougald. His own interest in Argus was exercised through his investment trust, which in 1975 held 22.4 per cent of Revelston Corporation Limited, the major shareholder of Argus. Meighen himself was president of Canadian General Investments from 1949 to 1969, chairman after 1970, and a director of Argus from 1961 to 1979, when he lost a struggle with Conrad Black for control, in the wake of McDougald's death.

Holding companies such as Argus differ from investment trusts in that their investments are concentrated in a relatively small number of firms. This more focused investment portfolio allows the holding company to exercise some influence and in many cases to exert control over the management of the held firm. The holding company is a vehicle for control of great amounts and various kinds of capital through ownership of lesser amounts of stock capital. In post-Second World War Canada, the leading example has been E. P. Taylor's creation, Argus Corporation. Park and Park (1973, 176) describe the genesis of this bastion of high finance:

Argus was designed as an investment holding company that would seek to exercise control over the companies in which it invested. The money with which to make the investments came from bank loans and the sale of shares to the public.

Taylor himself put into Argus his Canadian Breweries shares, receiving in return enough Argus shares to ensure him effective control of Argus in alliance with Phillips, McDougald, and McCutcheon.

Some 1,400,000 shares of Argus common have been issued circa 1960, owned by some 3,000 shareholders (many of whom are investment companies). However, Taylor and his three close associates hold, directly or through private investment companies, 40 percent of the outstanding common, with Taylor himself owning the larger fraction of this 40 percent.

Argus set about buying large blocks of shares in Massey-Ferguson (then Massey-Harris), in Dominion Tar and Chemical, in St. Lawrence Corporation, in B.C. Forest Products, etc.

It is clear from this example that holding companies further centralize the control of large capitals, effecting a complete interpenetration of financial and industrial interests. Just as it is misleading to describe holding companies as industrial "conglomerates," it is equally fallacious to assert that the controlling interests behind such companies are mere "financial capitalists" (Clement 1977, 24). In fact, holding companies institutionalize the financial control of industrial (and other) capital: they represent most concretely the modern form of large-scale capital that arose when the concentration of production and credit entailed their effective unification.

Quantitative criteria such as asset size are not especially illuminating in the identification of important investment companies. The practice of "pyramiding" intercorporate ownership to attain control of vast capitals, so central to the strategies of Taylor, Desmarais, the Bronfmans, and others, implies that the actual assets of their companies will be comparatively small. The Royal Commission on Corporate Concentration (1978), for instance, reports that Power Corporation ranked only 98th among the 100 largest Canadian corporations of 1976, while Argus Corporation did not qualify for the list at all, even though its affiliates, Massey-Ferguson, Dominion Stores, and Domtar, ranked 7, 10 and 36, consecutively.

Of course, these two investment companies posed no problems in this study: their generally acknowledged importance in the Canadian economy made their inclusion in the sample mandatory. The same may be said, with reference to recent times, of Canadian Pacific Investments, which in 1975 held controlling interest in such large firms as Cominco Limited, Algoma Steel, PanCanadian Petroleum, and Marathon Realty Company. Beyond these obvious examples of the country's most powerful and diversified investment companies, though, there were difficult questions surrounding the selection of firms in this sector.

Because of our focus on the Canadian political economy, it was decided to restrict the definition of "investment company" to those firms holding substantial stock in other large Canadian corporations, particularly in other firms in the sample. But this criterion was not sufficient in delineating the most important companies, since there are many privately held holding companies (and "charitable foundations"), each of which has only a nominal existence as a depository of a family's controlling interest in some other firm (see Niosi 1978, 172). Then, too, there are holding companies whose investments are restricted to one or a very few firms in the same industry, and whose function is essentially managerial. Dominion Stores Limited, for example, is the holding company through which Argus Corporation maintained control of Dominion Grocetarias until 1985, but it is not itself an important investment company. The accumulation strategies pursued by these different companies are quite distinct. The directors and executives of Dominion Stores and companies of its kind are primarily concerned with the technical conditions of commodity production and circulation, for example, with lowering costs and expanding markets. In contrast, the management of *bona fide* investment companies function as both financial and industrial capitalists in orienting toward operations of the capital market while maintaining a capacity to intervene directly in the technical management of the capitals they control.

These considerations led to the selection of ten publicly-traded investment companies holding substantial interests in other big Canadian firms at some time in the postwar period. In addition to the three obvious candidates mentioned above—Argus, Power and C.P.I.—these ten included the following: Ventures Limited (which controlled Falconbridge Nickel Mines Limited, Sherrit Gordon Mines, and Giant Yellowknife Mines, as well as a host of smaller firms until its absorption by Falconbridge in 1962 [Deverall et al., 1975]);[3] Canadian Chemical and Cellulose Company (a subsidiary of Celanese Corporation of America which controlled Columbia Cellulose Company Limited and Canadian Chemical Company Limited from its incorporation in 1951 until it wound up in 1958); Bowater Canadian Limited (formed in 1952 to control the North American assets of the Bowater Paper Corporation Limited of Britain, which continues to control Bowater's Newfoundland Pulp and Paper Mills Limited and Bowater Mersey Paper Limited); Anglo-Canadian Telephone Company (a subsidiary of General Telephone and Electronics Corporation of the U.S., controlling British Columbia Telephone Company (as well as subsidiaries in the Philippines and Dominican Republic); International Utilities Corporation (which operated as a Canadian corporation headquartered in Toronto from 1960 to 1970 and controlled Canadian Utilities Limited among other smaller Canadian subsidiaries); The Investors Group (which in 1976 controlled both Montreal Trust Company and Great West Life Assurance Company); and Canadian General Investments Limited (which has tended to maintain a more diversified and less concentrated investment portfolio, though it held quite substantial interests in Argus Corporation and Canada Trustco Mortgage Company in 1976).

Three additional firms were included as dominant industrial corporations in certain years and as investment companies in others. Both Genstar Limited and Reed Paper Limited were incorporated as investment companies but were later reorganized, fully consolidating their subsidiaries to become industrial corporations. This occurred in Genstar's case in 1965, when it amalgamated with its three operating subsidiaries, Brockville Chemicals Limited, Inland Cement Company Limited, and Iroquois Glass Limited. Reed similarly acquired full control of its major subsidiary, Anglo-Canadian Pulp and Paper Mills Limited, in 1974. Brascan Limited, on the other hand, managed an array of utilities in Brazil until it divested itself of these assets in December 1978. Its emergence as an indigenous investment company dates from 1967, however, when it acquired control of John Labatt Limited and Labatt's subsidiary, Ogilvie Flour Mills Limited.

In all, then, the sample of investment companies numbered thirteen, including three firms that were classified as industrial capitals in some years. Each investment company was included in the sample in all of the 1946–76 years, provided it was structured at the time as an investment company.

Dominant Merchandizers and Property Developers

Commercial capital presented a different situation from industry and finance. In 1946, only a portion of commercial capital was monopolized: namely the retail department store (and mail-order) sector in which Hudson's Bay Company, Simpsons Limited and T. Eaton Company Limited[4] were dominant. Other commercial capitals listed in the Financial Post *Survey of Corporate Securities* for that year were small and serviced regional markets only. By the mid-1950's, however, capital had concentrated in other areas of commerce, particularly in wholesale and retail food merchandizing, producing a much larger number of significant companies. The largest three commercial firms (ranked by assets) for 1946, the largest five for 1951 and the largest ten for 1956, 1961, 1966, 1971 and 1976 were therefore included in the sample.

Urban property development is another economic sector that was not highly monopolized in the early postwar era. Indeed, other than T. Eaton Realty Company and the substantial real estate assets of Canadian Pacific Railway (which were not managed by a separate company until the incorporation of Marathon Realty in 1963), there were few property developers of any size prior to the mid-1960's, at which time an intense movement of concentration and centralization began. Because this process was a recent one, and inasmuch as "property development" resembles industrial accumulation in creating differential ground rent through the incorporation of fixed capital into land, this sector was represented by firms with assets as large as the seventieth ranked industrial in any selection year.

A tabulation of the successive Top 100s selected by the above procedures is given in Table A1, where we can note stability over time in the number of industrials and financial intermediaries, and net increases in the number of investment, merchandizing and property development companies making up the Top 100. Indeed, by 1976, the "Top 100" has grown to include 116 corporations, an increase of 13 from 1946. The bottom rows of Table A1 indicate for each selection year the number of firms that were too small to qualify as dominant, as well as the number of firms that were not in existence at the time but that were included in the Top 100 in some other year.

Among the most important considerations in selecting a set of the largest corporations throughout an entire era is that of comparability with previous compilations of prominent firms. Quite an array of methods has been invoked by the several Canadian researchers who have assembled such lists. This variety of selection criteria makes it unrealistic to anticipate exact correspondence between this study's sample and other sets of large corporations. Still, it is not unreasonable to ask whether other standards generate "Top 100s" resembling the present ones, and, further, how close that resemblance is. Ideally, we would like to be able to assert that the present sample is not technique dependent, but overlaps substantially with other samples selected on the basis of differing criteria. A demonstration of considerable overlap would confer a degree of "concurrent validity" on the present sample, and would strengthen the claim that it includes the most important sections of monopoly capital in Canada.

In Table A2, the amount of overlap in the composition of the present sample and of samples selected in eight studies of large Canadian firms between 1944 and 1977 is assessed, both in terms of the number of firms common to both samples and the percentage of firms in one sample that also appear in the other. As was indicated in Table A1, in addition to the dominant firms of any given year there are in our sample of 194 corporations about 50 firms in operation that rank among the Top 100 of some other year. Different selection criteria may favour certain of these firms more than we have, raising the prospect of further overlap between the comparison sample and the present sample, viewed in longitudinal perspective. With this possibility in mind, each comparison sample in Table A2 is matched with the Top 100 (or an appropriate subset) of the selection year closest in time, as well as with all relevant firms in our total sample in the same year, regardless of whether or not they then numbered among the Top 100. In most cases the comparisons involve only nonfinancial firms or only financials, since researchers have generally drawn a distinction between these kinds of companies in the selection process.

One way of assessing the amount of overlap between the present sample and the various comparison samples in Table A2 is to consider the percentage of firms common to each pair of samples. For example, of the 74 nonfinancial corporations included in our 1946 Top 100, 58 were also identified by McCollum (1947) as members of the 100 largest nonfinancial corporations of 1944. Thus, 58 per cent of McCollum's sample overlaps with our 1946 dominant nonfinancials, and 78 per cent of the latter overlaps with McCollum's sample. Alternatively, of the 116 nonfinancial firms in our sample that were extant in 1946, 69 were also included in McCollum's; therefore 69 per cent of McCollum's sample overlaps with our entire nonfinancial sample for 1946, while 59 per cent of the latter is included in the former sample. Because this study's sample and the comparison sample in each instance may differ considerably in size, it is advisable to report both the largest and smallest of these four overlap percentages.

Table A1 "Top 100" Firms, by Industrial Sector, 1946–1976

Sector	1946	1951	1956	1961	1966	1971	1976
Industrials	70	70	70	70	70	70	70
Financial Intermediaries	23	23	23	23	23	23	23
Investment Companies	6	7	9	9	9	9	8
Merchandizers	3	5	10	10	10	10	10
Property Development	1	1	1	2	1	3	5
Subtotal	103	106	113	114	113	115	116
Not in "Top 100"							
but extant	45	49	52	56	53	51	45
Not extant	46	39	29	24	28	28	33
Total	194	194	194	194	194	194	194

Table A2 Comparisons of Sample with Other Compilations of Large Corporations, 1944–1977

Comparison Sample			Present Sample			Per cent in Common	
Source	Selection Criteria	N_1	Compared with:	N_2	N_3^*	$100\dfrac{N_3}{N_1}$	$100\dfrac{N_3}{N_2}$
McCollum (1947, 4–5)	largest corporations by assets, based on Financial Post Surveys, circa 1944, excluding financials	100	1946 Top 100 excluding financials	74	58	58	78
			All Sample Firms extant in 1946, excluding financials	116	69	69	59
Porter (1965, 581–90)	largest non-financial corporations, circa 1948–50 employing at least 500 workers and satisfying certain qualitative standards (see Porter 1965, 570–80), excluding two crown corporations	181	1946 Top 100, excluding financial intermediaries	80	60	33	75
			1951 Top 100, excluding financial intermediaries	83	65	36	78
			All Sample Firms, extant in 1951, excluding financial intermediaries	129	79	44	61
	9 chartered banks & 10 largest life insurers, by assets, circa 1950–51	19	1951 Top Financial intermediaries	23	17	89	74
			All sample financial intermediaries	26	18	95	69

Comparison Sample			Present Sample			Per cent in Common	
Source	Selection Criteria	N_1	Compared with:	N_2	N_3^*	$100\frac{N_3}{N_1}$	$100\frac{N_3}{N_2}$
Brecher and Reisman (1957, 257–85)	6 leading companies in 20 manufacturing and resource industries, 1954, according to a variety of criteria such as book value, total output, plant capacity and employment	106	1956 Top 70 industrials	70	38	36	54
			All sample industrials extant in 1956	107	42	40	39
Park and Park (1973, 239–46)	largest non-financial corporations of 1958, mainly on the basis of assets by industry	64	1956 Top 100, excluding financial intermediaries	90	58	91	64
			All sample firms, extant in 1956, excluding financial intermediaries	138	61	95	44
	8 chartered banks & trust and life insurance companies with assets of $100 million or more in 1958	35	1956 Top financial intermediaries	23	20	57	87
			All financial intermediaries extant in 1956	27	22	63	81
Porter (1965, 591–95)	non-financial corporations with assets of $100 million or more in 1960	64	1961 Top 100, excluding financial intermediaries	91	60	94	66
			All sample firms, extant in 1961 excluding financial intermediaries	143	62	97	43

N_3 = N of firms in both samples.

Table A2 Comparisons of Sample with Other Compilations of Large Corporations, 1944–1977

| Comparison Sample | | | Present Sample | | | Per cent in Common | |
Source	Selection Criteria	N_1	Compared with:	N_2	N_3*	$100\frac{N_3}{N_1}$	$100\frac{N_3}{N_2}$
Clement (1975, 400–428)	"dominant" corporations of 1971, ranked by assets and sales within different industries excluding financial inter-mediaries (banks, life insurers, sales finance, trust, mortgage and other finance companies) as well as Canadian National Railways (a crown corporation) and all "dominant subsidiaries."	94	1971 Top 100, excluding financial intermediaries	92	75	80	82
			All sample firms extant in 1971, excluding financial intermediaries	139	81	86	58
	"dominant" financial intermediaries of 1971, ranked by assets and gross income within different industries (exclusive of "investment companies")	36	1971 Top financial intermediaries	23	20	56	87
			All sample financial intermediaries extant in 1971	27	22	61	81
Royal Commission on Corporate Concentration (1978, 15–18)	largest non-financial intermediaries of 1975 by sales or revenues, excluding 6 crown corporations	94	1976 Top 100, excluding financial intermediaries	93	64	68	69
			All sample firms extant in 1976, excluding financial intermediaries	134	74	79	55
	largest financial institutions of 1975, by assets	25	1976 top financial intermediaries	23	20	80	87
			all sample financial [...] extant in 1976	27	23	92	85

Table A2 Comparisons of Sample with Other Compilations of Large Corporations, 1944–1977

Comparison Sample			Present Sample			Per cent in Common	
Source	Selection Criteria	N_1	Compared with:	N_2	N_3^*	$100\frac{N_3}{N_1}$	$100\frac{N_3}{N_2}$
Sweeny (1980, ch.20)	Canadian firms in *Financial Post Survey of Corporate Securities* or *Moody's Manual of Investments*, circa 1948, sharing at least three directors with a chartered bank** or with a firm which shared at least three of its directors with a chartered bank	76	1946 Top 100	103	32	42	31
			All sample firms extant in 1946	148	36	47	24
	As above, but using *Financial Post Directory of Directors* (1959) for data, circa 1958	104	1956 Top 100	113	44	42	39
			All Sample firms extant in 1956	165	52	50	32
	As above, circa 1967	104	1966 Top 100	113	44	42	39
			All sample firms extant in 1966	166	52	50	31
	As above, circa 1977	118	1976 Top 100	116	52	44	45
			All sample firms extant in 1976	161	60	51	37

*N_3 = number of firms in both samples.
**Excluding Banque Canadienne Nationale, Banque Provinciale du Canada, and Mercantile Bank of Canada.

The closest correspondences in Table A2 are with compilations based on the same selection criterion as this study's sample, namely asset rankings. There is an overlap of 58 per cent to 74 per cent between McCollum's "Top 100" non-financials of 1944 and the present sample at 1946. The overlap between Porter's dominant financial intermediaries of 1950–51 and our financial intermediaries of 1951 ranges from 69 per cent to 95 per cent, while Porter's largest non-financials of 1960 overlap 43 to 97 per cent of the time with our nonfinancial of 1961. Similarly, many of Park and Park's top nonfinancials (44 to 95 per cent) and financials (57 to 87 per cent) of 1958 also appear in our sample in 1956, as do a majority of Clement's dominant financial intermediaries (56 to 87 percent) and nonfinancials (58 to 86 per cent) at 1971. All these comparison samples were selected on the basis of some form of asset ranking and they tend to bear close resemblance to the present sample.

Other researchers have relied on rankings according to some other criterion of corporate size in compiling samples of prominent firms. The overlap between our sample and these collections is more moderate. With respect to Porter's largest nonfinancials of 1948–50 it ranges from 33 to 78 per cent; for Brecher and Reisman's leading manufacturing and resource extraction firms of 1954 it varies between 36 and 54 per cent, and for the Royal Commission on Corporate Concentration's largest nonfinancials of 1975 according to revenue, from 55 to 79 per cent.

Sweeny's (1980) prominent corporations of 1948, 1958, 1967 and 1977 were selected on quite different grounds from those described above. These are essentially "snowball samples" of firms sharing in the years just mentioned three or more directors with one or more of the country's biggest chartered banks, or with another corporation that shared at least three directors with a big bank. Sweeny's selection criterion is a structural one, stemming from the theoretical assumption that big banks form the nuclei of major financial groups in advanced capitalist economies. Compared with the samples just reviewed, there is less correspondence between the present sample and Sweeny's networks, particularly in 1948 when only slightly more than 30 firms (24 per cent to 47 per cent) are in common. But it is well worth noting that the amount of overlap increases between 1948 and 1958 (ranging from 32 to 50 per cent in 1958), even as the size of Sweeny's network expands from 76 to 104 and the size of our "Top 100" grows to 113. Then, between 1967 (31 to 50 per cent overlap) and 1977 (37 to 51 per cent) the correspondence improves again, as the size of the respective samples continues to increase. By 1977, 52 of the 118 firms in Sweeny's network of strongly interlocked corporations also appear in our Top 116 of a year earlier.

This trend is interesting on both methodological and substantive grounds. It indicates that, at least in recent years, the identification of major Canadian monopolies using two very different approaches yields somewhat similar results. Further, over time there is a greater overlap between the set of largest firms and the network of strongly interlocked corporations, a greater correspondence between "monopoly capital" operationalized on the *quantitative* basis of the amount of capital controlled and "monopoly capital" operationalized on the *qualitative* basis of position in a bank-centred network of structurally integrated capitals. In general, the comparisons of the present sample with other compilations indicate a good deal of commonality, suggesting that our sample captures the most significant sections of Canadian monopoly capital in the 1946–76 years.

DATA

Information on each firm in any of the Top 100s described in Table A1 was gathered from a variety of sources and, where possible, over the entire time period under investigation. The variables measured for each firm included gross assets, the names and positions of the firm's directors and executives, its principal industry, the country in which controlling interest was held, the year in which it was incorporated, and the year in which it surrendered its corporate charter (if prior to 1977). Sources employed in measuring these variables and the coding conventions adopted in their operational specification are discussed below.

Asset and directorship and executive data were collected on a yearly basis. The primary source of this information was company annual reports.[5] Whenever these documents were unavailable, the annuals published by The Financial Post and Moody[6] and the files of the Ontario Securities Commission were consulted. Directorship and executive information was also obtained from the Financial Post *Directory of Directors,* Standard and Poor's *Register of Corporations, Directors and Executives,* and the corporation files of the Ontario Ministry of Consumer and Commercial Affairs (Company Services Branch). These sources provided complete yearly information for 152 of the 194 sample firms. The remaining 42 corporations were approached directly and asked to supply the missing information on the composition of their directorate and executive, and/or financial statements for the relevant years. This request took the form of a letter to the corporate secretary or, if the secretary's identity was unknown, to some other high-ranking officer. The letter was followed up with a maximum of two phone calls to the addressee. Twenty-eight of the 42 companies responded to the request, with information of varying usefulness; fourteen companies refused to cooperate. Many of the refusals came from private companies unwilling to divulge financial information. In light of these gaps in the data, a request was made to the Federal Department of Consumer and Corporate Affairs for annual CALURA returns of 20 firms missing financial data in certain years. Usable financial information was obtained for 11 corporations, mostly in the later years of the study.

These sources in combination provided excellent coverage of sample firms in recent years, but left some gaps in the earlier period, especially for firms that entered the Top 100 only in later years. For example, of the 46 firms that existed in 1946 but did not rank among the Top 100 of that year, 14 were missing asset data and eight were missing data on directors and executives. The latter data, however, were found to be essentially complete for each set of dominant firms in a given year.[7] Since the bulk of our analysis centres on the composition of successive Top 100s, problems of bias because of missing data are, for the most part, localized to the designation of dominant firms in each year. The selection procedures discussed above probably mitigate the most significant of these biases: the exclusion of large, wholly-owned subsidiaries of foreign corporations.

Measuring Assets

Three major issues were faced in the measurement of corporate assets—an essential indicator of the accumulation trends charted in Chapter 4. In preparing several tabulations (namely Figure 4.2 and Table 4.9) it was important to obtain estimates of assets for the six privately owned industrial corporations. In calculating the aggregate concentration ratios depicted in Figure 4.2, for instance, were we to exclude asset figures for several large firms, the results could be influenced considerably. It was therefore necessary to retrodict the assets of the six large U.S.-controlled industrials in the years for which their balance sheets were unavailable. This was accomplished using a "benchmarking" procedure that determined for a given firm its asset ranking in the earliest available year, and then assigned to that company in earlier years the assets of firms with the same rank in the Top 70. This approach assumes that the six firms each grew at a pace just sufficient to maintain a constant ranking over the years for which financial data were unavailable.[8]

A second issue was the consistency of accounting practices over the three decades. While it was not feasible to standardize these methods fully across all firms in the study, it was deemed essential that no major change occur over time in the accounting of corporate assets; that is, that measured assets have the same substantive meaning at different times. Only one major change in accounting practices took place in the period of study. Most firms in the 1940's and through much of the 1950's treated accumulated depreciation (including "depletion reserves") as a liability but accounted such depreciation in later years as a contra-asset deducted from the value of fixed assets. The second convention was adopted in this study, and assets in the early years were adjusted accordingly, yielding a consistent time series for each firm. Similarly, in calculating the industrial concentration ratios in Figure 4.2, the modern convention was adopted by subtracting total depreciation from the aggregate industrial assets reported in *Taxation Statistics Part 2—Corporations* (Ottawa: Statistics Canada) for 1946, 1951, and 1956.

Thirdly, mention should be made of the measurement problems raised by intercorporate ownership. Many large corporations own shares in other firms, large and small, and their balance sheets often consolidate the assets of majority-owned subsidiaries. For instance, Bell Canada reports as its own the assets of its subsidiary, Northern Telecom. Our inclusion of both firms in the Top 100 raises the problem of bias from double-counting in the tabulation of dominant industrial assets. To avoid this bias, the assets of majority-owned subsidiaries were subtracted from those of the parent, whenever both firms were included in the Top 100. The resulting net asset values were used in compiling all tabulations in Chapters 4 and 7. In practice, however, data on intercorporate ownership relations were only systematically available in the most recent years; hence the tabulations for the 1940's and 1950's may contain some bias as a result of double-counting. In the light of these various methodological wrinkles, the results on capital accumulation in Chapter 4 should be interpreted very cautiously, as indicative of trends rather than definitive of some easily apprehended economic reality.

Three other accounting conventions deserve mention here. A few firms, such as Brascan Limited, reported assets in American currency. These figures were converted into current Canadian dollars using the yearly exchange rates given in Urquhart and Buckley (1965) and the *Bank of Canada Review* (December 1971 and April 1979). As mentioned earlier, the accounting of assets for trust companies was net of assets under administration (that is, estates, trusts and agency funds), again to provide a consistent time series. Finally, the assets of investment companies were accounted at market prices rather than at cost, to reflect the amount of stock capital actually at the disposal of these companies at any given time.

Corporate Directors and Executives

Collection of data on directors and executives of each corporation in the sample for each year of the study was a massive task requiring the assistance of several coders. The names and yearly positions of each firm's directors and executives were transferred from the listings in annual reports of other sources onto a coding form. Each director or executive was coded on a record uniquely identifying him or her according to the firm's identification number, a personal identification number within the firm, last name, first name and middle initials, and positions occupied between 1946 and 1976.

The manner in which these data were transformed into corporate interlocks is discussed in detail in the following section on data management. Simply put, a pair of firms was considered interlocked whenever an identical name was listed in the same year under both corporations' identification numbers, and the number of interlocks in a year was computed as the number of such name identities for a pair of firms.

Industrial Sectors

The categorization of each firm's main industry was fairly straightforward, though not without complications. In an era in which diversification and "conglomeration" occur as integral aspects of accumulation, it is sometimes difficult to assign firms to single industries or even to unique economic sectors. T. Eaton Company Limited, for instance, is quite clearly a commercial firm, yet it has long operated a number of consumer-goods factories and could in one sense be considered a vertically integrated industrial corporation. In general, though, the basic distinctions between industrial, financial and commercial capital can be

fairly easily drawn by considering whether a firm's net income derives principally from directly appropriated surplus value (as in the case of mining, manufacturing, transportation, communications and utilities companies, regardless of
whether they retail their own commodities or services), from interest or dividends on money capital lent out (whether it takes the form of direct loans or the
buying of stocks, bonds, and so on), or from an increment in selling price over
the price at which commodities are purchased. Thus, while Eaton's is involved
in a circuit of industrial capital, its primary activity and the source of most of its
profits, is the retailing of goods bought from other firms.

Industry was originally coded for each firm at five-year intervals beginning in
1946, using the Standard Industrial Classification (S.I.C.) for 1961 given in
Poor's *Register of Corporations, Directors and Executives* (1962). The
S.I.C. is comprised of several thousand four-digit numbers which represent the
principal products manufactured or services offered by a company or organiza-
tion. To simplify the coding task only the first three digits of the applicable
S.I.C. codes were recorded for each firm. The primary source of these data was
Standard and Poor's *Register of Corporations, Directors and Executives.*
Other sources, for companies not listed in Poor's *Register,* were the annuals
mentioned earlier, the Financial Post Corporation Service, *Canadian Trade
Directory, Dun and Bradstreet Million Dollar Directory,* and the files of
the Ontario Ministry of Consumer and Commercial Relations (Company Ser-
vices Branch).

For the present analysis, the S.I.C. numbers were collapsed to form three
very general industrial sectors plus four categories of nonindustrial capital. This
simplification was accomplished using the first two digits of the S.I.C. number,
which classify companies into nine major industrial groups. Industrial sectors of
Mining (S.I.C. 10 through 14, including the production of crude petroleum and
natural gas), Manufacturing (S.I.C. 19 through 39), and Transportation, Communication, and Utilities (S.I.C. 40 through 49) were thus created. The other
four categories of industry, which correspond exactly to the different sub-
samples of firms described earlier, are Wholesale and Retail Trade (S.I.C. 50
through 51), Financial Intermediation (S.I.C. 60 through 64), and Investment
Companies (S.I.C. 65).

Country of Control

Since the late 1960's a wealth of information has become available regarding
the countries in which major interests in large Canadian corporations are resident, particularly through the annual listings of large firms in *Canadian
Business* and the *Financial Post* and the occasional government publications
on intercorporate ownership (such as Canada 1979), which make systematic use
of company returns filed under the Corporations and Labour Unions Returns
Act of 1962. Even if the proportion of outstanding shares held in Canada is
known, however, the correct classification of a firm with respect to its nationality of control is not guaranteed, since control of corporate capital is not necessarily synonymous with share ownership per se. What matters most in the

determination of control is the relative distribution of shares among the stock-holders. When shares are widely held, a concentrated bloc of 10 or even 5 per cent may enable an interest to exert control (see, for example, Berle and Means 1932; Villarejo 1961, 1962; Porter 1965; Chevalier 1969; Burch 1972; Zeitlin 1974; Niosi 1978). But a bloc of the same size loses any claim to possible control if some other interest owns a majority of all issued equity. By implication, the country in which a majority of stock is held cannot by itself be taken as a general criterion of control. Canadian Pacific Limited, for instance, under indigenous control since its founding by leading Canadian capitalists in 1881 (Chodos 1973; Niosi 1978), was, until the 1960's, majority-owned outside of Canada, in the United Kingdom and United States. In 1946, only 9 per cent of its total stock was held in Canada, 59 per cent was held in the U.K. and 27 per cent in the U.S. In 1961, 30 per cent of the company's shares were held in Canada while 37 per cent and 23 per cent were held in the U.K. and U.S. By 1977, the percentages were 71 per cent, 7 per cent and 14 per cent, respectively. Yet indigenous control of Canadian Pacific throughout this period is widely acknowledged (MacGilchrist 1948; Brecher and Reisman 1957; Park and Park 1973; Porter 1965, 595; Chodos 1973, 136), precisely because the foreign-owned shares were widely dispersed among many passive investors.

Bell Canada presents an instructive counter-example. In 1933, American Telephone and Telegraph owned 24.3 per cent of Bell's shares, with most of the remaining stock (66.4 per cent) held by small Canadian investors. This situation gave A. T. & T. effective control of Bell, even though two-thirds of its shares were Canadian-owned. Over time the size of A. T. & T.'s bloc gradually diminished to 18 per cent in 1946, 11.8 per cent in 1949, 9.7 per cent in 1950, 4.2 per cent in 1957 and 3.5 per cent in 1960. Hence, while in 1946 the American parent clearly held controlling interest, Bell was just as clearly management-controlled in Canada by the late 1950's, even though throughout these years most of its stock was indigenously held.

The case of Bell Canada also provides an opportunity to point out the methodological imperative to identify the country in which controlling interest is ultimately held, rather than resting content with the knowledge of the nationality of a company's immediate controlling interest. Bell's longtime manufacturing subsidiary, Northern Telecom Limited, has been immediately controlled in Canada throughout the postwar period but obviously was controlled in the United States until control of its parent was transferred to Canada.

In the light of these considerations, national locus of control for each sample firm was assigned to the country where the largest single bloc of stock constituting more than 5 per cent of total outstanding shares, was held. Where no such concentrations of share ownership existed (such as in the case of Bell Canada after 1956) control was assumed to reside with the firm's Canadian management. This operationalization is similar to the approach taken by numerous researchers in the study of corporate ownership and control (see Berle and Means 1932; Porter 1965; Burch 1972; Niosi 1978). In practice, however, it became more of a guiding principle than an operational specification, since detailed data on the distribution of major corporate shareholdings are not generally available.

What were available were findings from several investigations of control of large Canadian corporations, and indications in the business press of the identity of controlling interests for many firms.[9] For each member of the sample, these sources were consulted and compared. Fortunately, the agreement among sources was excellent. The reason for this widespread concurrence is not obscure: the bulk of foreign direct investment in Canada has been owned by multinational corporations whose managements prefer to gain and maintain majority control of their foreign subsidiaries. Many of the most important foreign-controlled corporations in Canada are wholly owned subsidiaries; others have since their incorporation been majority-controlled by foreign-based multinationals.[10]

The less-certain cases of foreign control were for the most part restricted to minority holdings of individuals or firms not resident in Canada. But even here the secondary sources usually provided clear indications of the country of controlling interest. For a few firms in the early years of the study, when the sources provided ambiguous descriptions of control, the country of residence of corporate directors, particularly the chairman and president, was employed as an additional indicator (see Villarejo 1961, 1962; Chevalier 1969; Burch 1972). This procedure would not have been valid if applied to the recent past, because substantial Canadian representation on boards of directors has been legally required since 1975 (Statutes of Canada, 1974–75–76, vol. 1, Chapter 33, p.68). Nor would it have been valid to apply this criterion to Canadian branch plants, whose top managers are often recruited locally. But it is reasonable to assume that among non-branch plants in the 1940's and 1950's, prior to the emergence of widespread concern about the implications of foreign direct investment and before the enactment of legislation requiring Canadian representation on corporate boards, the country in which controlling interest resided was the country of residence of the directors who occupied top executive positions.

A few companies were found to be apparently under joint control by interests located in two countries. The most obvious examples are (1) Canadian Industries Limited (which before its segregation into two firms in 1954 was equally owned by Imperial Chemical Company Limited of the U.K. and E.I. DuPont of the U.S.); and (2) Simpson-Sears Limited (in which Simpsons Limited of Canada and Sears, Roebuck and Company of the U.S. each held 50 per cent interests from its incorporation in 1952 through 1976). These cases were classified according to the conventions adopted by CALURA: firms jointly controlled in Canada and some other country were categorized under foreign control, and firms jointly controlled in the U.S. and some other country were categorized under U.S. control (Canada 1980). This convention obviously tends to overstate the extent of foreign, particularly American, control in the sample of large corporations.

DATA MANAGEMENT

Figure A1 charts the collection and management of data from initial designation of corporations to be studied to creation of the files actually employed in the data analysis. The data were assembled into two parallel files: one contained information about corporate directors and executives, which was ultimately transformed into a file of interlocks, the other contained information on relevant corporate characteristics such as assets, industry, and country of control. After standard validity checks (steps 2, 3 and 5), the file of corporate characteristics was merged with the interlock data to enable analysis of interlocking between designated sets of firms (step 16).

The file of corporate directors and executives required more elaborate verification and manipulation. An interlock exists whenever the same person holds positions in two different corporations simultaneously. In the determination of interlocks from the names and yearly status of directors and executives, two kinds of errors were possible. The same person could be listed under two slightly different names, thus masking an interlock, or two different people could be listed under the same name, thus creating a spurious interlock.

Although in a file of some 25,000 names, it is not possible to eliminate all such errors, an effort was made to correct as many errors as possible within the practical constraints of time and available documentary information. After preliminary data cleaning (step 5), the records of directors and executives were alphabetically sorted and grouped according to an identity criterion including the first six characters of the last name, plus first and middle initial, producing a list of probable interlocks. This list of grouped names and yearly positions was scrutinized for possible errors. The checking procedures were aimed at identifying both spurious and masked interlocks, on the basis of available documentary information.

Cases having identical surname, first initial and middle initial were generally assumed to indicate the same person, except where other information cast doubt on this assumption. There were several kinds of questionable cases: (1) Two cases could have identical first initials but different first names (e.g., John S. Smith and James S. Smith). (2) Two cases could have identical names but refer to different generations of the same family. In these instances one might reasonably expect a period of several years between the careers of parent and offspring. Therefore, if in any set of grouped records there was a gap of ten or more years between the end of one incumbency and the beginning of the next, the cases were cross-checked against biographical descriptions in the Financial Post *Directory of Directors* and/or Standard and Poor's *Register of Corporations, Directors, and Executives*. Common surnames were considered the most likely sources of spurious interlocks. Since Canadian capitalists are overwhelmingly British in ethnic origin (Porter 1965, 285–87; Clement 1975, 231–39; Niosi 1978, 171), a number of very popular English and Scottish surnames were encountered. Obviously, the greater the frequency of cases having a given surname, the greater is the likelihood of mistaking two different people for a single individual. In light of this consideration, seventy-six surnames each subsuming thirty or more cases were intensively cross-checked against the biographical sources just mentioned. (3) In some grouped cases the credibility of career patterns was considered in determining whether to undertake documen-

Figure A1

Flow Diagram of Data Management

Select Initial "Top 100's" 1946–77 and assign Firm ID's

1. CODE each firm's directors and executives, 1946–1977. Assign firm ID and unique personal ID to each case and card numbers for director and executive data.

CODE industry, country of control, FINANCIAL INFORMATION and other corporate-level data, 1946–77. Assign firm ID to each case and card number within each case for different types of data.

2. Sight-check coded data.

Sight-check coded data.

3. Keypunch data and sight-check cards.

Keypunch data and sight-check cards.

4. Create card-image file.

Create card-image files for different types of data.

5. Initial data cleaning:
 – ensure that each case has proper firm ID & n of records.
 – check variable ranges & correct errors (in names & statuses).

Data cleaning:
 – ensure that each case has proper firm ID & n of records.
 – check variable ranges & correct errors.

6. Create file having 1 long record with a unique combination of firm and personal IDs for each case. Total n of cases = 25737. Check number of cases for each firm.

Merge corrected card-image files into a master file of firm characteristics, under the Statistical Analysis System.

7. Sort cases by first 6 characters of last name and first and middle initials. Group identical cases by this criterion and print out their IDs, names and positions, 1946–1977.

8. Cross-check these data against archival sources on the positions held by prominent Canadians, 1946–1977, ensuring that apparent interlocks actually existed and that each unique person

9. Correct file, modifying 9?? names, and deleting 1?? cases. Assign person IDs to each unique person according to updated name data.

10. Sort correct file by firm ID; output n of directors, n of executives, and n of missing cases for each year 1946–77. Check these values; flag unusual fluctuations in board size or n of executives.

11. Check firms showing fluctuations in board or executive size against *Directory of Directors* information; code appropriate revisions.

12. Correct file, modifying 204, adding 29, and deleting 1 case, yielding a file of 25,613 cases.

13. Create file of all combinations of firm memberships for each unique person—interlocks and personnel flows.

14. Create file of pairs of firms ever interlocked, i.e., having at least one unique person in common in at least one year. Each case gives ID of the two firms and the number of shared persons (directors and executives) in each year, 1946–1977.

15. Check for spurious interlocks between firms prohibited from interlocking (e.g., banks and trust companies, 1968ff). Correct the one case so identified, in files described in 12, 13 and 14 above.

16. Merge interlock file with select firm data (e.g., status vis-a-vis each "Top 100", industrial sector and country of control) for pairs of firms ever interlocked.

Rank firm by assets in the relevant selection years and create variables indicating each firm's status vis-a-vis each "Top 100".

tary cross-checking. Movement, for instance, from a high-status position with one firm to a lower status in another, or simultaneous occupancy of both positions, would raise suspicions concerning the validity of the interlock. (4) Whenever the first six characters of the surname did not yield unique groupings of names (such as J. S. Williams, J. S. Williamson) the middle initials of some of the grouped cases were altered to effect a unique identification of individuals.

The following methods were used in uncovering masked interlocks, that is, the listing of a single person under two or more names: (1) Questionable (unpronounceable) spellings of surnames were flagged, and these cases were checked against the documentary sources. Surnames having prefixes (such as De Grandpre) were also checked to ensure consistency in spelling within the file of directors and executives. (2) Cases having identical surnames and first initials but differing in that one had a middle initial while the other did not (for example, J. S. Smith, J. Smith) were cross-checked against the documentary sources. Whenever the sources confirmed that both names referred to the same individual, the proper middle initial was added to the case in which it had been missing. (3) Thirty-seven names containing honorific titles instead of given or family names (such as Lord, Viscount, Earl) were checked against standard biographical sources[11] to determine given and family names, and these latter names were then cross-checked against the same names in the file. This procedure resulted in very few unmasked interlocks, however. It would appear that the Canadian bourgeoisie is not especially dominated by British nobility.

These rules of thumb resulted in 942 name alterations in the file of directors and executives. The updated file was then checked for cases with identical names and company identification numbers, indicating a probable miscoding of one person as two. Again, the archival sources were consulted (principally, the *Directory of Directors*) to establish a correct coding of the person's career for each case. As a result, 171 revisions in career information were made, 10 names were revised, and 153 cases were deleted. In all, then, the detailed checking and cross-checking of directorship/executive data in step 8 produced over 1,000 revisions and 153 deletions.

The updated file was then cross-checked in another way. For each firm, the total number of directors and the total number of executives were computed in each year of the study. These values were compared for consistency over time, and firms showing odd fluctuations in board or executive size were cross-checked against listings of directors and executives principally found in the Financial Post *Directory of Directors* (second section, 1959ff). This procedure was adopted after the discovery of an erroneous decrease over time in the board size of one firm. It gave rise to the modifications mentioned in step 12 of Figure A1, which finally yielded a clean file of 25,613 names and corporate positions.

Next, a file of all combinations of firm memberships for each unique name was created. Each record in this file consisted of the identification numbers of the two firms, a number identifying the person holding memberships in both firms, and that person's yearly status in each firm. From this data structure it was a simple matter to aggregate over cases having the same identification numbers for both firms, whenever positions in both firms were concurrently held. In this way a file was created (step 14) whose cases were pairs of firms interlocked at some time, and whose variables were the identification numbers for the firms and the number of shared directors and executives in each year. After executing one final validity check on the resulting interlocks (step 15), variables from the file of corporation characteristics were merged with the interlock file to enable systematic analysis of interlock patterns over time.

APPENDIX 2

SOURCES OF DATA ON DOMESTIC AND FOREIGN OWNERSHIP AND CONTROL

A. STUDIES LISTING COUNTRY OF CONTROL FOR MAJOR CANADIAN CORPORATIONS (IN CHRONOLOGICAL ORDER)

MacGilchrist (1948). A survey of forty-five manufacturing industries in the 1940's. Companies of any size are listed and categorized according to financial control (domestic or foreign). Criteria of control are not specified, but a variety of business publications appear to have been consulted.

Brecher and Reisman (1957). A study of country of control for the six leading firms in twenty industries, circa 1954. Criteria of control are not specified.

Park and Park (1973 [1962]). Table II lists U.S. controlled companies by the Canadian banks with which their directorates interlock, circa 1958. The text contains numerous indications of the locus of controlling interest in major Canadian firms. Criteria of control are not specified.

Porter (1965). Table 15 lists ownership and control of Canadian corporations with assets over $100 million in 1960. Details as to the proportion of shares held by specific interests are given, along with a general assessment of the extent of Canadian participation in each firm. Criteria of control are indicated: private ownership and control, control by majority ownership, with small Canadian participation relative to size, minority control through ownership of an important minority block of stock, apparent management control, unclassifiable because of insufficient data.

Clement (1975). Appendix VII gives country of control, proportion of stock held, and identifies control centre, where possible, for dominant Canadian corporations of 1971. Criteria employed are those adopted by CALURA (Canada, 1975).

Niosi (1978). Tables II and III list 136 domestically-controlled companies with assets over $108 million in 1975, identifying the interests holding the largest bloc of stock and the proportion of all stock so held. Based on data from the Ontario and Quebec Securities Commissions *Bulletins*. Criteria of control are semi-absolute (80 per cent of stock or more), majority (50 per cent – 79 per cent), minority (5 per cent – 49 per cent), and managerial (less than 5 per cent).

B. RECURRENT PUBLICATIONS

Financial Post Corporation Service (various years). Frequently updated information cards detailing the history of each Canadian company, including its capitalization. Cards issued in the 1940's, 1950's, 1960's and early 1970's often identified the largest known shareholder, though not necessarily the proportion of stock held. These cards were an important source of yearly data in the early postwar years.

Intercorporate Ownership 1965, 1967, 1969, 1972, 1975 (Statistics Canada)
    An occasional publication which reports the proportions of stock held by other corporations, both domestic and foreign. Only holdings representing 10 per cent or more of issued equity are mentioned, and certain firms are excluded because they are exempt from filing CALURA returns. The 1972 and 1975 editions attribute country of control explicitly to each corporation listed.

Who Owns Whom International Subsidiaries of U.S. Companies (London: O. W. Roskill and Company (Reports) Limited. Various Years beginning in 1972).
    In the Canadian section the U.S. parent of each Canadian subsidiary is identified but no details on the percentage shareownership are provided.

Financial Post Survey of Industrials, Survey of Mines, Survey of Energy Resources.
    Indications of control centres for Canadian firms are often given in these annual reference manuals.

Moody's Industrials, Financials, Public Utilities, Railways.
    As above.

The Financial Post 300 (Summer 1978).
    Indicates for each firm the proportion of stock held outside of Canada, and in many cases identifies the exact locus of controlling interest.

The Canadian Business Top 400 (July 1978). Gives major shareholder percent of stock held and country of residences for each firm.

Articles in *Financial Post* and *Canadian Business* on foreign and domestic control: such as, *Financial Post*, 23 April 1973, 4.

APPENDIX 3

CORPORATIONS IN THE "TOP 100." 1946–1976

Name	Year Established	Year Defunct	Survivorship	STATUS 1946	1951	1956	1961	1966	1971	1976
ABITIBI PAPER COMPANY LTD.	1914	1977	TOP	INDUS	INDUS	INDUS	INDUS	INDUS	INDUS	INDUS
ALCAN ALUMINIUM LTD - ALCAN ALUMINIUM LTE	1928	1977	TOP	INDUS	INDUS	INDUS	INDUS	INDUS	INDUS	INDUS
ALGOMA CENTRAL RAILWAY	1899	1977	EXTANT	INDUS	INDUS	--	--	--	--	INDUS
AMOCO CANADA PETROLEUM COMPANY LTD.	1969	1977	NEW	--	--	--	--	--	INDUS	INDUS
ANGLO-CANADIAN PULP AND PAPER MILLS LIMITED	1924	1975	DEFUNCT	--	INDUS	INDUS	INDUS	INDUS	INDUS	--
ANGLO-CANADIAN TELEPHONE COMPANY	1934	1977	TOP	INVEST	INVEST	INVEST	INVEST	INVEST	INVEST	INVEST
ANGLO-NEWFOUNDLAND DEVELOPMENT CO. LTD.	1933	1977	EXTANT	--	INDUS	INDUS	--	--	--	--
ARGUS CORPORATION LIMITED	1963	1977	NEW	--	--	--	INVEST	INVEST	INVEST	INVEST
BANK OF MONTREAL	1945	1977	TOP	FINAN	FINAN	FINAN	FINAN	FINAN	FINAN	FINAN
BANQUE CANADIENNE NATIONALE	1873	1977	TOP	FINAN	FINAN	FINAN	FINAN	FINAN	FINAN	FINAN
BARCELONA TRACTION, LIGHT & POWER CO. LTD	1911	1948	DEFUNCT	INDUS	--	--	--	--	--	--
BATHURST PAPER LTD-LES PAPETERIES BATHURST	1948	1977	DEFUNCT	--	INDUS	INDUS	INDUS	INDUS	--	--
BELL CANADA	1880	1977	TOP	INDUS	INDUS	INDUS	INDUS	INDUS	INDUS	INDUS
BOWATER CANADIAN LIMITED	1952	1977	NEW	--	--	INDUS	INDUS	INDUS	INDUS	INDUS
BOWATER'S NEWFOUNDLAND PULP AND PAPER MILLS LIMITED	1938	1977	EXTANT	INDUS	INDUS	INDUS	INDUS	INDUS	--	--
BRASCAN LIMITED	1971	1977	NEW	--	--	--	--	--	INVEST	INVEST
BRITISH COLUMBIA FOREST PRODUCTS LIMITED	1912	1977	NEW	--	--	--	INDUS	INDUS	INDUS	INDUS
BRITISH COLUMBIA POWER CORPORATION LIMITED	1928	1961	DEFUNCT	INDUS	INDUS	INDUS	INDUS	--	--	--
BRITISH COLUMBIA TELEPHONE COMPANY	1916	1977	EXTANT	INDUS	INDUS	INDUS	INDUS	INDUS	INDUS	INDUS
BURNS FOODS LIMITED	1928	1977	EXTANT	INDUS	INDUS	INDUS	INDUS	INDUS	INDUS	INDUS
CADILLAC DEVELOPMENT CORPORATION LIMITED	1964	1974	NEW	--	--	--	--	--	PROP	PRCP
CALGARY POWER LTD.	1909	1977	TOP	INDUS	INDUS	INDUS	INDUS	INDUS	INDUS	INDUS
CAMPEAU CORPORATION	1968	1977	NEW	--	--	--	--	--	PROP	PRCP
CANADA CEMENT LAFARGE LTD.	1927	1977	TOP	INDUS	INDUS	INDUS	INDUS	INDUS	INDUS	INDUS
CANADA LIFE ASSURANCE CO.	1849	1977	EXTANT	FINAN	FINAN	FINAN	FINAN	FINAN	FINAN	FINAN
CANADA PERMANENT MORTGAGE CORPORATION	1927	1977	EXTANT	FINAN	INDUS	FINAN	FINAN	FINAN	FINAN	FINAN
CANADA PERMANENT TRUST COMPANY, 2	1961	1977	NEW	--	--	--	--	--	--	--
CANADA SAFEWAY LIMITED	1929	1977	EXTANT	INDUS	--	COMMER	COMMER	COMMER	COMMER	COMMER
CANADA STEAMSHIP LINES, LIMITED	1913	1977	EXTANT	INDUS	INDUS	INDUS	INDUS	--	--	--
CANADA TRUSTCO MORTGAGE COMPANY	1864	1977	NEW	--	--	--	--	--	FINAN	FINAN
CANADIAN CABLESYSTEMS LIMITED	1920	1977	EXTANT	INDUS	INDUS	INDUS	INDUS	INDUS	INDUS	INDUS
CANADIAN CANNERS, LTD.	1903	1977	EXTANT	INDUS	INDUS	INDUS	INDUS	INDUS	INDUS	INDUS
CANADIAN CAR & FOUNDRY COMPANY LTD.	1909	1962	DEFUNCT	INDUS	INDUS	INDUS	INDUS	--	--	--
CANADIAN CELANESE LIMITED	1926	1977	EXTANT	--	--	INDUS	INDUS	INDUS	INDUS	INDUS
CANADIAN GENERAL ELECTRIC COMPANY LTD.	1951	1977	DEFUNCT	INDUS	INDUS	INDUS	INDUS	INDUS	INDUS	INDUS
CANADIAN CHEMICAL & CELLULOSE COMPANY LIMITED	1930	1977	TOP	INDUS	INDUS	INDUS	INDUS	INDUS	INDUS	INDUS
CANADIAN GENERAL INVESTMENTS LIMITED	1932	1977	TOP	INVEST	INVEST	INVEST	INVEST	INVEST	INVEST	INVEST
CANADIAN IMPERIAL BANK OF COMMERCE	1961	1977	TOP	--	--	--	COMMER	COMMER	COMMER	COMMER
CANADIAN INDUSTRIES LIMITED. 1	1910	1953	DEFUNCT	INDUS	INDUS	--	--	--	--	--
CANADIAN INDUSTRIES LIMITED. 2	1954	1977	TOP	--	--	INDUS	INDUS	INDUS	INDUS	INDUS
CANADIAN INTERNATIONAL PAPER COMPANY	1916	1977	TOP	INDUS	INDUS	INDUS	INDUS	INDUS	INDUS	INDUS
CANADIAN INTERNATIONAL POWER COMPANY LIMITED	1956	1977	NEW	--	INVEST	INDUS	INDUS	INDUS	INDUS	INDUS
CANADIAN OIL COMPANIES LTD.	1908	1962	DEFUNCT	INDUS	INDUS	INDUS	INDUS	--	--	--
CANADIAN PACIFIC INVESTMENTS LIMITED	1962	1977	NEW	--	--	--	--	INVEST	INVEST	INVEST
CANADIAN REYNOLDS METALS COMPANY, LIMITED	1955	1977	NEW	INDUS	INDUS	INDUS	INDUS	INDUS	INDUS	INDUS

CORPORATIONS IN THE "TOP 100," 1946–1976

Name	Year Established	Year Defunct	Survivorship	1946	1951	1956	1961	1966	1971	1976
CANADIAN TIRE CORPORATION, LIMITED	1927	1977	EXTANT	--	--	--	--	--	INDUS	COMMER
CANADIAN UTILITIES LIMITED	1927	1977	EXTANT	--	INDUS	INDUS	INDUS	--	INDUS	INDUS
CARLING O'KEEFE LTD - CARLING O'KEEFF LTE	1930	1977	NEW	--	INDUS	INDUS	INDUS	INDUS	INDUS	--
CELANESE CANADA LIMITED	1963	1977	TOP	--	--	--	INDUS	INDUS	INDUS	--
CHRYSLER CANADA LTD	1925	1977	TOP	--	--	--	--	--	--	INDUS
CHURCHILL FALLS (LABRADOR) CORP LTD	1958	1972	DEFUNCT	--	--	--	--	--	INDUS	--
COLUMBIAN CELLULOSE COMPANY, LIMITED	1946	1977	TOP	--	--	--	--	INDUS	FINAN	--
COMINCO LTD.	1906	1977	TOP	--	--	--	--	--	--	INDUS
CONFEDERATION LIFE INSURANCE COMPANY	1930	1977	EXTANT	FINAN	FINAN	FINAN	FINAN	FINAN	FINAN	FINAN
CONSOLIDATED INTERNATIONAL LTD.	1871	1977	TOP	INDUS	INDUS	INDUS	INDUS	INDUS	INDUS	--
CONSOLIDATED-PAPER CORPORATION LIMITED	1931	1966	DEFUNCT	FINAN	FINAN	FINAN	INDUS	--	--	--
CONSOLIDATED-BATHURST LIMITED	1966	1977	NEW	INDUS	INDUS	INDUS	INDUS	INDUS	FINAN	INDUS
CROWN LIFE INSURANCE COMPANY	1900	1977	EXTANT	FINAN	INDUS	FINAN	FINAN	INDUS	FINAN	INDUS
CROWN ZELLERBACH CANADA LIMITED	1914	1977	EXTANT	INDUS	INDUS	INDUS	INDUS	INDUS	INDUS	INDUS
DOME PETROLEUM LIMITED	1950	1977	NEW	--	INDUS	INDUS	INDUS	INDUS	INDUS	INDUS
DOMINION BRIDGE COMPANY, LIMITED	1912	1977	EXTANT	INDUS	INDUS	INDUS	INDUS	INDUS	INDUS	INDUS
DOMINION FOUNDRIES AND STEEL LIMITED	1917	1977	EXTANT	INDUS	INDUS	INDUS	COMMER	COMMER	COMMER	INDUS
DOMINION STORES LIMITED	1918	1977	EXTANT	INDUS	INDUS	COMMER	COMMER	COMMER	COMMER	INDUS
DOMINION STORES LTD./UPERMARCHES DOMINION	1919	1977	DEFUNCT	--	INDUS	INDUS	INDUS	INDUS	INDUS	INDUS
DOMINION TEXTILE LIMITED	1922	1977	EXTANT	INDUS	INDUS	INDUS	INDUS	INDUS	INDUS	INDUS
DOMTAR INC.	1929	1977	EXTANT	--	--	--	--	--	INDUS	INDUS
DOW CHEMICAL OF CANADA LIMITED	1942	1977	NEW	--	--	INDUS	INDUS	INDUS	INDUS	INDUS
DUPONT OF CANADA LTD - DUPONT DU CANADA LTE	1954	1977	NEW	INDUS	INDUS	INDUS	INDUS	COMMER	COMMER	COMMER
EDDY PAPER COMPANY LIMITED	1946	1977	EXTANT	INDUS	INDUS	INDUS	INDUS	INDUS	INDUS	INDUS
F.W. WOOLWORTH CO. LIMITED	1907	1977	EXTANT	INDUS	INDUS	INDUS	INDUS	INDUS	INDUS	INDUS
FALCONBRIDGE NICKEL MINES LIMITED	1928	1977	EXTANT	--	INDUS	INDUS	INDUS	FINAN	FINAN	FINAN
FORD MOTOR COMPANY OF CANADA, LIMITED	1911	1977	EXTANT	INDUS	INDUS	INDUS	INDUS	INDUS	INDUS	INDUS
FRASER COMPANIES, LIMITED	1917	1977	EXTANT	INDUS	INDUS	INDUS	INDUS	INDUS	INDUS	INDUS
GAMBLES CANADA LIMITED	1926	1961	DEFUNCT	INDUS	INDUS	INDUS	INDUS	--	--	--
GATINEAU POWER COMPANY	1926	1977	NEW	INDUS	--	--	COMMER	--	--	--
GEN. METROPOLITAIN, INC.	1955	1977	NEW	--	--	INDUS	INDUS	INDUS	INDUS	INDUS
GEN. MOTORS ACCEPTANCE CORP. OF CANADA LTD.	1918	1977	TOP	INDUS	INVEST	FINAN	FINAN	FINAN	FINAN	FINAN
GENERAL MOTORS OF CANADA LIMITED	1951	1977	NEW	INDUS	INVEST	INVEST	INVEST	INDUS	INDUS	INDUS
GENSTAR LTD	1928	1977	EXTANT	INDUS	INDUS	INDUS	INDUS	INDUS	INDUS	INDUS
GEORGE WESTON LIMITED	1810	1977	EXTANT	FINAN	FINAN	FINAN	FINAN	FINAN	FINAN	FINAN
GOODYEAR CANADA INC.	1910	1977	TOP	INDUS	INDUS	INDUS	INDUS	INDUS	INDUS	INDUS
GREAT-WEST LIFE ASSURANCE COMPANY	1906	1977	EXTANT	INDUS	INDUS	INDUS	INDUS	INDUS	INDUS	INDUS
GULF CANADA LIMITED	1945	1977	EXTANT	INDUS	INDUS	INDUS	INDUS	INDUS	INDUS	INDUS
HAWKER SIDDELEY CANADA LTD.	1926	1977	EXTANT	INDUS	INDUS	INDUS	INDUS	INDUS	INDUS	INDUS
HIRAM WALKER-GOODERHAM & WORTS LIMITED	1926	1977	EXTANT	INDUS	INDUS	INDUS	INDUS	INDUS	INDUS	INDUS
HOLLINGER MINES LIMITED	1929	1971	DEFUNCT	INDUS	INDUS	INDUS	INDUS	INDUS	INDUS	--
HOME OIL COMPANY LIMITED	1928	1977	EXTANT	INDUS	INDUS	INDUS	INDUS	INDUS	COMMER	COMMER
HOWARD SMITH PAPER MILLS LIMITED	1927	1961	TOP	COMMER	INDUS	COMMER	COMMER	--	--	--
HUDSON BAY MINING AND SMELTING CO., LIMITED	1670	1977	EXTANT	INDUS	COMMER	INDUS	INDUS	INDUS	INDUS	INDUS
HUDSON'S BAY COMPANY	1926	1977	EXTANT	--	--	--	--	--	COMMER	COMMER
HUDSON'S BAY OIL AND GAS COMPANY LIMITED	1947	1977	NEW	--	--	INDUS	COMMER	COMMER	INDUS	INDUS
IAC LIMITED	1925	1977	EXTANT	FINAN	FINAN	FINAN	FINAN	FINAN	FINAN	INDUS
IBM CANADA LIMITED - IBM CANADA LIMITEE	1912	1977	EXTANT	INDUS	INDUS	INDUS	INDUS	INDUS	INDUS	INDUS
IMASCO LIMITED	1875	1977	DEFUNCT	FINAN	FINAN	FINAN	FINAN	FINAN	FINAN	INDUS
IMPERIAL BANK OF CANADA	1880	1961	TOP	INDUS	INDUS	INDUS	INDUS	--	--	--
IMPERIAL OIL LIMITED	1916	1977	EXTANT	INDUS	INDUS	INDUS	INDUS	INDUS	INDUS	INDUS
INCO LIMITED	1903	1977	EXTANT	INDUS	INDUS	INDUS	INDUS	INDUS	INDUS	INDUS
INTERNATIONAL HARVESTER CO. OF CANADA, LTD.	1920	1976	EXTANT	INDUS	INDUS	INDUS	INDUS	INDUS	INDUS	INDUS
INTERNATIONAL PETROLEUM CO., LTD.	1920	1976	DEFUNCT	INDUS	INDUS	INDUS	INDUS	INDUS	INDUS	--
INTERNATIONAL POWER COMPANY LIMITED	1926	1977	EXTANT	INDUS	INDUS	INDUS	INDUS	INDUS	INDUS	INDUS

CORPORATIONS IN THE "TOP 100." 1946–1976

Name	Year Established	Year Defunct	Survivorship	1946	1951	1956	1961	1966	1971	1976
INTERNATIONAL UTILITIES CORPORATION	1960	1970	NEW	---	INDUS	INDUS	INVEST	INVEST	INVEST	INDUS
INTERPROVINCIAL PIPE LINE LIMITED	1949	1977	NEW	---	INDUS	INDUS	INDUS	INDUS	INDUS	INDUS
IRON ORE COMPANY OF CANADA	1957	1977	EXTANT	---	---	---	INDUS	INDUS	---	INDUS
ITT CANADA LIMITED	1926	1977	EXTANT	---	---	---	---	---	---	INDUS
JOHN LABATT LIMITED	1930	1977	EXTANT	FINAN	FINAN	FINAN	FINAN	INDUS	INDUS	FINAN
LA BANQUE PROVINCIALE DU CANADA	1861	1977	TOP	FINAN	FINAN	FINAN	FINAN	COMMER	COMMER	COMMER
LOBLAW COMPANIES LIMITED	1921	1977	TOP	INDUS	INDUS	INDUS	INDUS	FINAN	FINAN	FINAN
LONDON LIFE INSURANCE COMPANY	1874	1977	EXTANT	---	---	---	---	---	---	---
MACLAREN POWER & PAPER COMPANY	1930	1958	DEFUNCT	FINAN	FINAN	INDUS	INDUS	INDUS	---	---
MACMILLAN & BLOEDEL LIMITED	1959	1977	NEW	INDUS	INDUS	INDUS	INDUS	INDUS	INDUS	INDUS
MACMILLAN BLOEDEL LIMITED	1887	1977	TOP	FINAN	FINAN	FINAN	FINAN	FINAN	FINAN	FINAN
MANUFACTURERS LIFE INSURANCE COMPANY	1863	1977	NEW	INDUS	INDUS	INDUS	INDUS	INDUS	---	PROP
MARATHON REALTY COMPANY LIMITED	1911	1977	EXTANT	INDUS	INDUS	INDUS	INDUS	INDUS	INDUS	INDUS
MASSEY-FERGUSON LIMITED	1911	1977	DEFUNCT	---	---	---	---	---	---	---
MCINTYRE MINES LIMITED	1964	1977	EXTANT	---	---	---	---	---	---	---
MINNESOTA AND ONTARIO PAPER COMPANY	1944	1950	DEFUNCT	INDUS	INDUS	---	INDUS	INDUS	INDUS	INDUS
MOBIL OIL CANADA LIMITED	1911	1977	TOP	FINAN	FINAN	FINAN	FINAN	FINAN	FINAN	FINAN
MONTREAL TRAMWAYS COMPANY	1895	1977	TOP	FINAN	FINAN	FINAN	INDUS	INDUS	INDUS	INDUS
MONTREAL TRUST COMPANY	1868	1977	TOP	FINAN	FINAN	FINAN	FINAN	FINAN	FINAN	FINAN
MOORE CORPORATION LIMITED - CORP. MOORE LTEE	1883	1977	TOP	INDUS	INDUS	INDUS	INDUS	INDUS	INDUS	INDUS
MUTUAL LIFE ASSURANCE COMPANY OF CANADA	1926	1977	EXTANT	FINAN	FINAN	FINAN	FINAN	FINAN	FINAN	INDUS
NATIONAL TRUST COMPANY, LIMITED	1879	1977	EXTANT	INDUS	INDUS	---	INDUS	INDUS	INDUS	INDUS
NORCEN ENERGY RESOURCES LIMITED	1954	1975	NEW	---	---	---	---	---	FINAN	INDUS
NORTH AMERICAN LIFE ASSURANCE COMPANY	1911	1977	TOP	INDUS	INDUS	INDUS	INDUS	INDUS	INDUS	PROP
NORTHERN AND CENTRAL GAS CORPORATION LIMITED	1967	1977	EXTANT	---	---	---	INDUS	INDUS	INDUS	PROP
NORTHERN TELECOM LIMITED	1957	1977	NEW	---	---	---	INDUS	INDUS	INDUS	INDUS
OXFORD DEVELOPMENT GROUP LTD.	1953	1958	DEFUNCT	INVEST	INVEST	INVEST	INVEST	INVEST	INVEST	INVEST
PACIFIC PETROLEUMS LTD.	1911	1962	DEFUNCT	INDUS	INDUS	---	---	---	---	---
PANCANADIAN PETROLEUM LIMITED	1925	1977	NEW	---	---	---	---	---	---	---
PETROFINA CANADA LTD. - PETROFINA CANADA LTE	1925	1977	NEW	---	---	---	---	---	INDUS	INDUS
PETROFINA CANADA LTD.	1930	1977	DEFUNCT	INDUS	INDUS	INDUS	INDUS	INDUS	INDUS	INDUS
POWER CORPORATION OF CANADA, LIMITED	1961	1977	EXTANT	---	---	INDUS	INDUS	INVEST	INVEST	INVEST
QUEBEC CORPORATION CANADA LTD	1956	1977	NEW	---	---	---	---	---	---	---
RAYONIER CANADA LTD	1924	1977	NEW	---	---	---	---	---	---	---
REDPATH INDUSTRIES LIMITED	1931	1970	DEFUNCT	INDUS	---	---	---	---	---	INDUS
REED PAPER LTD	1957	1977	EXTANT	---	COMMER	COMMER	COMMER	COMMER	COMMER	INDUS
RIO ALGOM LIMITED	1929	1977	EXTANT	---	---	INDUS	INDUS	INDUS	INDUS	INDUS
ROTHMANS OF PALL MALL CANADA LIMITED	1913	1977	NEW	---	---	INDUS	INDUS	INDUS	---	INDUS
SAGUENAY POWER COMPANY, LTD.	1939	1977	DEFUNCT	---	INDUS	COMMER	COMMER	COMMER	COMMER	---
SHELL CANADA LIMITED	1930	1962	EXTANT	COMMER	COMMER	COMMER	INDUS	INDUS	COMMER	INDUS
SIMPSONS-SEARS LIMITED	1930	1977	EXTANT	---	INDUS	INDUS	INDUS	COMMER	COMMER	INDUS
SIMPSONS, LIMITED	1865	1977	TOP	FINAN	FINAN	PROP	PROP	COMMER	COMMER	COMMER
SOUTHERN CANADA POWER COMPANY LIMITED	1923	1977	EXTANT	PROP	PROP	PROP	PROP	INDUS	INDUS	INDUS
ST. LAWRENCE CORPORATION LIMITED	1929	1977	EXTANT	INDUS	INDUS	INDUS	INDUS	COMMER	INDUS	INDUS
STEEP ROCK IRON MINES LIMITED	1927	1977	NEW	INDUS	INDUS	INDUS	INDUS	INDUS	INDUS	INDUS
STEINBERG INC.	1934	1977	NEW	---	---	INDUS	INDUS	INDUS	INDUS	INDUS
SUN LIFE ASSURANCE CO. OF CANADA	1832	1977	TOP	FINAN	FINAN	FINAN	FINAN	FINAN	FINAN	FINAN

CORPORATIONS IN THE "TOP 100," 1946–1976

Name	Year Established	Year Defunct	Survivorship	STATUS 1946	1951	1956	1961	1966	1971	1976
THE BANK OF TORONTO	1855	1954	DEFUNCT	FINAN	FINAN	---	---	---	---	PROP
THE CADILLAC FAIRVIEW CORPORATION LIMITED	1974	1977	NEW	---	---	---	---	---	FINAN	FINAN
THE CANADA TRUST CO.	1899	1967	DEFUNCT	FINAN	FINAN	FINAN	---	---	---	---
THE CANADIAN BANK OF COMMERCE	1867	1954	EXTANT	FINAN	FINAN	FINAN	---	---	---	---
THE CONSUMERS' GAS COMPANY	1848	1969	DEFUNCT	FINAN	FINAN	INDUS	INDUS	INDUS	INDUS	INDUS
THE DOMINION BANK	1869	1955	TOP	INVEST	FINAN	INVEST	INVEST	INVEST	INVEST	INVEST
THE INVESTORS GROUP	1940	1977	NEW	---	---	---	---	---	---	FINAN
THE MERCANTILE BANK OF CANADA	1953	1959	DEFUNCT	---	INDUS	INDUS	---	---	---	---
THE MEXICAN LIGHT & POWER COMPANY, LIMITED	1902	1966	EXTANT	INDUS	INDUS	---	---	---	---	---
THE MINING CORPORATION OF CANADA, LIMITED	1916	1977	NEW	---	---	---	---	---	---	---
THE MOLSON COMPANIES LIMITED	1930	1977	TOP	INDUS	INDUS	INDUS	INDUS	INDUS	INDUS	INDUS
THE OSHAWA GROUP LIMITED	1957	1977	TOP	FINAN	INDUS	COMMER	COMMER	COMMER	COMMER	COMMER
THE PRICE COMPANY LIMITED	1920	1977	TOP	INDUS	FINAN	FINAN	FINAN	FINAN	FINAN	FINAN
THE ROYAL BANK OF CANADA	1862	1977	TOP	FINAN	FINAN	FINAN	FINAN	FINAN	FINAN	FINAN
THE ROYAL TRUST COMPANY	1899	1977	TOP	INDUS	INDUS	INDUS	INDUS	INDUS	FINAN	FINAN
THE SEAGRAM COMPANY LTD. - LA CCMP. SEAGRAM	1928	1977	NEW	INDUS	INDUS	INDUS	INDUS	INDUS	INDUS	INDUS
THE SHAWINIGAN WATER AND POWER COMPANY	1898	1962	DEFUNCT	INDUS	INDUS	INDUS	COMMER	COMMER	COMMER	COMMER
THE STEEL COMPANY OF CANADA, LIMITED	1910	1977	TOP	COMMER	COMMER	COMMER	FINAN	FINAN	FINAN	FINAN
THE T. EATON CO., LIMITED	1891	1977	TOP	---	FINAN	FINAN	INDUS	INDUS	INDUS	INDUS
THE TORONTO-DOMINION BANK	1955	1977	NEW	---	---	FINAN	FINAN	FINAN	FINAN	COMMER
TRADERS GROUP LTD. - LE GROUPE TRADERS LTD.	1920	1977	EXTANT	---	---	---	FINAN	FINAN	FINAN	FINAN
TRANS MOUNTAIN PIPE LINE COMPANY LTD.	1951	1977	NEW	---	INDUS	INDUS	INDUS	INDUS	INDUS	INDUS
TRANSCANADA PIPELINES LIMITED	1951	1977	NEW	---	---	INDUS	PROP	PROP	PROP	PROP
TRIZEC CORPORATION LTD.	1960	1977	NEW	---	---	---	INDUS	INDUS	INDUS	INDUS
UNION CARBIDE CANADA LIMITED	1911	1977	EXTANT	INDUS	INDUS	INDUS	INDUS	INDUS	INDUS	INDUS
UNITED GRAIN GROWERS LIMITED	1911	1977	EXTANT	INDUS	INDUS	INDUS	---	---	---	---
VENTURES LIMITED	1928	1961	DEFUNCT	INVEST	INVEST	INVEST	INDUS	INDUS	INDUS	INDUS
WESTCOAST TRANSMISSION COMPANY LIMITED	1949	1977	NEW	---	---	---	COMMER	---	---	COMMER
WESTFAIR FOODS LTD.	1912	1977	EXTANT	INDUS	INDUS	COMMER	COMMER	---	---	---
WESTINGHOUSE CANADA LTD-WESTINGHOUSE CANADA	1903	1977	EXTANT	INDUS	INDUS	INDUS	INDUS	INDUS	INDUS	INDUS
WINNIPEG ELECTRIC CO.	1892	1952	DEFUNCT	INDUS	INDUS	---	---	---	---	---
WOODWARD STORES LIMITED	1947	1977	NEW	---	---	COMMER	COMMER	COMMER	---	---

NOTES

NOTES TO CHAPTER ONE

1. Among those who have explicitly applied Frank's dependency model to Canadian capitalism are Davis (1971), Watkins (1973), Clement (1977), and Marchak (1979).

NOTES TO CHAPTER TWO

1. One response to this problem is to adapt the concept of dependency to the specific features of Canadian society, as a means of highlighting Canada's distinctiveness (Matthews 1983, 94; see also Drache 1983, 44). Such an approach marks a retreat from theory to description. The resulting historiography may be free of theoretical distortion, but the possibility of comprehending Canada in the context of world capitalist development is also lost.

NOTES TO CHAPTER THREE

1. "Monopoly capital" is used here not in the neoclassical sense of complete control of a market, but in the more general sense of vast concentrations of capital that account for large proportions of whole industries, thereby affording their owners and managers enormous social power (see for instance Baran and Sweezy 1966, 57–58; Mandel 1975, 311; Aglietta 1979, 305, 381–83). Although absolute monopolies such as the Hudson's Bay Company, Canadian Pacific Railway, and Bell Canada have figured importantly in the development of Canadian capitalism, the more typical case is the "oligopolistic" sharing of markets among several large firms (Niosi 1985a, 41–43). "Monopoly capital" does not imply unlimited latitude for capitalists to fix prices and output, thereby escaping the general equalization of the rate of profit (see Marx 1967 III, pp.173–99; Mandel 1975, 529–50; Aglietta 1979, 273–327). Even absolute monopolies within protected national economies are subject in the long run to forms of competition on the world market.
2. In this period, credit was restricted to a "commercial" form in which industrialists and merchants granted each other promissory notes in their commodity exchanges; that is, written promises to pay for bought goods by a certain date. Although "commercial credit" did promote accumulation by reducing the size of each capitalist's reserve fund (Marx 1967, III, p.482), its historical importance is limited by its purely "circulatory function" in the realization of commodity capital.
3. I employ this term in preference to Lenin's "financial oligarchy" since the latter tends to have unfortunate connotations of operational "bank control over industry" (see Fitch and Oppenheimer 1970 for an example of this sort of misinterpretation). Lenin's concepts of finance capital and financial oligarchy refer in general to the increased importance of financial considerations and motivations in the accumulation of large-scale capital (Dobb 1967). In the era of finance capital, even the major "industrialists" controlling large corporations typically attain and maintain their positions by concentrating large proportions of share capital, itself a form of financial capital and an integral aspect of the credit system (see for instance Sweezy 1970, 258).

248   CORPORATE POWER AND CANADIAN CAPITALISM

4. Namely Britain, France, Germany and the United States.
5. An instructive example is furnished by the case of Massey-Ferguson, whose ambitious expansion, prior to a dramatic drop in world demand for agricultural equipment, placed it in serious financial straights by 1980. In this situation of enormous debt and depressed revenues, Massey's major shareholder, Argus Corporation, yielded to its largest creditor, the Canadian Imperial Bank of Commerce, by giving its three million shares to Massey employee pension funds. Simultaneously, seven Argus directors resigned from Massey's board, while the CIBC took a fourth seat, giving the bank three of the seven positions on Massey's reconstituted executive committee (Toronto *Globe and Mail*, 11 October 1980, B16).
6. Roy defined finance capitalists as directors of industrial companies who also held bank directorships (see also Soref 1980).
7. The failure to distinguish between these forms of financial power has marred a number of analyses of advanced capitalism. Paul Sweezy (1953; 1970, 267–68), for instance, identifies the decline of investment bankers' *operational* power over corporations with the decline of finance capital. He is ultimately led to view the American economy as dominated by a collection of mangement-controlled, self-financing corporations (Baran and Sweezy 1966). Jorge Niosi (1978, 1981), in his study of Canadian capitalism, similarly equates finance capital with the operational power of banks to control the management of industrial corporations. By ignoring allocative financial power, this methodology unacceptably reduces finance capital from a construct within a theory of monopoly capital to a purely descriptive category in the study of corporate ownership and control.
8. The following account is necessarily quite schematic. For a careful analysis of the economic and political contradictions that led to a substantial severing of colonial ties to Britain in 1849 see Cuneo (1982).
9. These included the Eastern Township Bank, Molson's Bank, Niagara District Bank, and Bank of Toronto, which were all established in 1855 (Ryerson 1973, 271).
10. According to Nelles (1974, 234), by 1905, "A web of interlocking directorships...linked the Electrical Development Company directly with the Bank of Commerce, which arranged its banking, the National Trust, which took up some of its bonds, the Toronto Electric Light and Toronto Railway companies, Toronto General Trusts, Canadian General Electric, the Canadian Northern and the life insurance companies [Sun Life, Canada Life and Manufacturer's Life]....More often than not the individuals holding bonds and stock of the Electrical Development Company had also invested in Havana Traction, Sao Paulo Tramway, Mexican Heat, Light and Power, Rio de Janeiro Tramway, Dominion Lands and the maritime coal and steel companies."
11. Piedalue's selection procedure led him to retain in the analysis for each year all firms accounting for a substantial proportion of the total assets in four major industrial sectors. Since the study period was one of great industrial concentration and centralization, the number of dominant corporations changed over time from 82 in 1900 to 138 in 1930, and the number of mining and manufacturing firms jumped from 18 to 88 (Piedalue 1976, 13), making comparisons of the average number of interlocks per firm difficult.

NOTES TO CHAPTER FOUR

1. Details about the methods employed in sampling, measurement and data management are given in Appendix 1.
2. To simplify the analysis, Comstock is categorized hereafter with the dominant manufacturing firms.
3. There is, of course, no logical contradiction in the proliferation of small businesses

and simultaneous concentration of capital in the largest firms. Sweezy and Magdoff (1969) argue that the many small capitals that persist and even thrive in the era of monopoly capitalism aid the corporate giants in at least three ways: (1) each big corporation buys from smaller businesses thousands of items, many of which offer too little prospect of high profit to attract monopoly capital; (2) smaller businesses provide stable markets for the products of giant corporations, often counteracting seasonal or cyclical variation in demand; and (3) smaller firms carry out much of the innovating function, absolving corporate giants from the need to take big risks while ultimately providing them with the benefits of such risk-taking.

4. The "benchmarking" procedure employed in Figure 4.2 and discussed in Appendix 1 was not deemed appropriate for this detailed analysis. Instead, the six industrials missing financial data were excluded from the analysis in all years.

5. Current dollars were converted to constant dollars using the wholesale price index. This procedure yielded an anomolous result in 1951, because of the high rate of inflation in the 1946–51 years and the deflation immediately thereafter to 1954. These price trends are not fully reflected by the size of industrial assets, much of which are tied up in fixed capital at any given point; hence the finding in Table 4.1 that industrial assets (in 1976 dollars) declined between 1946 and 1951.

6. Both asset values are net of Canadian Pacific's majority-owned subsidiaries, namely Cominco in 1946 and Canadian Pacific Investments in 1976. In this sense, the slow growth of Canadian Pacific Limited is partly an artifact of our accounting method. However, even without the subtraction of its subsidiaries, Canadian Pacific's share of dominant industrial assets fell from 23 per cent in 1946 to nine per cent in 1976. See Appendix 1 for details on the methods of accounting used in this study.

7. The names and survivorship status of all firms in the sample are given in Appendix 3.

8. The predecessor firms were Consolidated Paper Corporation Limited and Bathurst Paper Limited, which merged in 1966, MacMillan and Bloedel Limited and Powell River Limited, which merged in 1959, Northern and Central Gas Limited and Canadian Industrial Gas and Oil Limited, which merged in 1976, and BP Oil and Gas Limited and Supertest Petroleum Corporation Limited, which were consolidated in 1971.

9. See *Moody's Public Utilities* 1948, 603.

10. For example: Manitoba Hydro's takeover of Winnipeg Electric Company; Hydro Quebec's takeover of Gatineau Power Company, Quebec Power Company Limited, and Shawinigan Water and Power Company; the nationalization of Dominion Steel and Coal Corporation by Sidbec (a Quebec crown corporation); and the takeover of Columbia Cellulose Company Limited and formation of Canadian Cellulose Company Limited under ownership of the Province of British Columbia. The last of these was privatized in 1978 with the formation of British Columbia Resource Investment Corporation, a firm in which the Province of British Columbia retained only a minority interest.

11. Niosi (1981, 91–117) provides an interesting analysis of Canadian crown corporations which emphasizes the role of class contradictions, uneven regional development, and the need to promote indigenous industrialization as interrelated factors in the development of state capitalism in Canada.

12. Namely, Canada Permanent Trust Company, Canadian Imperial Bank of Commerce, and the Toronto-Dominion Bank.

13. This firm, most of whose assets were located outside Canada, moved its head office to Toronto in 1960 to avoid having to pay witholding tax on the profits of its Canadian subsidiaries, but in 1971 it returned to the U.S. to take advantage of fiscal opportunities there.

14. It should be emphasized that these advances and declines refer to differential *rates*

of growth, not to absolute quantities of capital controlled. With the exception of the 1954 recession, capital in Canada accumulated at a robust rate throughout the period of study. Also note that the percentages in Table 4.7 differ somewhat from results reported in an earlier analysis (Carroll 1982) which did not remove "double counting" from the measurement of corporate assets. For an account of how this problem was handled in this study, see Appendix 1.

15. See Appendix 1 for an explanation of the benchmarking procedure.
16. Irving Oil has been categorized as an American takeover, although voting equity after 1973 was equally shared by the Irving family of New Brunswick and Standard Oil of California.
17. The control of this firm is also somewhat ambiguous. In the 1970's, the two major blocs of voting stock were equally divided between Canadian (Noranda) and U.S. (Mead Corporation) interests (Clement 1975, 432).
18. Acquisition of smaller firms has been a common practice among indigenous and foreign-controlled monopolies alike: "From 1945 to 1961, 639 foreign acquisitions took place in Canada of which almost 500 were acquisitions of firms previously controlled in Canada. These international mergers may be compared with a total of 1187 domestic mergers and a total population of domestic firms that grew from 27,000 in 1945 to over 100,000 in 1961" (Reuber and Roseman 1969, 3). In the same period, most takeovers were concentrated in a small set of acquiring firms. Ten per cent of all acquiring firms under foreign control (29 firms) made 37.5 per cent of all foreign acquisitions; 18 per cent of acquiring firms under domestic control (69 companies) made 57.4 per cent of all domestic acquisitions (ibid., 59).
19. Moreover, the Anglo-Newfoundland Development Company Limited was taken over by the Price Company in 1962. It therefore fell under Canadian control when Abitibi took over Price in 1975.
20. One of these eleven strayed from indigenous control between 1946 and 1976. Algoma Steel Corporation was controlled by West German interests from the late 1950's to the early 1970's, when Canadian Pacific Investments bought controlling interest.
21. The two exceptions were the U.S.-controlled Ford Motor Company of Canada and Falcolnbridge Nickel. The latter was purchased in 1985 from Mobil Corporation by Dome Mines, an indigenous company (*Financial Post*, 8 June 1985, 12).

NOTES TO CHAPTER FIVE

1. The three consistently dominant merchandizers are excluded from this analysis.
2. As mentioned earlier, the density is simply the ratio of the number of interlocks among a set of firms to the total number of possible interlocks. For a subnetwork of size n the number of possible ties is $n(n-1)/2$; for two subnetworks of sizes n and m, the number of possible ties between them is nm.
3. To improve the table's legibility, and because of the small number of firms involved, corporate survivorship is not tabulated for companies controlled outside of North America.
4. To simplify the analysis, the three subsectors of industrial capital have been collapsed into a general category for foreign-controlled firms. The rightmost column represents the residual of nonindustrial, foreign-controlled companies, which number no more than ten at any given time and participate in very few interlocks throughout.
5. It is likely that some of these interlocks are based on an intertwining of share capital. For example, at year end 1974, Canadian life insurance companies held a total of 10.8 per cent of the shares of the Toronto-Dominion Bank, 9.7 per cent of the shares of the Bank of Nova Scotia, 8.5 per cent of the shares of the Canadian Im-

perial Bank of Commerce, and 3.8 per cent of the shares of the Bank of Montreal. These holdings were in addition to ownership by life insurers of $9.0 billion in corporate bonds and $1.2 billion in corporate shares (*Financial Post*, 15 November 1975, 17).

NOTES TO CHAPTER SIX

1. The extant firms are another possible source of network stability, but in fact they participated in only four stable ties. T. Eaton Realty, dominant in 1946, maintained a stable multiple-director tie with its parent T. Eaton Company Limited; Dominion Bridge, also dominant in 1946, was multiply-interlocked with Montreal Trust in 1946, 1976, and in twenty-three of the intervening years; Hudson's Bay Oil and Gas maintained a multiple interlock with Hudson's Bay Company (a minority shareholder) throughout the thirty-one years but only ranked as dominant in the later period; Canada Trustco Mortgage maintained a multiple tie with its subsidiary, Canada Trust Company, but neither was dominant in 1946.
2. These considerations resulted in four additional stable interlocks. The strong tie between Consolidated Paper and the Bank of Montreal was maintained after the former's merger with Bathurst Paper in 1966; three strong ties linking the Canadian Bank of Commerce with Brascan Limited, Canada Life, and Argus Corporation were continued after the Commerce's merger in 1961 with the Imperial Bank of Canada.
3. The four companies absent from the 1930 network are Consolidated Paper, Inco, Northern Electric, and Mutual Life. Piedalue only includes interlocks of three or more shared directors in his sociograms, so the correspondences may be understated.
4. Carroll, Fox and Ornstein (1981) in researching the same Canadian corporate network, adopt a more stringent criterion in their attempt to partition the network into mutually exclusive cliques. As I have pointed out elsewhere (Carroll 1984, 257) the suitability of a clique-detection algorithm depends on the theoretical concept for which it provides operational specification. Since the concept of a capitalist interest group does not preclude alliances and overlapping memberships *between* interest groups, Alba's less stringent criterion was deemed better suited to this study.
5. Excluded from the clique structure in 1946 were three small groupings of firms completely detached from the dominant component, namely (1) Anglo-Canadian Telephone Company and its subsidiary, B.C. Telephone Company; (2) T. Eaton Company and its subsidiary, T. Eaton Realty; and (3) Calgary Power Company, International Power Company, and the Price Company. In 1976, two corporate dyads were detached from the dominant component: George Weston and its subsidiary Loblaws, and Imperial Oil and its subsidiary Interprovincial Pipelines. It is clear that in both years there were no intercorporate groupings of any size other than the cliques within the network's dominant component.
6. The level of significance in this and subsequent tests is .01.
7. The plots are derived from non-metric multidimensional scalings (Schiffman et al. 1981) of three proximity matrices whose entries indicated the degree of overlap in the social circles of each pair of firms; that is, the number of firms with which both companies were interlocked *divided by* the total number of companies with which either firm was interlocked (Alba and Kadushin 1976). The more two firms share multiple directors with the same companies, the closer they appear in the MDS space.
8. Kruskal's stress coefficient, a measure of the discrepancy between input proximities and output distances, is 0.102, indicating a reasonably close correspondence between the 1946 dominant component and its two-dimensional representation in

Figure 6.3. The squared Pearson correlation between input disparities and output distances is 0.946 (see Schiffman et al. 1981, 175).

9. Kruskal's stress coefficient for this two-dimensional mapping of the 1976 dominant is 0.147; the squared Pearson correlation between input disparities and output distances is 0.898.

10. It was necessary to depict the 1976 network in two diagrams because of the extensive overlapping of clique peripheries, which precludes visual representation of boundaries in a two dimensional space. Kruskal's stress coefficient for this mapping of the network of clique members is 0.108; the corresponding squared Pearson correlation is 0.945.

NOTES TO CHAPTER SEVEN

1. This observation does not deny the considerable numbers of foreign takeovers of smaller firms, companies that have also been the prey of Canadian monopolies (Reuber and Roseman 1969). As I shall argue in the conclusion, foreign takeovers of big corporations that have occurred since the Second World War (such as Shell's takeover of Canadian Oil Companies, Lafarge's takeover of Canada Cement, and Gulf's takeover of British-American Oil) seem more consistent with a general "internationalization of productive capital" than with a particular silent surrender to U.S. capital.

2. This interpretation can be extended as far back as the early 1900's, when U.S.-controlled capital was "predominant in the electrical and chemical industries and also those industries based on the internal combustion engine," the sectors closely associated with the second industrial revolution (Hutcheson 1978, 95), and thus with rapid accumulation throughout the twentieth century.

3. *Financial Post* 23 April 1973, 4.

4. Observing that a net reflux of American foreign investment from Europe and Canada began in the 1970's, De Brunhoff speculates that changes in the international value of the U.S. dollar may have precipitated these flows. Before the early 1970's, an overvalued dollar encouraged export of American capital, but since devaluation in 1971 and 1973, the export of U.S.-produced commodities has been favoured, and capital export has concomitantly declined. De Brunhoff suggests that these trends "should serve as a warning against extrapolations, and against the prevailing notion of the inviolability of American hegemony" (1978, 116).

5. The three companies were Dominion Steel and Coal Corp. Ltd. (taken over from Hawker-Siddeley by Quebec's Sidbec in 1968), Columbia Cellulose Company, Limited (taken over from Celanese Canada by British Columbia's Canadian Cellulose Company in 1973), and Churchill Falls (Labrador) Corp. Ltd. (taken over from Brinco by Hydro-Quebec and Newfoundland-Labrador Hydro in 1974). It should be noted that our analysis of the national control of large-scale capital has systematically underestimated indigenous control by focusing exclusively on private-sector corporations. Thus, while the nationalization of several electric utilities in the 1950's and 1960's contributed to an observed decline in domestic control of the *private sector*, these state takeovers did not increase foreign control of the economy. See Niosi 1981, 69–117 for an insightful analysis of state capitalism in Canada.

6. An enterprise is defined by Statistics Canada as a group of corporations under common control. The 25 leading enterprises of 1975, for instance, are made up of 603 corporations grouped ultimately under 25 parent firms. Leading enterprises are ordered in terms of total unconsolidated sales. They *exclude* Federal agency crown corporations (such as the Canadian Wheat Board) as well as Provincial and Municipal crown corporations (such as Ontario Hydro). The asset tabulations in Table 7.2, therefore, underestimate the share of Canadian state capital in the economy.

7. Sources for this analysis included the *Financial Post 500* (June, 1985), *Canadian Business 500* (June 1985), and Niosi's list of major Canadian multinational corporations (1985a). Companies included in the 1976 Top 100 on qualitative grounds were excluded from the 1984/1985 list, as were crown corporations. Country in which controlling interest is held has been taken from the same sources, supplemented by more recent newspaper accounts. This variable represents the situation as of early August 1985.

8. The majority of these Canadian acquisitions were in the petroleum-producing sector, *viz*. Hudson's Bay Oil and Gas, Husky Oil, and Gulf Canada (purchased by Canadian capialists) BP Canada, Pacific Petroleum, and Petrofina Canada (purchased by PetroCanada), and Aquitaine Company of Canada (purchased by Canada Development Corporation). Canadian capitalists also gained control of one dominant mining company (Falconbridge), one manufacturer (Canadian International Paper), and three utilities (Canadian Utilities, Interprovincial Pipe Line, and Westcoast Transmission), all from American interests.

9. See *Financial Post*, 25 April 1981, 5; 16 May 1981, 5; 19 June 1982, 15; 4 August 1984, 3; Toronto *Globe and Mail*, 5 February 1981, B2; 20 June 1981, 1; 2 July 1981, B9; 3 July 1981, B14; 15 July 1981, 20; *Fortune*, 16 November 1981, 75–78.

10. Toronto *Globe and Mail* 2 June 1981, B1; 20 June 1981, 1, 2.

11. The position taken by the Communist Party of Canada resembles this sort of interpretation: "Monopoly capital not only exploits the working class, but through its dominant position in the economy and financial system and merger with the state, it rigs prices and taxes, manipulates credit, and extracts huge profits from the vast majority of Canadians." (Communist Party of Canada 1972, 10).

12. Recently documented examples of capitalist cartels operating in Canada include the other major oil companies (Lorimer 1981) and uranium producers (Toronto *Globe and Mail*, 8 July 1981, 1, 2).

13. Marchak (1979, 254) points out that foreign-controlled corporations in Canada borrow less of their total funds from external sources than do indigenous firms, relying instead of borrowings from affiliated companies controlled by the same foreign parents. In a study of forty-nine senior managers and directors of small and medium-sized corporations in southwestern Ontario, White (1979, 86–87) reports that most respondents from subsidiaries and foreign-controlled firms perceived their directorates to have no or hardly any influence over the affairs of the company, while respondents from independent and Canadian-controlled firms attributed some power to the board of directors.

14. See Toronto *Globe and Mail*, 16 July 1981, B1, B8; *Financial Times of Canada*, 28 January 1985, 29. Unless otherwise indicated, information in the remainder of this chapter was obtained from the Financial Post Corporation Service.

15. The interest in Canadian Pacific was recently sold. On the restructuring of the Power Corporation group see the *Financial Post*, 12 February 1983, 22; 21 April 1984, 4; Toronto *Star*, 14 October 1984, B1; Victoria *Times-Colonist* 23 March 1985, B5; and Toronto *Globe and Mail*, 11 August 1981, B1; 28 August 1985, B2.

16. On the restructuring of the Argus group, see the *Financial Post*, 3 March 1979, 12, 15; 19 June 1982, 15; 23 March 1985, 6; 22 June 1985, 1, 2; Toronto *Star*, 4 November 1984, B1, B6. Montague Black recently sold his interest in Revelston Corporation, leaving Conrad Black with 70 per cent of the holding company and Black's business associate Dixon Chant with 30 per cent, Toronto *Globe and Mail*, 3 August 1985, B11.

17. See *Financial Post*, 12 November 1983, 1.

18. Toronto *Star*, 30 September 1984, B1. Recently, Trizec purchased control of another major developer, Bramalea Ltd., which controls the Calgary-based Coseka Resources (Toronto *Globe and Mail*, 15 June 1985, B2).

19. See *Financial Times*, 9 January 1984, 1, 18, 19; also *Financial Post*, 25 April 1981, 5; 12 November 1983, 1–2; Toronto *Star*, 30 September 1984, B1.
20. See *Financial Times of Canada*, 28 January 1985, 3, 28.
21. See *Fortune*, 16 November 1981, 75–78; Toronto *Star*, 7 October 1984, B1. Niosi (1985, 148) describes the American parent as minority-controlled by Seagram.
22. Toronto *Star*, 23 September 1984, B1, B4; *Financial Times of Canada*, 28 January 1985, 1, 28–9.
23. Toronto *Star*, 21 October 1984, B1; *Financial Times of Canada*, 28 January 1985, 1, 28–29.
24. Toronto *Globe and Mail*, 27 June 1981, 5.
25. On the rise of the Reichmanns, see Toronto *Globe and Mail*, 27 June 1981, 1, 5; 3 August 1985, 1, 2; *Financial Post Magazine*, September 1981, 14–26; Toronto *Star* 28 October 1984, B1, B4; and *Financial Post 500* Summer 1985, 62.
26. See Toronto *Globe and Mail*, 3 August 1985, B1, B4.
27. See *Financial Post*, 11 February 1984, 21; 23 February 1985, 29–30; *Financial Times of Canada*, 28 January 1985, 1, 28–29.
28. See Toronto *Globe and Mail*, 27 June 1981, 1–2; *Financial Post*, 8 June 1985, 25.
29. See Toronto *Globe and Mail*, 24 December 1983, B1, B4.
30. See Victoria *Times-Colonist*, 20 March 1985, D12; *Financial Post*, 30 March 1985, 17; also Toronto *Globe and Mail*, 25 August 1984, B1; *Financial Times of Canada*, 28 January 1985, 1, 28–29; *Financial Post 500* Summer 1985, 58–62.
31. Toronto *Star*, 28 October 1984, B1; 23 September 1984, B1; *Financial Post Directory of Directors, 1985*.
32. See *Financial Post*, 3 March 1979, 12, 15.
33. Toronto *Star*, 4 November 1984, B1.
34. Toronto *Star*, 30 September 1984, B1. See also *Financial Post*, 12 November 1983, 2.
35. Toronto *Star*, 30 September 1984, B1.
36. *Financial Post*, 21 April 1984, 4; Toronto *Globe and Mail*, 28 June 1985, B1.
37. Toronto *Globe and Mail*, 15 June 1985, B2.
38. *Financial Post*, 12 March 1983, 1; *Financial Post 500*, Summer 1985, 62.
39. *Financial Post*, 12 November 1983, 2.
40. Toronto *Globe and Mail*, 3 August, 1985, B11.
41. These tendencies have, of course, been at work within capitalism for some time. In his discussion of the modern credit system and the centralization of capital, Marx observed that, "Conceptions which have some meaning on a less developed stage of capitalist development, become quite meaningless here. Success and failure both lead to a centralization of capital, and thus to expropriation on the most enormous scale. Expropriation extends here from the direct producers to the smaller and medium-sized capitalists themselves. It is the point of departure for the capitalist mode of production; its accomplishment is the goal of this production. In the last instance, it aims at the expropriation of the means of production from all individuals. With the development of social production the means of production cease to be private production, and can thereafter be only means of production in the hands of associated producers, i.e., the latter's social property, much as they are their social products." (1967, III, pp.439–40).
42. Toronto *Globe and Mail*, 11 October 1980, B16.
43. See *Financial Post*, 18 May 1985, 1, 2.
44. Toronto. *See Globe and Mail*, 2 August 1984, B1; Victoria *Times-Colonist*, 4 August 1984, B1.
45. Each of these companies has more than $100 million invested outside Canada. As a group these firms accounted for 65 per cent of Canadian direct investment in foreign countries in 1976.

NOTES TO CHAPTER EIGHT

1. See for instance Clement (1981, 1983); Ehrensaft and Armstrong (1981); Smythe (1981); Marchak (1983); Niosi (1983, 1985a); Williams (1983); Drache (1984); Laxer (1985); Panitch (1985).
2. Discussion of these conditions is beyond the scope of this analysis, but can be found in Kay (1975), Brenner (1977), Phillips (1977), Cypher (1979a), Szymanski (1981), and Weeks (1986).
3. See for instance Pastre's (1981, 141–262) detailed analysis of American finance capital and its establishment in France.
4. Panitch's account has been challenged by Drache (1983), who notes that from 1870 through 1930, American wage rates were consistently higher than Canadian wage rates. This observation, however, has no relevance to Panitch's central claim that the Canadian working class developed as a high wage proletariat "not only relative to the Third World but relative to the capitalisms of Europe" (1981, 16). More fundamentally, Drache grievously misrepresents the thrust of Panitch's argument, which is not that "the relatively high wage levels of the Canadian working class at the end of the nineteenth century retarded the rate of capital accumulation" (1983, 27), but that "industrial production in Canada had to expand on the basis of *relative* surplus value, the application of extensive fixed capital to the production process to expand labour productivity" (Panitch 1981, 19)—an undertaking for which large American corporations were favoured.
5. We ought not to push this account beyond its limited purpose in explaining the relatively large share of U.S. direct investment in certain Canadian industries. One legacy of the very extensive involvement of Canadian capitalists in the manufacturing sector after Canada's industrial revolution (Phillips 1979, 11) is the list of Canadian MNCs engaged principally in manufacturing: Seagrams, Northern Telecom, Massey-Ferguson, Moore Corporation, Bata Shoe Company, Canada Packers, and so forth. (Moore and Wells 1975, 79–90; Litvak and Maule 1981; Niosi 1985a).
6. Included in Canadian direct investment abroad are the investments of foreign-controlled Canadian companies. Since the proportion of such "go-between" investment has fallen dramatically in recent years (Litvak and Maule 1981, 8–9), the table underestimates the real rate at which indigenous capital has been expanding abroad.
7. A variant of this development strategy also seems evident in the current discussions of freer trade between the U.S. and Canada. Canadian capitalists and state managers do not fear more direct American competition, although there is no doubt that the accompanying restructuring of capital will create hardship and dislocation for many wage-earners. The concern is that the enormous U.S. deficit on trade in goods—an expression of American capital's poor international competitiveness—will intensify protectionism, closing the lucrative U.S. market to Canadian capitalists. See Harris 1984.
8. See *Financial Post*, 28 November 1981, 21.

NOTES TO APPENDIX 1

1. An unanticipated finding of this research was the considerable number of changes in corporation names. Throughout, I have referred to corporations by their names as of 1976 or, if they were defunct by that year, by their names immediately before disappearing. A useful source in tracing corporation names and reorganizations over time is the Financial Post's *Record of Defunct and Predecessor Companies* (1974, 1979, 1981, 1984).
2. Brecher and Reisman (1957, 280) list Iron Ore Company of Canada first among

the six largest iron ore producers of 1954.

3. The information that follows is taken from Financial Post Corporation Service, various years.

4. The T. Eaton Company was assumed to be among the dominant commercial firms for all of the selection year, although no financial statements are made public by that company. According to Royal Commission on Corporate Concentration estimates (Canada 1978, 15), Eaton's achieved sales of $1.3 billion in 1975, with assets of $1.15 billion.

5. Most of these were obtained at the Metropolitan Toronto Library, Business Department, whose collection covers many of the largest publicly traded Canadian corporations from the turn of the century forward.

6. Namely, the *Financial Post Survey of Industrials; Financial Post Survey of Energy Resources; Financial Post Survey of Mines; Financial Post Survey of Investment Funds;* Financial Post Corporation Service; *Moody's Industrials; Moody's Public Utilities; Moody's Railways;* and *Moody's Financials.* The *Canadian Real Estate Annual, Report* of the Superintendent of Insurance (Ottawa, annual), and *Report* to the Registrar of Loan and Trust Corporations, Ontario (annual) were also consulted in a few cases.

7. The only firms missing director/executive data in a year in which they were included in the Top 100 were International Harvester Company of Canada (in 1946, 1951 and 1956) and Genstar Limited (in 1951 and 1956, when the firm was called Sogemines Limited).

8. In the case of the Iron Ore Company of Canada, formed in 1949, it was assumed that the firm ranked below the Top 70 in 1951 but was dominant from 1956 onward.

9. The sources used are described in Appendix 2.

10. In the sample, wholly owned subsidiaries of foreign-based parents include Canadian International Paper Company; Chrysler Canada Limited; IBM Canada Limited; International Harvester Company of Canada, Limited; Mobil Oil Canada Limited; Sun Oil Company Limited; ITT Canada Limited; Bowater's Newfoundland Pulp and Paper Mills Limited; Canada Safeway Limited; Gambles Canada Limited; F.W. Woolworth Company Limited; General Motors Acceptance Corporation of Canada Limited; and Bowater Canadian Limited.

Companies that were majority-controlled by foreign interests in the study period include Imperial Oil Limited; Canadian General Electric Company Limited; Ford Motor Company of Canada Limited; Imasco Limited; Texaco Canada Limited; Petrofina Canada Limited; Goodyear Canada Incorporated; Canadian Utilities; Shell Canada Limited; Anglo-Canadian Telephone Company; Crown Zellerbach Canada Limited; Amoco Canada Petroleum Company Limited; Aquitaine Company of Canada Limited; Hawker Siddeley Canada Limited; Rothmans of Pall Mall Canada Limited; Union Carbide Canada Limited; Rio Algom Limited; Dupont of Canada Limited; Celanese Canada Limited; and B.P. Canada Limited.

11. Namely, in addition to the two manuals already mentioned, the *National Reference Book* (Toronto: Canadian Newspaper Services International Limited), *The Canadian Who's Who* (Toronto: Who's Who Canadian Publishers), *Who's Who in Canada* (Toronto: International Press Limited) and *Who's Who* (London, England: Adam and Charles Black).

BIBLIOGRAPHY

Aaronovitch, Stanley. 1961. *The Ruling Class: A Study of British Finance Capital*. London: Lawrence and Wishart.

Aglietta, Michel. 1979. *A Theory of Capitalist Regulation*. London: New Left Books.

Aitken, H.G.J. 1961 *American Capital and Canadian Resources*. Cambridge: Harvard University Press.

———. 1967 "Defensive Expansionism: The State and Economic Growth in Canada." *Approaches to Canadian Economic History*, ed. W.T. Easterbrook and M.H. Watkins. Toronto: McClelland and Stewart.

Alavi, Hamza. 1975 "India and the Colonial Mode of Production." *Socialist Register*: 169–97.

Alba, R.D. 1972. "COMPLT—a Program for Analyzing Sociometric Data and Clustering Similarity Matrices." *Behaviorial Science* 17:566.

———. 1973 "A Graph-Theoretic Definition of a Sociometric Clique." *Journal of Mathematical Sociology* 3:113–26.

Alba, R.D. and G. Moore. 1978 "Elite Social Circles." *Sociological Methods and Research* 7:167–88.

——— and Charles Kadushin. 1976 "The Intersection of Social Circles." *Sociological Methods and Research* 6:77–102.

Allen, Michael Patrick. 1974. "The Structure of Interorganizational Elite Cooptation: Interlocking Corporate Directorships." *American Sociological Review* 39.

———. 1978. "Continuity and Change within the Core Elite." *The Sociological Quarterly* 19, no. 4:510–21.

Amin, Samir. 1974. *Accumulation on a World Scale*. New York: Monthly Review Press.

———. 1976. *Unequal Development*. New York: Monthly Review Press.

Anderson, C.H. 1974 *The Political Economy of Social Class*. Englewood Cliffs, NJ: Prentice-Hall.

Anderson, J. 1973. "Ideology in Geography: An Introduction." *Antipode* 5, no. 3:1–16.

Anderson, Karen. 1985. "The State, the Capitalist Class, and the C.P.R." In *The Structure of the Canadian Capitalist Class*, ed. Robert J. Brym. Toronto: Garamond Press, pp. 117–28.

Andreff, Wladimir. 1984. "The Internationalization of Capital and the Reordering of World Capitalism." *Capital and Class* 22:58–80.

Angotti, Thomas. 1981. "The Political Implications of Dependency Theory." *Latin American Perspectives* 8, nos. 3 and 4:124–37.

Arrighi, Giovanni. 1978. *The Geometry of Imperialism*. London: New Left Books.

Ashley, C.A. 1957. "Concentration of Economic Power." *Canadian Journal of Economics and Political Science* 23:105–8.

Audley, Paul. 1983. *Canada's Cultural Industries: Broadcasting, Publishing, Records and Film.* Toronto: Lorimer.

Baer, W. 1962. "The Economics of Prebisch and E.C.L.A." *Economic Development and Cultural Change* 2, part 1:169–82.

Baran, Paul A. 1952. "The Political Economy of Backwardness." *Manchester School* (January).

————. 1957. *The Political Economy of Growth.* New York: Monthly Review Press.

————, and P.M. Sweezy. 1966. *Monopoly Capital.* New York: Monthly Review Press.

————. 1966. "Notes on the Theory of Imperialism." *Problems of Economic Dynamics and Planning: Essays in Honour of Michal Kalecki.* New York: Pergamon Press.

Barkin, David. 1981. "Internationalization of Capital: an Alternative Approach." *Latin American Perspectives* 8, nos. 3 and 4:156–61.

Barnet, Richard J. 1980. *The Lean Years.* New York: Simon & Schuster.

———— and Ronald E. Muller. 1974. *Global Reach.* New York: Simon & Schuster.

Barone, Charles A. 1983. "Dependency, Marxist Theory, and Salvaging the Idea of Capitalism in South Korea." *Review of Radical Political Economics* 15, no.1:41–70.

Barratt-Brown, Michael. 1958. "The Insiders." *Universities and Left Review* 5:26–32.

————. 1959. "The Controllers." *Universities and Left Review* 5:53–61.

Bearden, J., W. Atwood, P. Freitag, C. Hendricks, B. Mintz and M. Scwartz. 1975. "The Nature and Extent of Bank Centrality in Corporate Networks." Paper presented at the annual meeting of the American Sociological Association.

Becker, James. 1971. "On the Monopoly Theory of Monopoly Capitalism." *Science and Society* 35:415–38.

Belkaoui, Janice M. 1982. "The Mass Media in Canada." In *Social Issues,* ed. Dennis Forcese and Stephen Richer. Scarborough: Prentice-Hall Canada, pp. 440–68.

Bellamy, R. 1966. "Monopoly Capital—A Critical Review of a Contemporary Study." *Marxism Today* 10:333–40.

Berberoglu, Berch. 1984. "The Controversy over Imperialism and Capitalist Industrialization." *Journal of Contemporary Asia* 14:399–407.

Berkowitz, Stephen D. 1982. *An Introduction to Structural Analysis.* Toronto: Butterworths.

————, Yehuda Kotowitz, Leonard Waverman, et. al. 1976. *Enterprise Structure and Corporate Concentration.* Royal Commission on Corporate Concentration Study No. 17. Ottawa: Minister of Supply and Services.

Berkowitz, Stephen D., Peter J. Carrington, Yehuda Kotowitz, Leonard Waverman. 1979a. "The Determination of Enterprise Groupings through Combined Ownership and Directorship Ties." *Social Networks* 1, no. 4:391–413.

Berkowitz, Stephen D., Peter J. Carrington, June S. Corman, Leonard Waverman. 1979b. "Flexible Design of a Large-scale Corporate Data Base." *Social Networks* 2, no. 1:75–83.

Berle, A.A., and C.G. Means. 1932. *The Modern Corporation and Private Property.* New York: Macmillan.

Bertram, G.W. 1967. "Economic Growth in Canadian Industry, 1870–1915: the Staples Model." In *Approaches to Canadian Economic History,* ed. W.T. Easterbrook and M.H. Watkins. Toronto: McClelland and Stewart, pp. 74–98.

Bettelheim, Charles. 1972. "Appendix I. Theoretical comments by Charles Bettelheim." In Arghiri Emmanual, *Unequal Exchange: A Study in the Imperialism of Trade,* ed. Arghiri Emmanual. New York: Monthly Review Press, pp.271–322.

Bliss, Michael. 1970. "Canadianizing American Business: The Roots of the Branch Plant." *Close the 49th Parallel etc., The Americanization of Canada,* ed. Ian Lumsden. Toronto: University of Toronto Press, pp. 26–42.

———. 1974. *A Living Profit.* Toronto: McClelland and Stewart.

Bluestone, B., and B. Harrison. 1982. *The Deindustrialization of America.* New York: Basic Books.

Blumberg, P.I. 1975. *The Megacorporation in American Society: The Scope of Corporate Power.* Englewood Cliffs, NJ:Prentice-Hall.

Brecher, Irving and S.S. Reisman. 1957. "Some Statistical Notes on External Ownership and Control of Canadian Industry." Appendix B in *Canada-United States Economic Relations.* Ottawa: Queen's Printer, 278–90.

Brenner, Robert. 1977. "The Origins of Capitalist Development: Critique of Neo-Smithian Marxism." *New Left Review* 104:25–92.

Brett, E.A. 1983. *International Money and Capital Crisis, The Anatomy of Global Disintegration.* London: Heinemann.

Brewer, Anthony. 1980. *Marxist Theories of Imperialism.* Boston: Routledge & Kegan Paul.

Britton, J.N.H., and J.M. Gilmour. 1978. *The Weakest Link: A Technological Perspective on Canadian Industrial Underdevelopment.* Science Council of Canada Background Study No. 43. Ottawa: Minister of Supply and Services.

Browett, John. 1981. "Into the Cul-de-sac of the Dependency Paradigm with A.G. Frank." *Australian and New Zealand Journal of Sociology* 17: 14–25.

Brym, Robert J. 1985. "The Canadian Capitalist Class, 1965–1985." In *The Structure of the Canadian Capitalist Class,* ed. Robert Brym. Toronto: Garamond Press, pp.1–20.

Buck, Tim. 1948. *Canada: The Communist Viewpoint.* Toronto: Progress Books.

———. 1970. "Lenin and Canadian Independence." In *Lenin and Canada.* Toronto: Progress Books, pp. 79–91.

Bukharin, Nikolai. 1973. *Imperialism and World Economy*. New York: Monthly Review Press.

Bunting, D., and J. Barbour. 1971. "Interlocking Directorates in Large American Corporations, 1896–1964." *Business History Review*. 45:317–35.

Burch, P.H. 1972. *The Managerial Revolution Reassessed*. Lexington, Mass.: Lexington Books.

Burris, Val. 1980. "Class Formation and Transformation in Advanced Capitalist Societies: A Comparative Analysis." *Social Praxis* 7, nos. 3 and 4:147–79.

Burt, Ronald S. 1978. "Applied network analysis: An overview." *Sociological Methods and Research* 7:123–30.

———. 1983. *Corporate Profits and Cooptation*. Toronto: Academic Press.

———, K.P. Christman and B.C. Kilburn, Jr. 1980. "Testing a Structural Theory of Corporate Cooptation." *American Sociological Review* 45:821–41.

Calvert, John. 1984. *Government Limited: The Corporate Takeover of the Public Sector in Canada*. Ottawa: Canadian Centre for Policy Alternatives.

Cameron, Duncan, and Francois Houle. 1985. *Canada and the New International Division of Labour*. Ottawa: University of Ottawa Press.

Camilleri, Joseph. 1981. "The Advanced Capitalist State and the Contemporary World Crisis." *Science and Society* 45:130–58.

Canada. 1937. *Report* of the Royal Commission on Price Spreads. Ottawa: King's Printer.

———. 1975. Corporations and Labour Unions Returns Act, *Annual Report Part 1: Corporations*. Ottawa: Statistics Canada.

———. 1978. *Report* of the Royal Commission on Corporate Concentration. Ottawa: Minister of Supply & Services.

———. 1979. *Intercorporate Ownership*. Ottawa: Statistics Canada.

———. 1980. Corporations and Labour Unions Returns Act, *Annual Report 1978 Part 1: Corporations*. Ottawa: Statistics Canada.

———. 1983. Corporations and Labour Unions Returns Act, *Annual Report Part 1: Corporations*. Ottawa: Statistics Canada.

Cardoso, F.H., and E. Faletto. 1979. *Dependency and Development in Latin America*. Los Angeles: University of California Press.

Carey, Harold E. 1926. *Industrial Concentration in Canada*. Master's Thesis, University of Manitoba.

Carrington, P.J. 1981a. "Anti-competitive Effects of Directorship Interlocks." Working Paper Series No. 27. Structural Analysis Program, University of Toronto, Department of Sociology.

———. 1981b. *Horizontal Co-optation through Corporate Interlocks*. Ph.D. diss., University of Toronto.

Carroll, William K. 1982. "The Canadian Corporate Elite: Financiers or Finance Capitalists?" *Studies in Political Economy* 8:89–114.

———. 1984. "The Individual, Class, and Corporate Power in Canada." *Canadian Journal of Sociology* 9, no. 3.

———, John Fox and Michael D. Ornstein. 1981. "Longitudinal Analysis of

Directorate Interlocks." Paper presented at the annual meeting of the Canadian Sociology and Anthropology Association. Halifax, May.

———. 1982. "The Network of Directorate Links Among the Largest Canadian Firms." *Canadian Review of Sociology and Anthropology* 19:44–69.

Castells, Manuel. 1980. *The Economic Crisis and American Society.* Princeton: Princeton University Press.

Chandler, A.D. 1962. *Strategy and Structure: Chapters in the History of the Industrial Enterprise.* Cambridge: Harvard University Press.

Chevalier, Jean-Marie. 1969. "The Problem of Control in Large American Corporations." *Antitrust Bulletin* 14:163–80.

Chinchilla, Norma S., and James L. Dietz. 1981. "Toward a New Understanding of Development and Underdevelopment." *Latin American Perspectives* 8, nos. 3 and 4:138–47.

Chodos, Robert. 1973. *The CPR: A Century of Corporate Welfare.* Toronto: James Lewis and Samuel.

Clairmonte, Frederick. 1982. "Dynamics of Finance Capital." *Journal of Contemporary Asia* 12, no. 2:158–67.

Clarkson, Stephen. 1985. *Canada and the Reagan Challenge.* Rev. ed. Toronto: Lorimer.

Clawson, Patrick. 1976. "The Internationalization of Capital and Capital Accommodation in Iran and Iraq." *Insurgent Sociologist* 6, no. 2:64–73.

Clement, Wallace. 1975. *The Canadian Corporate Elite.* Toronto: McClelland and Stewart.

———. 1977. *Continental Corporate Power.* Toronto: McClelland and Stewart.

———. 1978. "A Political Economy of Regionalism in Canada." In *Modernization and the Canadian State,* ed. David Glenday, Hubert Guindon, and Alan Turowetz. Toronto: Macmillan, pp. 89–110.

———. 1981. *Hardrock Mining.* Toronto: McClelland and Stewart.

———. 1983. *Class, Power and Property.* Toronto: Methuen.

Cliffe, Lionel, and Peter Lawrence. 1977. "Editorial." *Review of African Political Economy* 8:1–6.

Communist Party of Canada. 1972. *The Road to Socialism in Canada.* Toronto: Progress Books.

Craven, Paul and Tom Traves. 1979. "The Class Politics of the National Policy 1872–1933." *Journal of Canadian Studies* 14, no. 3:14–38.

Crean, S.M. 1976. *Who's Afraid of Canadian Culture.* Don Mills: General Publishing.

Creighton, Donald G. 1937. *The Commercial Empire of the St. Lawrence, 1760–1850.* Toronto: The Ryerson Press.

Cueva, Agustin. 1976. "A Summary of 'Problems and Perspectives of Dependency Theory.' " *Latin American Perspectives* 3, no. 4:12–16.

Cuneo, Carl J. 1980. "State Mediation of Contradictions in Canadian Unemployment Insurance, 1930–1935." *Studies in Political Economy* 3:37–65.

———. 1982. "The Politics of Surplus Labour in the Collapse of Canada's Dependence on Britain, 1840–49." *Studies in Political Economy* 7:61–87.

————. 1983. "Transition in Canada's Class Structure 1901–81." Paper presented at the Marx Centenary Conference, University of Manitoba, March.

Currie, David. 1983. "World Capitalism in Recession." In *The Politics of Thatcherism*, ed. Stuart Hall and Martin Jaques. London: Lawrence and Wishart, pp. 79–105.

Cypher, James M. 1979a. "The Internationalization of Capital and the Transformation of Social Formations: A Critique of the Monthly Review School." *Review of Radical Political Economics* 11, no. 4:33–49.

————. 1979b. "The Transnational Challenge to the Corporate State." *Journal of Economic Issues* 13:513–42.

Dann, James. 1979. "U.S. Hegemony over the Three Worlds." *Review of Radical Political Economics* 11, no. 4:64–77.

Davis, Arthur K. 1971. "Canadian Society and History as Hinterland versus Metropolis." In *Canadian Society: Pluralism, Change and Conflict*, ed. Richard J. Ossenberg. Scarborough: Prentice-Hall, pp. 6–32.

De Brunhoff, Suzanne. 1978. *The State, Capital and Economic Policy.* London: Pluto Press.

De Cormis, Anna. 1983. "So Much for 'the American Way' in Auto and Steel." *Guardian* (New York) 35, no. 32:11.

De Grass, Richard P. 1977. *Development of Monopolies in Canada from 1907–1913.* Master's Thesis, University of Waterloo.

De Vroey, Michel. 1975. "The Separation of Ownership and Control in Large Corporations." *Review of Radical Political Economics* 7, no. 2:1–10.

Desrosiers, Richard and Julian Sher. 1980. "Who owns Canada?" *October* 9:5–97.

Deverell, John, and the Latin American Working Group. 1975. *Falconbridge: Portrait of a Canadian Mining Multinational.* Toronto: James Lorimer.

Dhingra, Harbans L. 1983. "Patterns of Ownership and Control in Canadian Industry: a Study of Large Non-financial Institutions." *Canadian Journal of Sociology* 8:21–44.

Dobb, M. 1967. "Some problems under discussion." *Marxism Today* 11:88–89.

Dooley, P. 1969. "The Interlocking Directorate." *American Economic Review* 59.

Dore, Elizabeth, and John Weeks. 1977. "Class Alliance and Class Struggle in Peru." *Latin American Perspectives* 4, no. 3.

Dow, Alexander. 1984. "Finance and Foreign Control of Canadian Base Metal Mining, 1918–55." *The Economic History Review* 37, no. 1:54–67.

Drache, Daniel. 1970. "The Canadian Bourgeoisie and its National Consciousness." In *Close the 49th Parallel etc., The Americanization of Canada*, ed. Ian Lumsden. Toronto: University of Toronto Press, pp. 3–25.

————. 1977. "Staple-ization: A Theory of Canadian Capitalist Development." In *Imperialism, Nationalism, and Canada*, ed. Craig Heron. Toronto: New Hogtown Press and Between the Lines, pp. 15–33.

————. 1983. "The Crisis of Canadian Political Economy: Dependency Theory versus the New Orthodoxy." *Canadian Journal of Political and Social*

Theory 7, no. 3:25–49.

———. 1984. "The Formation and Fragmentation of the Canadian Working Class: 1820–1920." *Studies in Political Economy* 15:43–89.

Droucopoulos, Vassilis. 1981. "The Non American Challenge: A Report on the Size and Growth of the World's Largest Firms." *Capital and Class* 14:36–46.

Drummond, Ian. 1962. "Canadian Life Insurance Companies and the Capital Market, 1890–1914." *Canadian Journal of Economics and Political Science* 27:204–24.

———. 1978. "Review of R.T. Naylor, History of Canadian Business." *Canadian Historical Review* 59:90–93.

Easterbrook, W.T. and H.G.J. Aitken. 1956. *Canadian Economic History*. Toronto: MacMillan.

Ehrensaft, P., and W. Armstrong. 1981. "The Formation of Dominion Capitalism: Economic Truncation and Class Structure." In *Inequality: Essays on the Political Economy of Social Welfare*, ed. A. Moscovitch and G. Dover. Toronto: University of Toronto Press, 99–155.

Eitzen, D.S., D.A. Purdy and M. Jung. 1985. "Interlocking Ownership among the Major Banks." *Insurgent Sociologist* 12, no. 4:45–50.

Emmanuel, Arghiri. 1972. *Unequal Exchange*. New York: Monthly Review Press.

Evans, Eric. 1980. "As Aggressive Backers, Banks at the Heart of Takeover Battles." *Financial Post*, 6 December 1980, 54.

Fanon, Frantz. 1966. *The Wretched of the Earth*. New York: Grove Press.

Fennema, Meindert. 1974. "Car Firms in the European Communities, A Study of Personal Linkages, Joint Ventures and Financial Participation." Paper presented at the ECPR Workshop on Internationalization of Capital, Strasbourg.

———. 1982. *International Networks of Banks and Industries*. Boston: Martin Nijhoff.

——— and P. De Jong. 1978. "Internationale Vervlechting van Industrie en Bankwezen." In *Herstrukturering van de Nederlandse Industrie*, ed. A. Tevlings. Alphen a/d Rijn: Samsom.

———. and Huibert, Schijf. 1979. "Analysing Interlocking Directorates: Theory and Methods." *Social Networks* 1:297–332.

Fienberg, Stephen E., and S.S.Wasserman. 1981. "Categorical Data Analysis of Single Sociometric Relationships." In *Sociological Methodology*, ed. Samuel Leinhardt. San Francisco: Jossey-Bass, pp. 162–92.

Fine, Ben. 1986. "Banking Capital and the Theory of Interest." *Science and Society* 49:387–413.

Fisher, A.G.B. 1935. *The Clash of Progress and Security*. London: MacMillan.

———. 1952. "A Note on Tertiary Production." *Economic Journal* 62:820–34.

Fitch, R. 1971a. "Reply to 'Question: Who Rules the Corporation. Answer: The Ruling Class.' " *Socialist Revolution* 2, no. 1:150–70.

———. 1971b. "Sweezy and Corporate Fetishism." *Socialist Revolution* 2, no.

5:93–127.

———— and Mary Oppenheimer. 1970. "Who Rules the Corporations?" *Socialist Revolution* 1, no. 4:73–107, no. 6:33–94.

Fournier, Pierre. 1980. "The New Parameters of the Quebec Bourgeoisie." *Studies in Political Economy* 3:67–92.

Francis, Diane. 1981. "Swallowed Alive." *Canadian Business* 54, no. 7:56–60.

————. 1984. "Is Canada Heading for New Feudalism?" *Toronto Star*, 27 September 1984:A1, A8.

Frank, Andre Gunder. 1966. "The Development of Underdevelopment." *Monthly Review* 18, no. 4:17–31.

————. 1967. *Capitalism and Underdevelopment in Latin America*. New York: Monthly Review Press.

————. 1972. *Lumpenbourgeoisie. Lumpendevelopment*. New York: Monthly Review Press.

————. 1979. *Dependent Accumulation and Underdevelopment*. New York: Monthly Review Press.

————. 1980. *Crisis: In the World Economy*. New York: Holmes & Meier.

Franko, Lawrence G. 1978. "Multinationals: The End of U.S. Dominance." *Harvard Business Review* (November/December 1978):93–101.

Frieden, Jeff. 1977. "The Trilateral Commission: Economics and Politics in the 1970s." *Monthly Review* 29, no. 7:1–18.

Friedman, Jonathan. 1978. "Crises in Theory and Transformations of the World Economy." *Review* 2:131–46.

Furtado, Celso. 1964. *Development and Underdevelopment*. Berkley: University of California Press.

Galaskiewicz J., and S. Wasserman. 1981. "Dynamic Study of Change in a Regional Corporate Network." *American Sociological Review* 46:475–84.

Galtung, Johan. 1971. "A Structural Theory of Imperialism." *Journal of Peace Research* 8, no. 2:81–117.

Glasberg, Davita S. 1981. "Corporate Power and Control: the Case of Leasco Corporation vs. Chemical Bank." *Social Problems* 29, no. 2:104–16.

————. and Michael Schwartz. 1983. "Ownership and Control of Corporations." *Annual Review of Sociology* 9:311–332.

Glynn, Lenny. 1981. "Bronfman Diviners: Investors Try to Guess the Family's Next Moves." *Canadian Business* 54, no. 7:15–17.

Godfrey, Dave, and Mel Watkins, eds. 1970. *Gordon to Watkins to You*. Toronto: New Press.

Goff, Colin H. and Charles E. Reasons. 1978. *Corporate Crime in Canada: A Critical Analysis of Anti-Combines Legislation*. Scarborough, Ont.: Prentice-Hall.

Gogel, R., and T. Koenig. 1981. "Commercial Banks, Interlocking Directorates and Economic Power: An Analysis of the Primary Metals Industry." *Social Problems* 29, no. 2:116–28.

Goldfrank, Walter L. 1977. "Who Rules the World? Class Formation at the International Level." *Quarterly Journal of Ideology* 1, no. 2:32–37.

Gonick, C.W. 1970. "Foreign Ownership and Political Decay." In *Close the 49th Parallel etc., The Americanization of Canada*, ed. Ian Lumsden. Toronto: University of Toronto Press, pp. 43–73.

Govett, M.H. 1975. "The Geographic Concentration of World Mineral Supplies." *Resources Policy* 1:357–70.

Gunnarsson, Christer. 1985. "Development Theory and Third World Industrialization." *Journal of Contemporary Asia* 15:183–206.

Hacker, Andrew. 1964. "Power to do What?" In *The New Sociology*, ed. I.L. Horowitz. New York: Oxford University Press, pp. 134–46.

Hacker, Louis M. 1970. *The Course of American Growth and Development*. New York: John Wiley.

Halliday, Fred. 1983. *The Making of the Second Cold War*. London: Verso.

Halliday, J., and G. McCormack. 1973. *Japanese Imperialism Today*. London: Penguin.

Harary, Frank, Robert Norman and Dorwin Cartwright. 1965. *Structural Models: An Introduction to the Theory of Directed Graphs*. New York: John Wiley.

Harding, Timothy F. 1976. "Dependency, Nationalism and the State in Latin America." *Latin American Perspectives* 3, no. 4:3–11.

Harris, Catherine. 1984. "U.S. Deficit Hurts Rest of World." *Financial Post Report on the Nation*, November: 51.

Harvey, David. 1982. *The Limits to Capital*. Chicago: University of Chicago Press.

Hawley, Jim. 1979. "The Internationalization of Capital: Banks, Eurocurrency and the Instability of the World Monetary System." *Review of Radical Political Economics* 11, no. 4:78–90.

Hawley, James P. and Charles Noble. 1982. "The Internationalization of Capital and the Limits of the Interventionist State: Towards an Explanation of Macroeconomic Policy Failure." *Journal of Political and Military Sociology* 10:103–20.

Helmers, H.M. et al. 1975. *Graven Naar Macht. Op Zoek Naar de Kern van de Nederlandse Ekonomie*. Amsterdam: Van Gennup.

Henfrey, Colin. 1981. "Dependency, Modes of Production, and the Class Analysis of Latin America." *Latin American Perspectives* 8, nos. 3 and 4:17–54.

Hermansson, C.H. 1971. *Monopol und Storfinans-de 15 Familierna*. Stockholm: Raben and Sjogren.

Hilferding, Rudolph. 1923. *Das Finanzkapital*. Wien: Wiener Volksbuchhandlung.

———. 1981. *Finance Capital*. London: Routledge and Kegan Paul.

Hobson, J.A. 1965. *Imperialism*. Ann Arbor: University of Michigan Press.

Holland, Paul W., and Samuel Leinhardt. 1981. "An Exponential Family of Probability Distributions for Directed Graphs." *American Statistical Association Journal* 76:33–50.

Holloway, John, and Sol Picciotto. 1978. "Introduction: Towards a Materialist

Theory of the State." In John Holloway and Sol Piccotto (eds.) *State and Capital: A Marxist Debate*. London: Edward Arnold, pp. 1–31.

Houle, François. 1983. "Economic Strategy and the Restructuring of the Fordist Wage-Labour Relationship in Canada." *Studies in Political Economy* 11:127–47.

Howe, Gary N. 1981. "Dependency Theory, Imperialism, and the Production of Surplus Value on a World Scale." *Latin American Perspectives* 8, nos. 3 and 4:82–102.

———. and A. Sica. 1980. "Political Economy, Imperialism, and the Problem of World System Theory." In *Current Perspectives in Social Theory*, ed. S.G. McNall and G.N. Howe, Vol. I. Greenwich, Conn.: JAL Press, pp. 235–86.

Hussein, Athar. 1976. "Hilferding's Finance Capital." *Bulletin of the Conference of Socialists* 5, no. 1:1–18.

Hutcheson, John. 1978. *Dominance and Dependency*. Toronto: McClelland and Stewart.

Hymer, Stephen. 1972. "The Internationalization of Capital." *Journal of Economic Issues* 6, no. 1:91–111.

Information Canada. 1972. *Foreign Direct Investment in Canada*. Ottawa: Queen's Printer.

Innis, Harold A. 1956. *Essays in Canadian Economic History*. Toronto: University of Toronto Press.

———. 1970. *The Fur Trade in Canada*. Rev. Ed. Toronto: University of Toronto Press.

Jalee, Pierre. 1972. *Imperialism in the Seventies*. New York: The Third Press.

Jeidels, O. 1905. *Das Verhaltnis der Deutschen Grossbanken zur Industrie mit Besonderer Biruckichtigung der Eisenindustrie*. Leipzig: Demaker and Humbolt.

Johnson, Carlos. 1981. "Dependency Theory and the Processes of Capitalism and Socialism." *Latin American Perspectives* 8, no. 3 and 4:55–81.

———. 1983. "Ideologies in Theories of Imperialism and Dependency." In *Theories of Development*, ed. R.H. Chilcote and D.L. Johnson. Beverly Hills: Sage, pp. 75–106.

Johnson, Leo A. 1972. "The Development of Class in Canada in the Twentieth Century." In *Capitalism and the National Question in Canada*, ed. Gary Teeple. Toronto: University of Toronto Press, pp. 141–84.

Kadushin, Charles. 1968. "Power, Influence and Social Circles. A New Methology for Studying Opinion Makers." *American Sociological Review* 33:685–99.

Kaufman, Michael. 1985. "The Internationalization of Canadian Bank Capital (With a Look at Bank Activity in the Carribean and Central America)." *Journal of Canadian Studies* 19, no. 4:61–81.

Kay, Geoffrey. 1975. *Development and Underdevelopment: A Marxist Analysis*. New York: St. Martin's Press.

Kealey, Gregory S. 1982. "Toronto's Industrial Revolution, 1850–1892." In

Canada's Age of Industry, 1849–1896, ed. Michael S. Cross and Gregory S. Kealey. Toronto: McClelland and Stewart, pp. 20–61.

Kemp, Tom. 1978. *Historical Patterns of Industrialization*. London: Longman Canada.

Knowles, James C. 1973. "The Rockefeller Financial Group." In *Superconcentration/Supercorporation*, ed. R. L. Andreano. Andover, Mass.: Warner Modular Publications.

Koenig, Thomas, John Sonquist and Robert Gogel. 1978. "Interlocking Directorates as a Social Network." *Journal of Sociology and Economics*.

Kolko, Gabriel. 1963. *The Triumph of Conservatism: A Reinterpretation of American History, 1900–1916*. New York: Free Press.

Kolko, Joyce. 1977. "Imperialism and the Crisis of Capitalism in the 1970s." *Journal of Contemporary Asia* 7, no. 1:9–21.

Kotz, David M. 1978. *Bank Control of Large Corporations in the United States*. Berkeley: University of California Press.

Laclau, Ernesto. 1971. "Feudalism and Capitalism in Latin America." *New Left Review* 67:19–38.

Lall, S. 1975. " Is 'Dependence' a Useful Concept in Analyzing Underdevelopment?" *World Development* 3, nos. 11 and 12:799–810.

Landsberg, Marty. 1976. "Multinational Corporations and the Crisis of Capitalism." *Insurgent Sociologist* 6, no. 3:19–33.

Laxer, Gordon. 1985. "The Political Economy of Aborted Development: The Canadian Case." In *The Structure of the Canadian Capitalist Class*, ed. Robert J. Brym. Toronto: Garamond Press, pp. 67–102.

Laxer, Jim. 1973a. "Canadian Manufacturing and U.S. Trade Policy." In *Canada Ltd., The Political Economy of Dependency*, ed. Robert Laxer. Toronto: McClelland and Stewart, pp. 127–152.

———. 1973b. "Introduction to the Political Economy of Canada." In *(Canada) Ltd., The Political Economy of Dependency*, ed. Robert Laxer. Toronto: McClelland and Stewart, pp. 26–41.

———, and Doris Jantzi. 1973. "The De-industrialization of Ontario." In *(Canada) Ltd., The Political Economy of Dependency*, ed. Robert Laxer. Toronto: McClelland and Stewart, pp. 147–52.

Laxer, Robert. 1973. *(Canada) Ltd., The Political Economy of Dependency*. Toronto: McClelland and Stewart.

Leaver, Richard. 1977. "The Debate on Underdevelopment: 'On Situating Gunder Frank.' " *Journal of Contemporary Asia*, 7, no. 1:108–15.

Leinhardt, Samuel. 1977. "Social Network Research: Editor's Introduction." *Journal of Mathematical Sociology* 5:1–4.

Lenin, V.I. 1970 [1917]. "Imperialism, the Highest Stage of Capitalism." In V.I. Lenin, *Selected Works*, Vol. 1. Moscow: Progress Publishers, pp. 667–768.

Levine, Joel. 1972. "The Sphere of Influence." *American Sociological Review* 37:14–27.

Levitt, Kari. 1970. *Silent Surrender*. Toronto: MacMillan of Canada.

Leys, Colin. 1977. "Underdevelopment and Dependency: Critical Notes."

Journal of Contemporary Asia, 7, no. 1:92–107.

———. 1978. "Capital Accumulation, Class Formation and Dependency—the Significance of the Kenyan Case." *Socialist Register*, pp. 241–66.

Lindsey, C.W. 1982. "Lenin's Theory of Imperialism." *Review of Radical Political Economics* 14, no. 1:1–9.

Lintner, John. 1959. "The Financing of Corporations." In *The Corporation in Modern Society*, ed. E.S. Mason. Cambridge: Harvard University Press, pp. 166–201.

Lipietz, Alain. 1982. "Towards Global Fordism?" *New Left Review* 132: 33–47.

———. 1984. "Imperialism or the Beast of the Apocalypse." *Capital and Class*, 22:81–109.

Little, I.M.D. 1975. "Economic Relations with the Third World—Old Myths and New Prospects." *Scottish Journal of Political Economy*, 22:223–35.

Litvak, I.A., and C.J. Maule. 1981. *The Canadian Multinationals*. Toronto: Butterworths.

Lorimer, James, ed. 1981. *Canada's Oil Monopoly*. Toronto: James Lorimer.

Lower, A.R.M. 1967. "The Trade in Square Timber." In *Approaches to Canadian Economic History*, ed. W.T. Easterbrook and M.H. Watkins. Toronto: McClelland and Stewart, pp. 28–43.

Lumsden, Ian. 1970. "American Imperialism and Canadian Intellectuals." In *Close the 49th Parallel etc., The Americanization of Canada*, ed. Ian Lumsden. Toronto: University of Toronto Press, pp. 321–36.

Luxemburg, Rosa. 1951. *The Accumulation of Capital*. New York: Monthly Review Press.

McCollum, W.H. 1947. *Who Owns Canada?* Ottawa: Woodsworth House Publishers.

McCrorie, James N. 1980. *Canadian Review of Sociology and Anthropology* (Special issue on dependency, underdevelopment and regionalism.) 17, no. 3.

MacDonald, L.R. 1975. "Merchants Against Industry: An Idea and its Origins." *Canadian Historical Review* 56:263–81.

MacEwan, Arthur. 1984. "Interdependence and Instability: Do the Levels of Output in the Advanced Capitalist Countries Increasingly Move Up and Down Together?" *Review of Radical Political Economics* 16, nos. 2 and 3:57–79.

MacGilchrist, R.G. 1948. *Canadian Manufacturing—A Survey of the Major Industries with Respect to Financial Control*. Master's Thesis, University of Pennsylvania.

McLennan, J.L. 1929. *The Merger Movement in Canada Since 1880*. Master's Thesis, Queens University.

McNally, David. 1981. "Staple Theory as Commodity Fetishism: Marx, Innis and Canadian Political Economy." *Studies in Political Economy* 6:35–63.

Mandel, Ernest. 1968. *Marxist Economic Theory*, London: Merlin Press.
――――. 1970. *Europe vs America*. New York: Monthly Review Press.
――――. 1973. *Capitalism and Regional Economic Disparities*. Toronto: New Hogtown Press.
――――. 1975. *Late Capitalism*. London: New Left Books.
Marchak, Patricia. 1979. *In Whose Interests*. Toronto: McClelland and Stewart.
――――. 1983. *Green Gold*. Vancouver: University of British Columbia Press.
Marcussen, H.S., and J.E. Torp. 1982. *The Internationalization of Capital: The Prospects for the Third World*. London: Zed Press.
Mariolis, Peter. 1983. "Interlocking Directorates and Financial Groups: a Peak Analysis." *Sociological Spectrum* 3:237–52.
―――― and M.H. Jones. 1982. "Centrality in Corporate Interlock Networks: Reliability and Stability." *Administrative Science Quarterly* 27, no. 4:571–84.
Markusen, Ann R. 1978. "Class, Rent and Sectoral Conflict: Uneven Development in Western U.S. Boomtowns." *Review of Radical Political Economics* 10 (3), 117–129.
Marshall, Herbert, Frank Southard and Kenneth W. Taylor. 1936. *Canadian-American Industry: A Study of International Investments*. New Haven: Yale University Press.
Marx, Karl. 1967. *Capital*. 3 vols. New York: International Publishers.
Matthews, Ralph. 1983. *The Creation of Regional Dependency*. Toronto: University of Toronto Press.
Mathias, Phillip. 1976. *Takeover: The 22 Days of Risk and Decision that Created the World's Largest Newsprint Empire, Abitibi-Price*. Toronto: Financial Post.
Matthews, Ralph. 1983. *The Creation of Regional Dependency*. Toronto: University of Toronto Press.
Mellos, Kovla. 1979. "Critical Remarks on Critical Elite Theory." *Journal of Canadian Studies* 13, no. 4:72–88.
Menshikov, S. 1969. *Millionaires and Managers*. Moscow: Progress Publishers.
Mepham, John. 1979. "The Theory of Ideology in *Capital*." In *Issues in Marxist Philosophy*, ed. John Mepham and D.H. Ruben. Vol. III. Brighton: Harvester, pp. 141–74.
Mintz, Beth, and Michael Schwartz. 1978. "The Role of Financial Institutions in Interlock Networks." Paper presented at the Conference on New Directions in Structural Analysis. University of Toronto, March.
――――. 1981a. "Interlocking Directorates and Interest Group Formation." *American Sociological Review* 46:851–69.
――――. 1981b. "The Structure of Intercorporate Unity in American Business." *Social Problems* 29, no. 2:87–103.
Mitchell, James C., ed. 1969. *Social Networks in Urban Situations*. Manchester: Manchester University Press.
Mittelstaedt, Martin. 1985. "Banks and Trust Companies." *Report on Busi-*

ness Magazine 2, no. 1:34–40.

Mizruchi, M.S. 1982. *The American Corporate Network 1904–1974.* Beverly Hills, CA.: Sage.

—— and D. Bunting. 1981. "Influence in Corporate Networks: An Examination of Four Measures." *Administrative Science Quarterly* 26:475–89.

Moore, Steve, and Debi Wells. 1975. *Imperialism and the National Question in Canada.* Toronto: privately published.

Moreno, Jacob L., ed. 1960. *The Sociometry Reader.* Glencoe, Ill.: The Free Press.

Myers, G. 1972. *A History of Canadian Wealth.* Toronto: James Lewis and Samuel.

Nabudere, D.W. 1977. *The Political Economy of Imperialism.* London: Zed Press.

——. 1979. *Essays on the Theory and Practice of Imperialism.* London: Onyx Press.

Naylor, R.T. 1972. "The Rise and Fall of the Third Commercial Empire of the St. Lawrence." In *Capitalism and the National Question in Canada,* ed. Gary Teeple. Toronto: University of Toronto Press, pp. 1–41.

——. 1973. "The History of Foreign and Domestic Capital in Canada." In *(Canada) Ltd., the Political Economy of Dependency,* ed. Robert Laxer. Toronto: McClelland and Stewart.

——. 1975a. *The History of Canadian Business 1867–1914.* 2 vols. Toronto: James Lorimer.

——. 1975b. "Commentary." *Our Generation* 11, no. 1:17–24.

Nelles, H.V. 1974. *The Politics of Development.* Toronto: Macmillan.

Neufeld, E.P. 1969. *A Global Corporation, A History of the International Development of Massey Ferguson Ltd.* Toronto: University of Toronto Press.

——. 1972. *The Financial System of Canada: Its Growth and Development.* New York: St. Martin's Press.

Newman, Peter, C. 1975. *The Canadian Establishment,* Vol. 1. Toronto: McClelland and Stewart.

Niemeijer, R. 1973. "Some Applications of the Concept of Density." In J. Boissevain and J.C. Mitchell (eds.), *Network Analysis: Studies in Human Interaction.* The Hague: Mouton.

Niosi, Jorge. 1978. *The Economy of Canada.* Montreal: Black Rose Books.

——. 1981. *Canadian Capitalism.* Toronto: James Lorimer.

——. 1983. "The Canadian Bourgeoisie: Towards a Synthetical Approach." *Canadian Journal of Political and Social Theory* 7, no. 3:128–49.

——. 1985a. *Canadian Multinationals* Toronto: Garamond Press.

——. 1985b. "Continental Nationalism: the Strategy of the Canadian Bourgeoisie." In *The Structure of the Canadian Capitalist Class,* ed. Robert J. Brym. Toronto: Garamond Press, pp. 53–66.

Offe, Claus. 1984. *Contradictions of the Welfare State.* Cambridge, MA: MIT Press.

Organization for Economic Cooperation and Development. 1981. *Main Eco-*

nomic Indicators. Paris, April.
Ornstein, Michael D. 1976. "The Boards and Executives of the Largest Canadian Corporations: Size, Composition, and Interlocks." *Canadian Journal of Sociology* 1:411–37.
———. 1980. "Assessing the Meaning of Corporate Interlocks: Canadian Evidence." *Social Science Research* 9, no. 4:287–306.
———. 1984. "Interlocking directorates in Canada: Intercorporate or class alliance?" *Administrative Science Quarterly* 29:210–31.
———. 1985. "Canadian Capital and the Canadian State: Ideology in an Era of Crisis." In (ed.) *The Structure of the Canadian Capitalist Class*, ed. Robert J. Brym. Toronto: Garamond Press, pp. 129–66.
Overbeek, Henk. 1980. "Finance Capital and the Crisis in Britain." *Capital and Class* 2:99–120.
Palloix, Christian. 1975. "The Internationalization of Capital and the Circuit of Social Capital." In *International Firms and Modern Imperialism*, ed. Hugo Radice. Markham: Penguin, pp. 63–88.
———. 1977. "The Self-expansion of Capital on a World Scale." *Review of Radical Political Economics* 9, no. 1:1–28.
Palmer, Bryan D. 1983. *Working-Class Experience*. Toronto: Butterworths.
Palmer, Donald. 1980. "Broken Ties: Some Political and Interorganizational Consequences of Interlocking Directorates among American Corporations." Paper presented at the annual meeting of the American Sociological Association, New York.
———. 1983. "Interpreting Corporate Interlocks from Broken Ties." *Social Science History* 7:217–23.
Panitch, Leo. 1981. "Dependency and Class in Canadian Political Economy." *Studies in Political Economy* 6:7–33.
———. 1985. "Class and Power in Canada." *Monthly Review* 36, no. 11:1–13.
Panitch, Leo, and Donald Swartz. 1985. *From Consent to Coercion: The Assault on Trade Union Freedoms*. Toronto: Garamond Press.
Park, Libbie, and Frank Park. 1973 [1962]. *Anatomy of Big Business*. Toronto: James Lewis and Samuel.
Pastre, Olivier. 1981. *Multinationals: Bank and Corporation Relationships*. Greenwich, CN: JAI Press.
Penner, Norman. 1977. *The Canadian Left*. Scarborough ONT: Prentice-Hall.
Pennings, Johannes M. 1980. *Interlocking Directorates*. San Francisco: Jossey-Bass.
Pentland, H. C. 1981. *Labour and Capital in Canada 1650–1860*. Toronto: James Lorimer.
Perlo, Victor. 1957. *The Empire of High Finance*. New York: International Publishers.
Perry, Robert L. 1979. "Local Enterpreneurs 'Repatriating the Branch-plant City'." *Financial Post*, 18 August 1979:10.
Petras, James. 1984a. "Marxism and World-Historical Transformations." *Contemporary Marxism* 9:18–34.

————. 1984b. "Towards a Theory of Industrial Development in the Third World." *Journal of Contemporary Asia*. 14:182–203.

————. and Robert Rhodes. 1976. "The Consolidation of U.S. Hegemony." *New Left Review* 97:37–53.

————. and Morris Morley. 1982. "The New Cold War: Reagan's Policy Towards Europe and the Third World." *Studies in Political Economy* 9:5–44.

Phillips, Anne. 1977. "The Concept of Development." *Review of African Political Economy* 8:7–20.

Phillips, James. 1980. "Renovation of the International Economic Order: Trilateralism, the IMF, and Jamaica." In *Trilateralism: The Trilateral Commission and Elite Planning for World Management*, ed. Holly Sklar. Boston: South End Press, 468–91.

Phillips, Paul. 1979. "The National Policy Revisited." *Journal of Canadian Studies* 14, no. 3:3–13.

Phillips, Ron. 1983. "The Role of the International Monetary Fund in the Post-Bretton Woods Era." *Review of Radical Political Economics* 15, no. 2:59–81.

Piedalue, Gilles. 1976. "Les groupes financiers au Canada 1900–1930." *Revue d'Histoire de l'Amerique Francaise* 30, no. 1:3–34.

Porter, John. 1956. "Concentration of Economic Power and the Economic Elite in Canada." *Canadian Journal of Economics and Political Science* 22:199–220.

————. 1965. *The Vertical Mosaic*. Toronto: University of Toronto Press.

Portes, Alejandro and John Walton. 1981. *Labor, Class, and the International System*. Toronto: Academic Press.

Postone, Moishe. 1985. "Jean Cohen on Marxian critical theory." *Theory and Society* 14:233–46.

Poulantzas, Nicos. 1974. "Internationalization of Capitalist Relations and the Nation-state." *Economy and Society* 3:145–79.

Prebish, R. 1950. *The Economic Development of Latin America and its Principal Problems*. Lake Success, NY: U.N. Department of Economic Affairs.

Radice, Hugo. 1984. "The National Economy: a Keynesian Myth?" *Capital and Class* 22:14–140.

Ratcliff, Richard E. 1980. "Banks and Corporate Lending: An Analysis of the Impact of the Internal Structure of the Capitalist Class on the Lending Behaviour of Banks." *American Sociological Review* 45:553–70.

Reddick, Jackie. 1984. "Crisis, 'Seigniorage' and the Modern World System: Rising Third World Power or Declining U.S. Hegemony?" *Capital and Class* 23:121–34.

Resnick, Philip. 1977. *Land of Cain*. Vancouver: New Star Books.

————. 1982. "The Maturing of Canadian Capitalism." *Our Generation* 15, no. 3:11–24.

Reuber, Grant L., and Frank Roseman. 1969. *The Take-Over of Canadian Firms, 1945–61*. Economic Council of Canada Special Study No. 10. Ottawa: Queen's Printer.

Richardson, R.J. 1982. "Merchants Against Industry: An Empirical Study." *Canadian Journal of Sociology* 7:279–96.

————. 1985. "A Structural-Rational Theory of the Functions of Directorship Interlocks between Financial and Non-financial Corporations." In *The Structure of the Canadian Capitalist Class*, ed. Robert J. Brym. Toronto: Garamond Press, pp. 103–16.

Roberts, Dick. 1969. "The Financial Empires of America's Ruling Class." *International Socialist Review* 30 (May-June 1969):24–35.

Rochester, A. 1936. *The Rulers of America*. New York: International Publishers.

Rosenblum, Simon. 1975. "Economic Nationalism and the English-Canadian Socialist Movement." *Our Generation* 11, no. 1:5–15.

Rosenbluth, Gideon. 1961. "Concentration and Monopoly in the Canadian Economy." In *Social Purpose for Canada*, ed. M. Oliver. Toronto: University of Toronto Press.

Rowthorn, B. 1975. "Imperialism in the 1970's—Unity or Rivalry?" In *International Firms and Modern Imperialism*, ed. Hugo Radice, Markham, Ont: Penguin, pp. 158–80.

Roy, William G. 1983. "The Unfolding of the Interlocking Directorate Structure of the United States." *American Sociological Review* 48:248–57.

Rush, Gary B. 1983. "State, Class, and Capital: Demystifying the Westward Shift of Power." *Canadian Review of Sociology and Anthropology* 20:255–89.

Russell, Bob. 1984. "The Politics of Reproduction: Funding Canada's Social Wage, 1917–1946." *Studies in Political Economy* 14:43–73.

Ryerson, Stanley B. 1973. *Unequal Union*. Toronto: Progress Books.

————. 1976. "Who's Looking after Business?" *This Magazine* 9:41–6.

Schiffman, S.S., M.L. Reynolds and F.W. Young. 1981. *Introduction to Multidimensional Scaling*. Toronto: Academic Press.

Schmidt, Ray. 1981. "Canadian Political Economy: A Critique." *Studies in Political Economy* 6:65–92.

Schumpeter, Joseph. 1949. *The Theory of Economic Development*. Cambridge: Harvard University Press.

Scott, John. 1979. *Corporations, Classes and Capitalism*. London: Hutchison.

Seidman, Ann, and Phil O'Keefe. 1980. "The United States and South Africa in the Changing International Division of Labor." *Antipode* 12, no. 2:1–16.

Semmler, Will. 1982. "Competition, Monopoly, and Differentials of Profit Rates: Theoretical Considerations and Empirical Evidence." *Review of Radical Political Economics* 13, no. 4:39–52.

Singelmann, Joachim. 1978. *From Agriculture to Services*. Beverly Hills, CA: Sage.

Sklar, Holly ed. 1980. *Trilateralism: The Trilateral Commission and Elite Planning for World Management*. Boston: South End Press.

Smout, T.C. 1980. "Scotland and England: Is Dependency a Symptom or a Cause of Underdevelopment?" *Review* 3:601–630.

Smythe, Dallas W. 1981. *Dependency Road: Communications, Capitalism, Consciousness and Canada*. Norwood, NJ: Ablex Publishing Corp.

Sonquist, J.A., and T. Koenig. 1975. "Interlocking Directorates in the Top U.S. Corporations: A Graph Theory Approach." *Insurgent Sociologist* 5, no. 3:196–229.

Soref, Michael. 1980. "The Finance Capitalists." In Maurice Zeitlin (ed.), *Classes, Class Conflict and the State*. Cambridge, MA: Winthrop Publishers.

Stanworth, P. and A. Giddens. 1975. "The Modern Corporate Economy: Interlocking Directorships in Britain, 1906–1970." *Sociological Review* 23:5–28.

Stapells, H.G. 1927. *The Recent Consolidation Movement in Canada*. Master's Thesis, University of Toronto.

Stening, Bruce, and Wan Tai Wai. 1984. "Interlocking Directorates among Australia's Largest 250 Corporations 1959–1979." *Australian and New Zealand Journal of Sociology* 20, no. 1:47–55.

Stevenson, Paul. 1983. "The State in English Canada: The Political Economy of Production and Reproduction." *Socialist Studies/Etudes Socialistes* 1:88–128.

Swainson, Nicola. 1977. "The Rise of a National Bourgeoisie in Kenya." *Review of African Political Economy* 8:39–55.

Sweeny, Robert. 1980. *The Evolution of Financial Groups in Canada and the Capital Market Since the Second World War*. Master's Thesis, Université du Quebec à Montreal.

Sweezy, Paul M. 1939. "Interest Groups in the American Economy." In U.S. Natural Resources Committee, *The Structure of the American Economy, Part 1*. Washington, pp. 309–17.

———. 1953. "Recent Developments in American Capitalism". In *The Present as History*. New York: Monthly Review Press.

———. 1970. *The Theory of Capitalist Development*. New York: Monthly Review Press.

———. 1972. "Power Elite or Ruling Class?" In *Modern Capitalism and Other Essays*, ed. Paul M. Sweezy. New York: Monthly Review Press, pp. 92–109.

———. 1980. "The Crisis of American Capitalism." *Monthly Review* 32, no. 5: 1–13.

———. and Harry Magdoff. 1969. "The Merger Movement: A Study in Power." *Monthly Review* 21, no. 6:1–19.

Szymanski, Albert. 1981. *The Logic of Imperialism*. New York: Praeger.

Teeple, Gary. 1972. "Land, Labour, and Capital in Pre-Confederation Canada." In *Capitalism and the National Question in Canada*, ed. Gary Teeple. Toronto: University of Toronto Press, pp. 43–66.

Therborn, Goran. 1978. *What does the Ruling Class do When it Rules?* London: New Left Books.

————. 1983. "Why Some Classes are More Successful than Others." *New Left Review* 138:37–55.

Thompson, Grahame. 1977. "The Relationship between the Financial and Industrial Sector in the United Kingdom Economy." *Economy and Society* 6:235–83.

Traves, Tom. 1979. *The State and Enterprise: Canadian Manufacturers and the Federal Government, 1917–31.* Toronto: University of Toronto Press.

Tugendhat, C. 1973. *The Multinationals.* London: Penguin.

Urquhart, M.C. and K.A.H. Buckley. 1965. *Historical Statistics of Canada.* Cambridge: Cambridge University Press.

Useem, Michael. 1978. "The Inner Group of the American Capitalist Class." *Social Problems* 25:225–40.

————. 1979. "The Social Organization of the American Business Elite." *American Sociological Review* 44:553–71.

————. 1980. "Corporations and the Corporate Elite." In *The Annual Review of Sociology*, ed. Alex Inkeles et al. Vol. 6. Palo Alto, CA.: Annual Review, Inc., pp. 41–78.

————. 1984 *The Inner Circle.* New York: Oxford University Press.

Villarejo, Don. 1961. "Stock Ownership and the Control of Corporations, Part 1." *New University Thought* 2 (Autumn).

————. 1962. "Stock Ownership and the Control of Corporations, Part 2." *New University Thought* 2 (Winter).

Walker, Richard A. 1978. "Two Sources of Uneven Development under Advanced Capitalism: Spatial Differentiation and Capital Mobility." *Review of Radical Political Economics* 10, no. 3:28–38.

————. 1985. "Is There a Service Economy? The Changing Capitalist Division of Labor." *Science and Society* 49, no. 1:42–83.

Wallerstein, Immanuel. 1974. *The Modern World System: Capitalist Agriculture and the Origins of the European World Economy in the Sixteenth Century.* New York: Academic Press.

Warren, Bill. 1973. "Imperialism and Capitalist Industrialization." *New Left Review* 31:3–44.

————. 1975. "How International is Capital?" In *International Firms and Modern Imperialism*, ed. Hugo Radice. Markham, ONT: Penguin, pp. 135–40.

————. 1980. *Imperialism: Pioneer of Capitalism.* London: New Left Books.

Watkins, Mel H. 1963. "A Staple Theory of Economic Growth." *Canadian Journal of Economics and Political Science* 29:141–58.

————. 1970. "Preface." In *Silent Surrender*, ed. Kari Levitt. Toronto: MacMillan, pp. ix-xvii.

————. 1973. "Resources and Underdevelopment." In *(Canada) Ltd., The Political Economy of Dependency*, ed. Robert Laxer. Toronto: McClelland and Stewart, pp.107–126.

————. 1977. "The Staple Theory Revisited." *Journal of Canadian Studies* 12, no. 5:83–95.

―――. 1981. "Perspectives on Nationalism." *This Magazine* 15, no. 4:26–28.

―――. 1983. "The NEP and the Left: A Commentary on Sher and Others." *Socialist Studies/Etudes Socialistes* 1:151–57.

―――. et. al. 1968. Task Force on the Structure of Canadian Industry *Report*. Ottawa: Queen's Printer.

Weeks, John. 1977. "The Sphere of Production and the Analysis of Crisis in Capitalism." *Science and Society* 41:281–302.

―――. 1981. "The Differences between Materialist Theory and Dependency Theory and Why They Matter." *Latin American Perspectives* 8, nos. 3 and 4:118–23.

―――. 1986. "Epochs of Capitalism and the Progressiveness of Capital's Expansion." *Science and Society* 49:419–36.

―――. and Elizabeth Dore. 1979. "International Exchange and the Causes of Backwardness." *Latin American Perspectives* 6, no. 2:62–87.

White, H.C., S.A. Boorman and R.L. Breiger. 1976. "Social Structure from Multiple Networks. I. Blockmodels of Roles and Positions." *American Journal of Sociology* 31:730–80.

White, T.H. 1979. "Boards of Directors: Control and Decision-making in Canadian Corporations." *Canadian Review of Sociology and Anthropology* 16:77–95.

Whitely, Richard. 1974. "The City and Industry: The Directors of Large Companies and their Characteristics and Connections." In *Elites and Power in British Society,* ed. P. Stanworth and A. Giddens. Cambridge: Cambridge University Press, pp. 63–80.

Wibaut, F.M. 1913. "De nieuwste ontwikkeling van het kapitalisme." *De Nieuwe Tijd* 18:284–349.

Wilkens, Mira. 1970. *The Emergence of Multinational Enterprise: American Business Abroad from the Colonial Era to 1914.* Cambridge: Harvard University Press.

―――. 1974. *The Maturing of Multinational Enterprise: American Business Abroad from 1914 to 1970.* Cambridge: Harvard University Press.

Williams, Glen. 1983. *Not for Export: Toward a Political Economy of Canada's Arrested Industrialization.* Toronto: McClelland and Stewart.

Wolfe, David A. 1984. "The Rise and Demise of the Keynesian Era in Canada: Economic Policy 1930–1982." In *Modern Canada 1930–1980s,* ed. M.S. Cross and G.S. Kealey. Toronto: McClelland and Stewart, pp. 46–80.

Young, Bert. 1974 "Corporate Interests and the State: Anti-Combine Activity in Canada—1900 to 1970." *Our Generation* 10 (Winter/Spring):70–83.

Zeitlin, Maurice. 1974. "Corporate Ownership and Control: The Large Corporation and the Capitalist Class." *American Journal of Sociology* 79:1073–1119.

INDEX